GETTING BUSINESS

TO

COME TO YOU

EVERYTHING YOU NEED TO KNOW
TO DO YOUR OWN ADVERTISING, PUBLIC RELATIONS,
DIRECT MAIL, AND SALES PROMOTION,
AND ATTRACT ALL THE BUSINESS
YOU CAN HANDLE

PAUL and SARAH EDWARDS

and Laura Clampitt Douglas

A Jeremy P. Tarcher/Putnam Book
published by
G. P. Putnam's Sons
New York

A Jeremy P. Tarcher/Putnam Book
Published by G. P. Putnam's Sons
Publishers Since 1838
200 Madison Avenue
New York, NY 10016

Library of Congress Cataloging-in-Publication Data

Edwards, Paul, date.
  Getting business to come to you: everything you need to know to do your
own advertising, public relations, direct mail, and sales promotion, and
attract all the business you can handle / Paul and Sarah Edwards, Laura
Clampitt Douglas.—1st ed.
    p.   cm.
  ISBN 0-87477-629-5
  1. Home-based businesses 2. Advertising. 3. Marketing. I. Edwards, Sarah
(Sarah A.) II. Douglas, Laura Clampitt. III. Title.

HD2341.E38   1990
658.8—dc20   91-23196
                                                              CIP

Jeremy P. Tarcher, Inc.
5858 Wilshire Blvd., Suite 200
Los Angeles, CA 90036

Manufactured in the United States of America
20 19 18 17 16 15 14 13 12 11

CONTENTS

■■■■■■■■■■■■■■■■■■■■

ACKNOWLEDGMENTS

■■■■■■■■■■■■■■■■■■■■■■

We're told that it's unusual for authors to have three books published at the same time by the same publisher. Yet this book is proof that it can happen and it is due to the extraordinary team of people at our publisher, Jeremy P. Tarcher, Inc. To Jeremy Tarcher we owe a continuing debt for his vision that resulted in his publishing *Working From Home* when it was regarded as something short of a fad in 1985, because he recognized that people are seeking alternatives to the 9-to-5 routine and that it's both possible and profitable to make it on your own working from home.

We thank Rick Benzel, our editor for our three new books, *Best Home Businesses for the 90s, Getting Business to Come to You,* and *Making It on Your Own.* Rick's support, creativity, good sense, and problem-solving ability has come through many times in the course of developing these books.

We are especially grateful to Robert Welsch for his special vision and role in bringing these books about. We don't know how many hours of sleep Paul Murphy and Susan Harris will have lost to get these books out on time, and we are grateful. To Mike Dougherty, Lisa Ives, Michael Graziano, Lisa Chadwick we say "thank you" for helping us to get our message out that there are positive alternatives for people in a rapidly changing world.

We appreciate the hundreds of people we interviewed for these books, many of whom came to us by way of the Working From Home Forum on CompuServe and our radio shows.

CHAPTER
ONE

■ ■

What Works: The Marketing Strategies of Successful Home-Based Businesses

Just imagine: You wake up every Monday morning raring to get to work, because you're working for yourself. You're the boss. You call the shots, set the hours, and work when you want to, doing what you want to do and making good money. You are enjoying the lifestyle you've created for yourself. You are among the rapidly growing number of self-employed individuals operating very small or home-based businesses or working as free-lancers, consultants, or subcontractors. And you are living the dream of up to 70 percent of all Americans . . . or you would like to be.

You are one of a select few because, while seven out of ten of us dream of being our own boss, only one in seven actually are. And of those who try to make it on their own, only two out of five make it past the first five years. Often this is simply because they don't have enough business to stay in business, or fear they won't. They fear or actually find that when they get up on Monday morning, there isn't any work to do, or at least not enough to pay the bills. So instead of providing the products or services they went into business to provide, they are faced with having to spend their time trying to bring in some business or just waiting for the phone to ring.

If you are like most of today's growing ranks of self-employed individuals, you're not excited about running a business; you're excited about being on your own. You probably don't think of yourself as having a sales personality. Chances are you dislike having to sell and perhaps even dread it. But you are good at what you do and want to succeed as your own boss, and you know that if you can't somehow get enough business fast enough and regularly enough, you are doomed to work for someone else just to maintain a reasonable lifestyle. So you are determined to find practical, effective ways to attract

1

a steady flow of business, and you would rather have it come to you than have to go out and get it. After all, how can you spend your time both getting business and doing business?

We know how this dilemma feels. Among the three of us we have been on our own for over thirty-one years. We each remember dry spells, times when we ached for an opportunity to work and we wondered whether leaving the security of a paycheck had been a mistake. But we also know about the excitement and exhilaration of having the phone ring off the hook with eager customers and finding the mailbox stuffed with orders and, better yet, checks!

Through the years we have learned that over the long haul having plenty of business is not a matter of luck or happenstance. One magical word can put you in charge of making sure that you have all the work you need: *marketing.* Marketing refers to all the activities involved in making sure you have enough business flowing through your door and that it keeps flowing in.

When we left the security of a paycheck for the freedom of being our own boss, we didn't know what the word *marketing* meant. We didn't have business backgrounds. Sarah was a psychotherapist. Paul was a lawyer. Laura was somewhat more fortunate: "I had a substantial sales background and a wealth of diverse experience in various phases of marketing. But that didn't really make developing an appropriate framework for my skills any easier. And I, too, had to hustle in order to get business." We each knew we wanted to be on our own, and we quickly learned that we had to generate some business fast if we didn't want to be back on the payroll. We also learned quickly that much of what is written and taught about marketing and how to get business simply doesn't apply to us. We were not a big business or retail operation with funds for market research, a sales force, and an advertising and public relations budget, but three individuals in business for ourselves, working from our homes. Initially, we didn't even think of our work as a business: we were consultants, professionals in private practice, independent contractors, or freelancers. To us, business was something conducted in a retail store or office with employees. And that is exactly what the books we found on marketing talked about, in abstract business terms—large-scale marketing operations appropriate for companies with large budgets for an array of sales and promotional activities, from television to mass-market direct-mail campaigns.

Since that time we have learned that many of today's self-employed individuals feel as we did. They don't always define themselves as a business, yet they do have to get business and usually have to do so on a shoestring, without a staff of professionals or the help of a marketing, public relations, or advertising agency. And unfortunately, while much of the information available about marketing is excellent, applying it to what we need to do to make sure we have work to do on Monday mornings is like trying to make a good impression in a hand-me-down suit: it is not a comfortable fit.

Often over the years we wished there were some type of guide for building business that could help us circumvent the time and expense involved in retailoring the basic principles of marketing into approaches that would work for us. But there wasn't, so we, like others who have ventured out on their own, had to handcraft our own strategies for getting business. Now, there are some twelve million self-employed individuals. Many of them are tremendously successful, bringing in incomes well beyond the national average.

Among the three of us, we have talked at some depth with hundreds of these successful self-employed men and women, and we have discovered that there is a marketing technology suitable for the self-employed. When we met via computer on the Working From Home Forum on CompuServe Information Service, we decided it was time to write the very guide we had wished for so long ago. We distilled what actually works from the results of collective years of trial and error and blood, sweat, and tears—years of tailoring and retailoring what is known about how to get business to fit the needs of people like yourself in homes and small offices across the continent who no longer want just to dream about being their own boss, but want to live that dream.

The One Essential Element

In reality, virtually everyone in this country can get into business. We have even talked to prisoners who are doing business from their jail cells. In fact, getting into business is the easiest thing about being in business. With a desk, a file cabinet, a telephone, some letterhead and stationery, and, if funds allow, a personal computer, printer, and fax, you are ready to provide your product or service to the world.

Even these basics aren't always essential. We have a friend who has been in business for nine years who has neither a desk nor stationery although she does have a business card. She doesn't even have an office. She works from home, seeing clients in her living room and using her personal phone to make appointments. Although such an arrangement may not be ideal or even recommended, this woman is a business success who, over those nine years, has had a steady stream of clients.

Two other acquaintances of ours were not so fortunate. They invested their personal savings and retirement funds in a luxurious office, elegantly designed stationery, and the most advanced equipment. They opened the office in September with a lavish party. Although they seemed to have everything a business could need, the office closed before Thanksgiving. The one thing they didn't have was clients.

The only truly essential element for a successful business is having enough people to buy your product or service, week after week, month after month, year after year. You aren't truly *in* business until you *have* business. No matter what other accoutrements you have, as catalog publisher Tim Mullen so aptly pointed out, "Customers are your only true source of funding!" Even if you can raise cash from some other source, it still must ultimately be repaid with money produced from customers. Customers put you in business and keep you in business. A lack of customers can put you out of business.

If you are in business for yourself, you undoubtedly are acutely aware of this reality. If you are thinking about going out on your own, you hopefully are equally aware of the need to get business. Concern over whether there will be enough business to replace a paycheck is the primary reason most people still have jobs.

Getting Business to Come to You Instead of Having to Go Out and Get It

Traditionally, getting business has meant having to get out and sell. But for the majority of men and women who want to be their own boss, selling is the dreaded "S" word. Most people fear the rejection and frustration selling can entail. We have all heard too many horror stories of having to make fifty sales calls a week to get just one appointment that doesn't pan out.

Many of today's most successfully self-employed individuals don't like selling any more than the rest of us do. They didn't go into business in order to spend most of their time asking for a chance to do it, and they have found they don't have to. These successful individuals have found ways to *get business to come to them*.

That is why we called this book *Getting Business to Come to You* rather than simply *Marketing for Free-lancers and for Small and Home-Based Businesses*. The purpose of this book is to provide practical skills, information, and techniques you can use to get business to come to you so you can minimize the time and psychic energy you spend doing the dreaded task of cold calling. You will find that once these techniques begin working for you, you'll be able to spend your time doing the work you have chosen to do instead of trying to get a chance to do it.

Five Lessons from $100,000-Plus Home-Based Businesses

When we set out to discover how successful home-based businesses get business, we decided to begin our search with those who get a lot of business. So we began by analyzing the marketing strategies of the most successful home-based businesses—those making over $100,000 a year. We found that they do one or more of five things that others usually do not do, and as a result we decided to build this book around those five business-getting strategies. In fact, this book can be considered a primer for generating or increasing the amount of business that comes to you by following in the footsteps of these successful businesses.

1. Get people to beat a path to your door. This, of course, is what all newly self-employed individuals want. They hope that if they provide a good enough product or service, customers will somehow materialize automatically. That rarely happens. Over the years we have told countless numbers of would-be entrepreneurs not to expect people to beat down their doors. So you can imagine our surprise to discover that in some cases the most successful home-based businesses did indeed have people beating a path to their door from the very moment they opened!

Eleanor Duggan is a good example of someone who had clients right from the start. When she began her business, she already had a solid reputation as one of the best focus-group leaders in her field, and word that she had gone out on her own spread rapidly through the grapevine. She was busy from the first year on. And so it was with Mike Greer, one of the best instructional designers in Los Angeles. When he left to form his own firm, clients eagerly followed him.

That such a path formed for these two people was clearly not the whim of luck. If, like Eleanor and Mike, you are good at what you do, *with proper marketing* you can put together the elements that will draw people to you. You can:

- offer something people want so badly that they would do almost anything to get it.
- become so well known among the people who want what you offer that plenty of them know that you're offering it.
- do the highly valuable things you do so well that everyone who uses you can't wait to tell everyone else about you.

Clearly, the better you are at what you do and the better known you are for it, the more easily and quickly you will attract business. This suggests the need to limit your business to those things you do best or to take the time to master something well before venturing on your own. It also suggests applying what you do best to real needs and emphasizes the importance of developing as high a profile as possible with those who need your skills.

2. Establish a niche. The most successful home-based individuals are highly specialized. They have a product or service that serves a particular market segment or niche that no one else is serving adequately or that is not provided elsewhere. They don't do general management consulting, for example; they are consultants to the fashion industry on collection problems. They don't have a general billing service; they do billing for anesthesiologists. Or perhaps they have a temporary agency exclusively for design professionals or escrow officers, or do public relations only for high-tech or environmentally conscious companies.

This would suggest that whatever stage your business is in, focusing it as tightly as possible on one or, possibly, two specialty areas will make it easier for you to attract clients or customers. The fear in doing this, of course, is that by narrowing your market you will have fewer people to draw from and therefore fewer people will buy. In reality, the opposite is true. As long as the special area you have chosen has enough potential customers, the more specialized your business, the more people will be able to recognize the benefit of what you offer them.

For the self-employed individual, finding a niche is somewhat like establishing job security. It means clearly identifying a group of people who need a product or service that you are distinctively able to provide. If you are offering a service that is in high demand such as medical billing or medical transcribing, you may not need to rely on finding a special niche; but the more competitive the field you are in, the more important it is for you to find what you are uniquely qualified to do.

Your niche needs to be small enough that you don't have a lot of competition and can reach most of your potential clients within the limits of your time and budget. And the niche needs to be large enough to provide sufficient customers to support your business. For example, Chip Morgan of Sacramento, California has found the right balance: he provides full-service design and management for radio-station owners who are remodeling or building. Although there are fewer than one hundred such stations in the country at any time, that is enough to keep him busy.

Usually, finding a niche is based on matching your education or specific job experience to a particular industry. But it can also be based on a lifelong interest, or hobby, or even a personal tragedy. For example, computer programmer and consultant David Brace's daughter suffered a serious brain injury. In helping her recover, David developed the software for computer-based therapy for brain-trauma patients. This has led to his developing a specialty working on projects that are retraining accident victims with brain traumas.

We each have or can develop our own unique qualifications. Finding them is a matter of relating experiences from your personal history to people's current needs and then building new experiences that make you even better qualified. For example, when Larry Barnett completed graduate school to begin his video production business, he began marketing to restaurant chains, because although he had never done a professional video project, he had worked his way through school as a manager for such a chain. This experience made it possible for him to qualify to produce a small low-budget video for a restaurant's training film. This first project gave him the experience he needed to find additional clients in the field, and each restaurant project he got made it easier to obtain the next.

Barnett wisely avoided the trap in which so many new entrepreneurs get caught. Although he has an interest in providing many different production functions and would like to explore providing them to many different industries, he did not try to be all things to all people, especially not until he was firmly established in his niche of doing commercial films for the restaurant industry.

Others we have met were not so wise. When two personnel managers left their jobs at a large department store to become management consultants, they, like many entrepreneurs, had a wide variety of skills and interests. They structured their business to feature as many of these skills and interests as possible. Their brochure listed five different services from editorial work to financial counseling. This material, however, conveyed no clear idea what they actually did or for whom they could do it.

A poet made a similar mistake. She wanted to earn her living selling poetry, but fearing she wouldn't be able to earn enough money in this field, she created a business card that listed everything she could do including singing, doing calligraphy, selling gift items, and coordinating parties, as well as writing poetry. Needless to say, not only were others confused in looking at her card, she became confused herself about what she should say when anyone asked what she did. To overcome this confusion she developed a pat answer, "It depends on which hat I'm wearing." Of course, people weren't interested in helping her put on the right hat.

The solution is not for these people to give up their varied interests and skills, rather to focus their interests to find a specialized platform upon which to provide their skills. For example, the personnel managers might form a business called Boutique Management, providing a wide variety of personnel functions for clothing stores that are too small to have a personnel department. The poet, on the other hand, might focus her business by becoming Lyrics for Love's Special Occasions, creating invitations, songs, gifts, ceremonies, and events for weddings, engagement parties, anniversaries, and bridal showers.

Suppose you want to find a niche for using your varied background in the health field. Consider these possibilities:

- Establish a temporary agency that specializes in providing medical transcription personnel to hospitals, clinics, and doctors' offices.
- Create a temporary agency that provides hygienists for dental offices.
- Work with social services and hospitals to provide a central database on pediatric records.
- Provide medical billing services for doctor's offices and small clinics.
- Produce a newsletter that synthesizes the information from all the medical journals about a particular medical specialty—a kind of medical *Reader's Digest,* with each series targeted toward a different specialty.

No matter what products or services you provide, you can carve out a niche for them based on your experience, skills, and interests and then build up that niche as you work to serve it. Ask yourself questions like:

- What do I do best?
- Who needs that the most?
- Where can I provide that product or service that will give me a chance to expand what I do to utilize my other interests?

- What industries or types of companies do I already have experience in?
- What industries or companies do I have access to now?
- Whom do I already know?
- What jargons or industry-specific acronyms am I already familiar with?

3. Gain entrance through gatekeepers. Many of the most successful home-based businesses have achieved success because they had access to key sources of business. For example, David Freed obtains his business as a housing consultant through leads and referrals he gets from the lawyers, lenders, and personnel he knows in the nonprofit housing industry in Washington, D.C. Robert Livingston is a successful New York cabinetmaker, much of whose business comes as a result of referrals from an architectural designer he works with. Los Angeles-based graphic designer Tom Dower gets most of his business from his publicist wife, Kim Freilich.

Some of the most successful businesses are started with such contacts securely in place, which makes getting business easier and quicker. But even if you are already in business and feel like you don't know a soul, there are specific ways you can go about meeting and establishing successful relationships with the very gatekeepers you need. In chapters 2 and 3 we discuss in detail how to find and use gatekeepers as a source of regular business.

4. Position yourself as preeminent in your field. The better you are known for being a leader in your field, the easier it will be to attract business.

Ways to Carve Out a Niche

Here are a few of the ways you can slice up your market and find your niche:

Market Slice	Examples
Geography	West Side, East Side, MacArthur Park, statewide
Industry	Medicine, construction, law, real estate, banking, insurance
Size of company	Fortune 1000, Under $50,000,000, five to ten employees
Demographics	Age, sex, marital status, lifestyle, income
Price sensitivities	Premium quality, best value, bargain basement
Special interests	Antiques, history, sports, self-improvement, travel
Hobbies	Animals, cars, collecting, cooking, gardening, music
Life events	Birth, marriage, divorce, death, retirement
Corporate function	Finance, sales, personnel, training, purchasing
Problem	Collections, turnover, cash flow, drug abuse

However, most of the $100,000-plus business owners we spoke to were not well known when they started out. Many became well known by *positioning* themselves to become recognized leaders in their field.

You probably have noticed that some of the best known and most successful individuals in any given field are not necessarily the most brilliant or the most knowledgeable. They were able to place themselves in a position that gave them prominence by one of three routes:

- furthering the knowledge in their field
- assuming a leadership role in their field
- pioneering a new field

Management consultant Dave Jamison became prominent in his field by serving as the president of first a local chapter, then the national and international levels of his professional organization. Psychologist Dr. Linda De Villars became a leading authority on the relationship between sexual satisfaction and exercise by undertaking a groundbreaking study. Pat Hardy became a prominent bed-and-breakfast innkeeper by editing a newsletter, co-founding and serving as executive director of a trade association, and co-authoring a definitive book for innkeepers.

Anyone who is the first to offer a product or service in an area of need is a pioneer and thereby can become a leader in the field. Gene Call became the first private-practice consultant in the country, helping professionals market their businesses. Howard L. Shenson became one of the first to provide information about how to become a professional consultant and became known as the "consultant's consultant." Judy and Shell Norris started the first reunion-planning business and remain preeminent despite the new proliferation of such services. When Boyd and Felice Willat created the *DayRunner Time Management System,* they became the pioneers and leaders of what was to become the burgeoning field of personal organization systems.

Becoming preeminent in your field means people think of you first. It is an ideal marketing strategy for anyone who doesn't like marketing, because it gives you access to gatekeepers, establishes you in a niche, and can create the momentum you need to get people to beat a path to your door—all while you are doing the things you're most interested in doing.

5. Become a premier marketeer. While only a few of the $100,000-plus home-based business people we spoke with were superb salespeople, some were superb marketeers in that they consistently used a variety of methods to attract customers. They knew the importance of these tools and had the knowledge to use them creatively and with flair.

They didn't take out run-of-the-mill ads; their ads sparkled. They didn't send out the customary mailings, rather gifts or brochures with unique colors and folds. They didn't simply attend a lot of networking meetings; they spoke forcefully and engagingly before such groups and started their own networking groups. Many of the ideas and examples we have used throughout this book draw upon the experiences of these premier marketeers.

We are convinced that all that stands between a premier marketeer and other entrepreneurs is access to the knowledge of how to use the tools of marketing in more personalized and specialized ways. With proper knowledge, anyone who is willing to invest the time can become a superb marketeer. And with the right marketing effort, any of the other four lessons of attracting business becomes possible.

Marketing can open doors to gatekeepers, establish you as preeminent in your specialized niche, and ultimately generate a stream of customers who are eagerly seeking what you and only you can offer. In this book, we have set out to provide you with the tools to become a superb marketeer. As you will discover, superb does not mean extravagant.

Premier marketeers Gene Call and Helen Berman both fill their training classes by giving free seminars. Gene holds free preview nights, where he gives professionals a chance to get a taste of what they will learn in his six-week marketing training program for professionals. Helen conducts sales seminars at professional meetings, teaching executives in her field how to boost their sales. Seeing the effectiveness of her methods, participants hire her to train their sales forces.

To launch his book-indexing service, Ted Laux of Ithaca, New York looked through bookstores to find books that didn't have adequate indices. To demonstrate how much more effective these books would be had the publishers used his services, he indexed the books using his TRS Model I computer and sent copies to the publishers. Several liked the results, and he was in business.

Daniel Cassidy of San Francisco built his scholarship-matching service from calls that came in response to an interview he did on a local radio talk show. Radio interviews continue to be a major source of business for him. Judy and Shell Norris of Chicago launched their business, Class Reunions, with an article in the *Wall Street Journal.*

None of these methods were costly, but they were effective. Our research happily shows that the best ways to let potential customers and clients know about a home business are not the most expensive. Far too many home-based businesses try to rely on costly advertising and direct-mail efforts only to be highly disappointed with the response. Consequently some businesses run out of money unnecessarily or just give up, assuming there is no market for what they do.

So how do you know where to begin? How do the successful marketeers discover which methods will actually work for them? And what are the best methods for you as a home-based business or self-employed individual to let people know about what you offer? Can a home-based business really get business from direct mail? Will advertising be a waste of your money? Or will other routes be more desirable? These are the questions we wanted to answer, and here is what we discovered.

Developing a Marketing Campaign Tailored for You

Since home businesses are usually offering a personal service or a customized specialty item, we have found the best marketing methods—at least initially—involve a personal and customized approach. The most successful businesses act as their own best promoter. The elements of a successful marketing campaign are:

- your personality
- your budget
- your business
- your time

If you have selected a business that solves a problem or answers an unmet need, you have potential customers this very minute. But they probably don't know where you are, and you may not know where they are either, at least not in sufficient numbers to keep your business busy. Somehow you must find each other. Of course, that is what marketing is designed to address. Marketing serves as your flag, your bullhorn, your neon sign. It shows those who need you where to find you. Furthermore, in today's world there are probably many businesses similar to yours, so marketing also helps distinguish you from your competition. It enables you to stand out from the crowd.

The premier marketeers we found are successful in attracting business because they have a concerted marketing effort that doesn't leave this process to chance. They set in place a variety of promotional activities that support and enhance one another to provide them with the most possible customers within their time and money limits.

Campaign is the ideal word to describe these efforts. The *Random House Dictionary* defines a campaign as "a systematic course of aggressive activities for some specific purpose." Indeed that is exactly what a marketing campaign is: a systematic course of aggressive activity for the purpose of getting business to come to you.

A Marketing Mindset

What all premier marketeers have in common in developing their marketing campaign is what we call a *marketing mindset*—a way of thinking about what they have to offer in terms of how it benefits others and an excitement about finding ways to let people know about it. This mindset has enabled them to come up with creative, cost-effective ways to *attract* business, rather than having to *sell* in the traditional sense.

In talking with successfully self-employed individuals of all types, we found that even when they had no marketing or business background, even when they were opening a business in a brand-new community without access to gatekeepers, and even when they were competent but not initially outstanding in their work, by operating with a marketing mindset they were able to create effective ways to attract business.

Meeting these successful marketeers was inspiring and informative because we realized that anyone can become a premier marketeer by making three mental shifts in thinking about his or her business. Instead of focusing only on providing a quality product or service, shift your attention to include these three issues as well:

How does what you do benefit those you serve? How are their lives or businesses improved? The procedures, materials, formats, and other features of your product or service are important to you. But those who need your product or service care only about such things as far as what these features *will do for them*. Your job is to answer the question, What's In It For Me?, a.k.a. WIIFM. Clients want to know that who, how, and what you provide will meet their needs; what they can count on from you; and what they will get for their money in terms of improvements or benefits to their life, job, or business.

Can you save your customers money, time, or effort? Can you increase their ability to compete in their market? Can you make the buyers look good to their bosses? Can you help clients correct someone's mistake and save their jobs? Can you give them peace of mind? Put yourself in the customer's shoes, then if you talk about, promote, and advertise from that perspective, your potential customers will be more likely to take notice, become interested, and decide to buy.

To help you shift your thinking from seller to buyer, pretend you are buying the service or product you provide from someone else. Or talk with people who need and use your service. Hold an informal focus group with your customers. Attend conferences, meetings, and events where your customers gather to discuss their issues. Don't talk; listen. Read trade journals and magazines. These tend to reflect your customer's current needs and concerns. What subjects do the articles cover? How does what you offer address those needs and concerns?

What do you have to offer that is special or unique? What makes you or your product or service different from what others do? Somehow your potential customers and clients have to be able to determine why they should select your product or service over similar ones. Usually they won't see the advantages automatically. To help reorient their thinking, study your competition. Find out what they provide, to whom, and how they do it. Who don't they serve? What don't they do? How does this compare to what you do? Chances are there are significant differences between your product or service and theirs. Within these differences lie the reasons someone should choose you over your competition.

How will you spread the word about the benefits you offer to those who need them? Successful marketeers feel a sense of urgency about wanting people to know about their product or service. They're not willing to wait or to hope they will get some business. They may be shy, or even retiring, but they feel compelled to let people know about what they offer. It is this internal drive that spurs their creativity to find imaginative ways to get the word out.

To ignite this drive within yourself, remind yourself why you went out on your own. How much do you want to do the work you're doing? How important is it to you? Why? Why not just go back to work for someone else? If your answers to these questions don't compel you to want to get the word out about what you do, rethink the nature of your business. Without the funds to pay for elaborate marketing efforts and the ability to hire top-notch professionals, your own compelling sense of passion becomes the essential element that will attract business. That kind of passion is contagious. It will come through in all your spoken and written communication from simply introducing yourself to describing what you do in a yellow-pages or classified ad. Like the many successful marketeers we've interviewed, your desire to achieve will propel you to find the best marketing methods available to you and to create innovative and inexpensive ways to to use them.

The Four Most Effective Low-Cost Methods

We found that the most successful self-employed marketeers are getting the best results from directing their time, energy, and money into four primary marketing methods.

1. Word-of-mouth. Without reservation we can say that word-of-mouth marketing can be the single best way to start and build a home-based personal or professional service business. Word-of-mouth marketing is often called networking. It refers to using face-to-face contact to establish relationships that can lead to business. It is based on talking with people about what you do and listening to find out how you might serve them. It also means meeting mentors, gatekeepers, and community leaders who can open doors of opportunity to you.

Once a business is established, word-of-mouth is defined as getting referrals from satisfied customers who talk about you. But until a business is self-sustaining, *you* do the talking. You tell people about your business. You speak with everyone you already know (family, friends, vendors, and colleagues) and you make a concerted effort to meet and talk with many new people too. Word-of-mouth marketing means you use your mouth to follow through on contacts and build relationships.

In Part One of this book, you will find out more about why word-of-mouth marketing is actually the most cost-effective way to get business to come to you. We will introduce you to the specific techniques used to get business from networking and to people who have used them effectively. You will learn how they have been able to meet mentors and gatekeepers and develop business by becoming involved in their community.

We will discuss three specific methods successful home-based businesses use once they're established to get a steady flow of referral business from customers. Then you'll find out how they magnify their word-of-mouth efforts by turning their business name, cards, stationery, and other printed materials into mini-billboards that draw business to them.

2. Public relations. If you don't already have a reputation that draws business to you, public relations is the surest and fastest way to get the visibility and exposure you need to set yourself out as a leader in your field. Public relations in this case refers to any publicity that puts you in the limelight as the expert, resource, authority, or leader. It involves getting yourself and your business featured in the media—on radio or television, in newspapers or magazines, or at events. It involves such things as being interviewed on talk shows, written up in articles, and invited to appear on panels at conferences, to present at trade shows, to write articles, books, and newsletters, or to teach courses and seminars.

We found that many successful home-based businesses rely heavily on public relations as a primary source of business. Like networking, it is something you can do yourself, and the costs can be kept low. It is a particularly effective means to market a business that is unusual enough to arouse interest or that is based on your unique expertise and knowledge.

In Part Two you will learn more about when and how to use public relations. You'll meet many people who have used it to establish a formidable reputation that brings them business. You'll learn how to gain access to free and low-cost publicity opportunities and how to make use of them to enhance visibility of your business in your market.

3. Direct marketing. Much to our surprise, one of the most effective ways for a home business to attract customers turns out to be a variety of methods that are referred to as *direct marketing*. No one we spoke with actually referred to these methods by this term, however. They spoke about the variety of things they do to get their message across directly in such a way that stimulates a customer to buy right then and there.

They talked about sampling as one of the most effective of these methods. Sampling allows people to experience an example of your product or service as a means to get them to buy. Sampling is an ideal way for those who love what they do to market their business; it is simply a demonstration of what they do; demonstrations speak for themselves.

They also told us about special promotions and about discounts and other strategic pricing incentives. Such offers are hard to refuse. In fact, we found strategic pricing can work for any home business and is especially useful in slow times or when just starting out, because it tends to produce business quickly. Such a strategy can be one of the fastest routes to draw business to you.

Many businesses find that nothing sells like going the extra mile, giving more than is expected, or producing more for less. All these incentives get people to take notice quickly and make them want to tell others about you. Suddenly you may get a volunteer sales force. Charlotte Mitchell takes going the extra mile literally. As Notary on Wheels and Fingerprinting on Wheels, she takes her business where her clients need her. Home-based marketing consultant Linda Jagoda describes her extra effort this way: "Treat your clients, no matter what their size, to royal service. Your smallest customer can bring you one of your biggest clients later on."

The successful home-based marketeers also talked about using a very specialized form of direct mail that can make the mail and delivery services a cost-effective means for a small or home-based business to advertise.

In Part Three, you'll discover when and how you can get your phone ringing with these varied, cost-effective, direct-marketing tools.

4. Inventive advertising. Although everyone is familiar with advertising, we found that successful home-based businesses use it cautiously, placing well-designed ads in carefully selected media targeted to their specialized customers or clients. In order to afford the frequency and duration of advertising they need to get a response, they have to be inventive. In other words, when you don't have a big budget you have to use your brain.

These businesses select cost-effective media that enable them to run their ads consistently. For example, Earl and Pam Weston, of At Home Professions, found classified ads to be their best avenue. Edward Salazar, however, found public-access cable television to be the best medium for advertising himself as a hair stylist. Cheryl Myers gets the best results for her office support services from yellow-pages advertising.

In Part Four, you will learn how to use inventive low-cost advertising approaches like these to cement your name in the minds of those who need your product or service so that you are the one they call when they need what you've got.

We have found there is clearly no single route guaranteed to work for everyone or every type of business. Actually, there are probably several that will work well for you. In fact, marketing is an ongoing, experimental process. It is most effective when multiple methods are employed in concert with one another. For example, personal networking and other word-of-mouth efforts help you create a consistently positive general image and help you build individual relationships that turn into business. Sales promotions and pricing incentives provide an added boost for customers to buy immediately. With public relations you hope to garner support for your company that will be reflected in a positive response to your product or service. Creative advertising introduces the specific product or service to a potential customer and urges the customer to take action either to contact you or to place an order. So your marketing campaign should consist of coordinating several marketing activities that complement one another.

A Sample Marketing Campaign

Consider what the poet introduced earlier might do for her marketing campaign. First, she might promote Lyrics for Love's Special Occasions by developing a six-month campaign on the theme of "Love Is in the Air." She could co-sponsor a Love Is in the Air fashion show with a local bridal boutique. Together, Grace and the boutique should begin their campaign to promote the show three months in advance. They could jointly take out ads in the local paper, set up an in-store promotional display, line up donated prizes of romantic dinners from local restaurants and get the restaurants to give away coupons for the fashion show. Then, of course, they should send a news release to the local media about the upcoming show.

During the show itself, Grace would disseminate gift cards with love lyrics to those present, sing the lyrics as the bridal models walk down the runway, and generally promote her services, offering a special price for anyone registering for the new class she will be offering entitled *Keeping Romance Alive.* With luck the joint effort will draw a feature story either before or after the show in the local paper.

During the three months after the show, Grace might send a series of special offers to all those who attended. A certain number of those who signed up for her class would also want her to plan events or provide other services for them. At the end of the six months, she should review the return on her efforts and make plans for the next six months' campaign.

Selecting Your Promotional Mix

In this example, Grace uses the power of multiple marketing methods to implement a coordinated effort to reach potential customers. The particular combination you choose for your marketing campaign is referred to as your *promotional mix.*

In selecting your mix, we recommend reading the pros and cons of each of the marketing methods available to you in the following chapters. Then select several methods to begin experimenting with which you think would be best suited to your market, personality, interests, skills, time, and budget. In making your selection, keep in mind this fundamental rule of successful marketing:

The measure of a successful marketing campaign is the extent to which it reaches at the lowest possible cost the greatest number of people who can and will buy your product or service.

Here are a few guidelines for finding a marketing mix that brings you the most business for the least money.

1. Choose methods that you will look forward to trying out. Since you probably will be the one to implement your marketing program, you need to enjoy doing the tasks involved. Don't force yourself to use methods that will be unduly stressful; you'll probably just end up abandoning them. If, for example, you hate public speaking, don't talk yourself into using seminars as a key marketing tool. There are most likely several workable methods which will suit your personality and talents.

2. Choose the methods that will provide you the easiest and least costly access to the specific people you want to reach. Do some investigation to

---

Principal Promotional Methods

Throughout this book we'll introduce you to the following thirty-five promotional methods. At the end of each section is a chart suggesting which of the methods discussed in that section are best suited to the type of business activity you do.

Part 1: Word-of-Mouth

1. Networking
2. Mentors and gatekeepers
3. Volunteerism
4. Sponsorships
5. Charitable donations
6. Referrals
7. Business name
8. Letterhead and business card
9. Product packaging
10. Point-of-sale display

Part 2: Public Relations

11. Writing articles
12. Letters to the editor
13. News releases
14. Speeches and seminars
15. Publicity:
    Newspaper
    Magazine
    Radio and TV
    Business and trade publications

Part 3: Direct Marketing

16. Sampling
17. Incentives
18. Discount Pricing
19. Contests and giveaways
20. Newsletters
21. Circulars and flyers
22. Trade shows and exhibits
23. Sales seminars
24. Demonstrations
25. Direct mail

Part 4: Inventive Advertising

26. Classified ads
27. Business directories
28. Yellow-page advertising
29. Bulletin boards and tear pad
30. Your own radio show
31. Your own TV show
32. Online networking
33. FAX
34. Direct response ads
35. Card decks

The Time/Money Marketing Continuum

Generally speaking, the more of your time a marketing activity requires, the less money it costs you, and vice versa.

More Time		More Money
	Public Direct	Money
Networking	Relations Mail	
Less	Referrals Sales Advertising	Less
Money	Promotions	Time

discover in what ways you will most likely be able to reach the people you want to contact with the least amount of effort. What do they read? Where do they gather? What would likely catch their attention?

3. *Never rely on only one method at a time.* Since marketing is an experiment, you could easily run out of money before you find out which method or methods will work best for you. This is the old all-the-eggs-in-one-basket warning. Allocate what money you have to several methods simultaneously

Type of Business

To find the best marketing strategies for your business, identify which type of business you are and whether your primary market is consumers or other businesses. You can use the following examples as a guide. Then review the Measure of Marketing Success Chart at the end of each section of the book.

Service Businesses

Consumer	**Business**
Bed and breakfast	Answering service
Bridal makeup service	Appraisal service
Carpet cleaning/Window washing	Bookkeeping/Accounting service
Day care for children or adults	Computer programmer
Hair styling/Beautician	Equipment repair
Lawn/Landscape maintenance	Information brokering
Personal shopping service	Medical transcription
Plumbing/Electrician	Office organization service
Repairs/Refinishing	Public relations/Publicity
Résumé service	Sales training
Tax preparation service	Translating
Wedding planning	Word processing

to find out which ones produce the best results. If money is limited, don't forget your other major marketing asset: time.

4. Select activities that will complement one another. For example, if you are speaking at a major conference attended by many of your prospective clients, plan to advertise in the conference program guide. Send a news release about your appearance to the newsletter of your appropriate trade associations. Do a mailing inviting key individuals you want to meet to attend your speech. You might send them your news release. Hand out materials at the speech that provide information about your product or service and include some special offer good for the week of the conference.

5. Review the methods your competition is using, and find out what seems to be working best for them. If they continue to use one or two methods

---

Service/Product Businesses

Consumer	Business
Balloon delivery	Architecture/Building contracting
Cabinetmaking	Commercial art
Calligraphy	Computer consulting
Catering	Desktop publishing
Couturier	Import/Export
Gift-basket service	Industrial video production
Guidebook publishing	Instructional design
Home remodeling	Newsletter publishing
Jewelry design	Security consulting/Installation
Landscape design	Temporary help agency
Photography	Trade-show-exhibit building

Product Businesses

Consumer	Business
Antiques	Audio and video training programs
Button sales	Corporate gifts
Crafts	Customized business cards
Embroidery	Customizing cameras
Greeting cards	Customized office furniture
Herb growing	Manufacturing anything
Jewelry making	Office supplies
Knitting supplies	Small clothing manufacturing
Mail-order specialty catalog	Software publishing
Mushroom growing	Toolmaking
Perfume	Wholesale catering
Toy making	Wholesale nursery

---

over others, this is generally a sign that these methods are working. Investigate what people in your field both locally and from other parts of the country are doing.

6. Track the results of your marketing efforts. Set up some way to find out how each new client learned about you. Then invest more of your time and money in those methods that are producing the best results.

How Much Time and Money to Spend on Marketing

Marketing methods vary significantly as to how much time, money, and energy they require. Networking and building a referral program require considerably more time and energy, for example, than using direct mail and advertising, but they cost less.

Marketing methods also vary as to how quickly they will produce business. Going out to get business usually produces results more quickly than getting business to come to you. Writing personal letters, sitting down at the phone or calling on prospective customers door-to-door will probably be quicker than using networking or public relations.

Often new marketers are so averse to selling, however, that they would rather insulate their egos and use methods that take a little more time. Sales promotions are probably their best bet, because they encourage people to buy *immediately!* Here's a comparison of how the various methods addressed in this book relate on the time/money continuum.

The best methods of promoting your business initially will tend to require a relatively low investment of cash in exchange for a greater investment of your personal time and energy.

Until your business is well under way, you should be willing to spend at least 40 percent of your time and money on marketing. This means that since the average home-based business operates sixty-one hours a week, you could spend twenty-four of those just marketing. Even when you get busy, we recommend setting aside at least 20 percent of your time and money for marketing. The wisest time to market is when you have business, because if you wait until a slow time, you may have to endure a long dry spell while your marketing efforts take effect.

As your business grows and you have ample customers to fill your time, you may want to shift the balance of your marketing efforts, selecting approaches that may cost a little more but will save your time for billable activities.

Using This Book to Bring in Business

In the chapters that follow, you will find the basic how-to's you need to implement the lessons learned from successful home-based businesses in order to get business to come to you. The book is designed so that you can read through it either cover-to-cover or topic-by-topic.

Reading through the entire book will provide you with a complete perspective on how you as a self-employed individual can use word-of-mouth marketing, public relations, sales promotions, direct mail, and advertising to turn on and then sustain a steady stream of business. But since people who are on their own often have virtually no time to spare, you can also simply turn to whatever section of the book applies to specific methods you want to undertake and follow the guidelines outlined.

If you spend the time and energy now to do the things described in this book, you will soon find you need to spend less of your time on getting business and more will be spent doing the work you want to do and getting paid for it. Eventually your business will become self-sustaining—that is, it will generate all the business you need. And you'll truly be able to say, "I get almost all of my business from referrals."

Five Ways to Get Business Fast

If you need business right now, here are five stop-gap ideas for getting business fast.

1. **Turn your ex-employer into your client.** Your former employer already knows your capability and has a proven need for it. Often you can negotiate to do on a part-time or contractual basis what you had been doing full-time, or you can negotiate a contract to train your replacement. This can be a viable strategy even if you are going into another type of business.

2. **Subcontract or do overload.** Your competitors can be an excellent source of business. Howard Shenson reports that 11 to 21 percent of new business comes from the competition.

3. **Work as a temporary in the field in which you will be doing business.** Working for a temporary agency can provide invaluable experience and excellent contacts. At the same time it provides a flexible source of immediate income while building your business.

4. **Make them an offer they can't refuse.** Some money beats no money. So identify people who need your skills and make them a special offer so tempting they simply can't say no. But do be sure you at least cover all your costs and ask them to serve as a reference for you in the future.

5. **Volunteer.** Some work beats no work, and work does tend to beget work. There's nothing worse for morale than having no work to do. Volunteer efforts may become paid efforts, and many volunteers turn their experiences into paying contracts or orders. At the very least, volunteer efforts can be a source of experience and references that you can leverage into getting future business.

Should slow times occur, you will be able to act with confidence to turn them around promptly. If you wish, you may be able to hire an outside firm to do your marketing and public relations for you. Having successfully done much of it yourself, you will be able to work with them more knowledgeably and know whether they are doing a professional job for you. But best of all, you will be able to get all the business you need to come to you in the normal course of doing the work you enjoy doing.

C H A P T E R
T W O

■■■■■■■■■■■■■■■■■■■■■■

Networking: Making Contacts
That Turn Into Business

Your mouth is your most valuable marketing tool. In the next three chapters, we will outline how you can consciously set out to use this tool to turn contacts into contracts and clients into more clients.

It has long been said that success lies not so much in *what* you know as in *whom* you know. Implicit in that adage is the belief that this is in some way unfair. In truth, our experience has shown that, in business, knowing *what* you need to know is a given. If you are not qualified to do what you do, if you cannot provide the basic level of competence required, you won't be in business for long, no matter whom you know. However, as a popular television commercial once reminded us, business is about relationships. Knowing people who believe in you and your work, people who will recommend you, refer to you, and open doors for you, can make the difference between a marginal and a stunning success.

But that is actually good news, because it means your success is not tied to how much money you spend on expensive advertising or costly direct-mail campaigns. It means you can use your own mouth to make the business contacts you need to succeed. We no longer live in a society where one's set of acquaintances is fixed by one's family upbringing or education. In today's information-intensive world, you can contact virtually anyone you need to know through *networking*.

No matter how large an enterprise becomes, business is still about relationships. It's done person to person, not company to company, organization to organization, nor agency to agency. Corporations can't hold conversations; people do. Ultimately, business is always a people-to-people proposition. Networking recognizes this fact by using person-to-person contacts to establish relationships that will lead to business. Through networking anyone can become well connected.

Networking is simply a matter of meeting people and developing business with them. In fact, our research with successful home-based businesses shows that it is the single best way to start and build a one- or two-person personal or professional service business.

Recently a friend invited us to lunch with Kathryn Dager, founder and head of Profitivity, a customer-service training firm. Kathryn had been seeking for some time to do a radio show and establish a 900 customer-service number but didn't know whom to contact. We were so excited about Kathryn's work that we immediately introduced her to someone who offered her the opportunity to be the permanent host on a consumer call-in radio show. We were also able to refer her to someone who was eager to set up a 900 telephone number with her for customer complaints.

Today dramatic results like these need not be limited by geography—they take place across the nation and around the world. When information broker John Everett from Dallas, Texas, was looking for someone to co-author a book with him, he looked no further than to his computer. Using a modem and communications software, he tapped into an electronic network and left a message describing the type of person he needed on the Working From Home Forum on CompuServe Information Service. He quickly had a response from writer Libby Crowe from Huntsville, Alabama and together they wrote a successful book entitled *Information for Sale*. To this day they have yet to meet in person; the whole book was written through phone and computer contact.

Another individual visiting the Working From Home Forum left a message announcing a multimillion-dollar contract he had secured in the Soviet Union. He stated that every contact he had made to conclude this deal came from networking through the Forum. In fact, the very book you are reading is the result of networking through that organization.

Many of the most promising business opportunities come about from being in the right place at the right moment—when you encounter serendipitously someone in need of your produce or service. One of our favorite networking stories is about a sales representative who was flying home from a disappointing week in the field. Despite feeling tired, rejected, and discouraged, he decided to strike up a conversation with the person sitting next to him on the plane. To his surprise and delight, this seatmate turned out to be in the market for exactly what he was selling, and the encounter rewarded him with a new five-figure client! While such providence can occur anywhere, you can increase the odds it will happen to you by increasing the number of contacts you make.

Wherever you are in today's global village, when you're in the right place at the right time, things once thought to be difficult become amazingly simple. Networking, in person or electronically, is one of the most certain means for making sure you are in the right place at the right time.

We call networking word-of-mouth marketing because it is a means of building contacts by talking with people about what you do and listening carefully to find out how you might assist each other in doing business. Once a business is up and running, word-of-mouth marketing expands to mean getting referrals from satisfied customers who talk about you.

Think about it. Wouldn't you prefer to do business with someone you know and trust or someone who has come recommended to you by such a person? Most of us would. For this reason it is obvious that the more people you meet, the more likely you are to find people to do business with. And, of course, out of sight is out of mind. So the more you keep in touch with the people you know, the more likely they will turn into customers and clients.

Expanding Your Business Relationships

Every community offers both formal and informal networking opportunities to help you expand your business contacts. Formal methods involve attending gatherings created specifically for the purpose of networking. These organizations arrange meetings and other functions that members attend for a fee for the primary purpose of referring business to one another. One such group is the Small Business Network in Davis, California. Founded by Marilyn Gayler, this group is designed to assist its members build their businesses through communications. Another such group is the Women's Referral Service, which has multiple chapters in several Southern California locations. A perusal of local business journals and professional magazines will often yield the names of similar organizations in your community.

Some formal networking groups are national organizations that have local chapters coast to coast. Sometimes called *leads clubs,* many of these groups meet weekly and limit membership to only one member from each type of business, thereby assuring cooperation instead of competition among members.

Informal networking can be and is done just about everywhere, including churches, social gatherings, sports events, and so forth. Sometimes it happens quite coincidentally, as with the aforementioned sales rep on the airplane. But even informal networking need not be left to chance. Simply identify places and events where your customers and clients gather and arrange to frequent them yourself.

That is exactly what artist Carol Steinberg did to get her career underway. She developed a plan to attend as many shows at local art galleries as possible and was amazed at the business contacts she was able to make. A career

National Networking Organizations

Business Network International
268 South Bucknell Avenue
Claremont, CA 91711
(800) 825-8286

American Business Associates
475 Park Avenue South, 16th Floor
New York, NY 10016
(212) 689-2834

LEADS
279 Carlsbad
Carlsbad, CA 92018
(619) 434-3761
(800) 783-3761

LeTip, International
4907 Marina Blvd., Ste. 13
San Diego, CA 92117
(800) 255-3847

Call or write to find out about the chapter nearest you of any of these organizations or for information on starting a new chapter.

counselor developed a similar plan to build her business. She attended every introductory personal-growth seminar she could, because people who attend such events are often seeking to change careers. During each seminar, she made a point of asking a question or making a comment that allowed her to introduce herself and her work. When a seminar ended, several people invariably approached her to ask about her services.

Both of these networking strategies are ideal for a business that is starting out on a shoestring. The only investment they require is time and the willingness to speak out. And since both these networkers enjoy going to such events anyway, it is a pleasant way to get business.

There are an infinite number of other informal avenues for networking, ranging from joining professional and trade organizations to participating in civic groups such as the Rotary; clubs like the Eagles, the Elks, or the Lions; or such business associations as the Chamber of Commerce. Of course, your competitors may be members of these groups as well, but that's all the more reason for you to build a civic profile.

One way to locate such organizations in your community is through the Gale Research *Encyclopedia of Associations* or Finderbinder and Sourcebook Directories, which list local media sources and clubs, groups, and associations in major metropolitan areas (see Resources).

Networking at Professional, Trade, and Civic Organizations

Any solid program of networking will most likely incorporate both formal and informal methods for turning the people you meet or know casually into customers, colleagues, or business associates. In today's mobile society, communities have grown so large and transient that we no longer have the relationships and knowledge that come with growing up in the same community. We must make a concerted effort to meet and stay in contact with people who can use our products and services. Usually, you won't find yourself building profitable relationships just by joining one organization and showing up at occasional meetings; effective networking requires participation, effort, and some funds. But if it is done well, you can get results without unduly taxing your calendar or your budget. Here are several guidelines for developing an effective networking strategy:

Join one or two key civic, professional, or trade organizations that have members with whom you can do business.   Make sure to join organizations whose members are either potential clients themselves or who serve your potential clients. Networking requires too much time and energy to become involved in groups that only marginally or peripherally address your market. For example, if, like clinical psychologist Art Weingaertner, you do psychological testing, you might want to join an organization whose members include educators or lawyers, both of whom regularly make referrals for such testing. If you sell health and fitness products, you might wish to become active in a sports club or health organization.

Attend meetings regularly.   Simply being listed in a membership directory or showing up at the annual awards dinner is rarely the basis for making lasting business contacts. You need to have repeated interaction to build rapport.

Set aside time on your calendar to attend at least two organizational meetings a week. Sometimes individuals who are newly self-employed worry about spending their time in so-called *socializing*. But remember, business is a social process. If you have joined suitable organizations, there is nothing frivolous about such activity. It is a legitimate marketing task. Also costs involved are business expenses and are tax deductible if you've kept proper records.

Even at times when you have plenty of business, you are best advised to remain active in at least one such group, because generating business takes time. If you wait until you need it, you may face a long dry spell while you get back into circulation and attract more business. And since out of sight is out of mind, you need to be around when someone you talked with six months ago suddenly needs what you offer. If you're not and someone else is, you know who will end up with the business.

Become an active member in the organizations you join by participating in activities, serving on committees, and assuming leadership roles.   The best way to build relationships is to interact frequently with other people in goal-directed activities. Attend meetings to make contacts, but get involved in goal-directed group activities to build relationships. This is why people who work inside a company often build strong and lasting bonds with co-workers. As a self-employed individual, you have to make your own opportunities for such long-term group interaction. If a group has a sports team, a community project, a fundraising event, or a committee structure, participate in their events. You'll earn respect and trust from the team effort and from sharing a history of accomplishment.

And when you participate, don't settle for being a faceless body in the crowd; make a noticeable contribution. Stand out from the crowd by taking a leadership role. Work your way into the power structure of the group and establish yourself as a valued resource. If you ever doubt the rewards of this approach in terms of increased business, just keep track of what happens to someone's business when that person becomes president of a major charity or trade organization. Follow the person's progress over a year or two and you will see why we advise this strategy.

Make a point of meeting new people who attend the organization's functions. Once you become active in a group or organization, don't fall into the rut of talking or sitting only with your buddies. The more people you meet, the more people you can build business relationships with. Balance your time between reconnecting with people you've met before and meeting others. Set a goal to meet at least five new people before you settle in with old friends.

By making this effort to meet new people at every event, you will generate a steady stream of new contacts. Encourage your organization to launch an active membership-recruitment drive or guest program. You might even volunteer to serve as chair of the membership committee or act as a greeter at meetings, welcoming first-time visitors and new members.

Schedule one or two business meals a week to follow up on the new contacts you've made. When you are actively seeking business, we suggest scheduling no less than two business meals each week; have breakfast, lunch, or dinner with people you've met through networking. At these meetings, find out how *you can help them succeed in their business.* Take the time to ask questions, and listen to find out more about what they do. Your interest *in* them is what will make you interesting *to* them and make them more open to learning about what you do.

If your time is temporarily restricted, you can follow up on networking contacts by phone or by mail. For personal and business services, however, these contacts are rarely as fruitful as personal ones. Some small business owners decide to do as Chellie Campbell does. Whenever her bookkeeping service, Cameron Diversified Management, grows to the point that she has no time left for networking and follow-up, she adds new personnel. And her service has grown from a two-person to a six-person business in six years.

Join or start one formal leads club or networking group where members meet weekly for the sole purpose of referring business to each other. Such a group may consist of anywhere from five or six members up to thirty or more, but it works best when each member is in a position to support the business of all others. For example, a technical writer might join a group composed of a graphic designer, a computer trainer, a freelance programmer, and a printer, because each of these members serves clients that need the services of the others. Thus there is no competition, only cooperation, and everyone can win when anyone wins.

Actively refer business regularly to those you meet. This is the most important point of networking. People refer business to those who refer business to them. Make a list of every other business service your clients and customers need. Locate people in each area of need to whom you can make referrals *with confidence.* Establish a relationship with these people whereby you will refer clients to one another. Then, whenever someone you are talking with needs a service in your network, volunteer to put them in touch with the resource you know. You'll become a walking yellow pages. And the more you give, the more you'll get.

Fourteen Tips for Getting Results from Networking

Sometimes people wonder why they don't get better results from their networking efforts. Usually it is because they are not making the most of networking opportunities. Here are fourteen things you can do to improve your track record.

1. Arrive at meetings and group activities at least fifteen minutes early. Always attend the social hour if there is one. This is the time when the most networking occurs. Once the program for the evening has started there is usually little time for networking.

2. Stop waiting for something to happen. Sometimes we hear people complain that they have attended various events hoping to network but "nothing happened." They didn't meet anyone. In probing further, we find these people are approaching the networking event as if they were a *guest,* waiting for someone to introduce them. Instead, approach the event as if you are the *host,* greeting people yourself. Strike up a conversation. If you smile and extend your hand, 99 percent of people you meet will smile back and introduce themselves in return. If not, you can simply add, "I don't think we've met."

3. Introduce yourself with a sixteen-second sizzler. Have you ever been introduced to someone and, when told what the person did, been completely at a loss for words because you had no idea what he or she was talking about? Such conversations end quickly because no one wants to appear foolish and ignorant. Overly technical and professional jargon can put an instant end to any conversation.

To make sure you don't fall into this trap, practice introducing yourself in a simple twenty-five word statement that provokes interest; use terms an eighth grader will understand. For example, instead of saying, "I am the President of LegalTech. I install third-party vendor systems for vertical markets," say something like, "My company is called LegalTech. We help lawyers and their staffs make friends with computers."

Your introduction should include your name and company name if you have one, the market you serve, and how you benefit your clients. For example:

- "I'm Jennifer Greg. I have a twenty-four-hour word-processing service for screenwriters. I specialize in meeting impossible deadlines."
- "I'm Ahman Beals. My company is called the Indoor Forest. We provide large, luscious mushrooms to the finest restaurants in town."
- "I work with people who are tired of dieting. I'm Dr. Nancy Bonus and I have a no-diet, no-exercise weight-loss program called the Bonus Plan."

On the other hand, when you meet someone whose self-description leaves you in the dark, don't back away like everyone else does. Ask the person, "What does that mean exactly?" Not only will you possibly find a hidden prospect by sticking around, you may also make a friend and learn something new as well.

4. Carry a large stack of business cards at all times. Keep them wherever it is most convenient, but always have them handy. An efficient system for exchanging business cards is to keep your cards in one coat pocket and put those you receive in the other.

5. Make sure you get a business card from every appropriate contact you make. Then you can follow up by calling your contacts later. The primary reason for giving out your business card is so you can get the cards of others in return. Never leave it up to those you want to talk with further to contact you—always take the initiative yourself.

6. Have a pen or pencil handy. Make notes on the cards you collect about where and when you met the people, any special information about them, and what you want to discuss with them in the future. Don't rely on memory. Since most business cards are undistinguished, chances are two weeks after getting a card you'll have no idea who gave it to you or why you kept it.

7. Make your name tag work for you. Don't just put your first name on the tag. In large, clear letters, print your full name and the name of your company. Wear your name tag on your right side so people can easily see it when they shake hands with you.

8. Concentrate on talking with one person at a time. Don't rush madly from person to person. If you are too much of a go-getter, people will get up and go—away. Over the long term, you will do far better talking sincerely with a few people.

9. Wrap up conversations graciously. There is a normal conversational cycle; as soon as it winds down of its own accord, feel free to move on. You can conclude conversations with a customary exit line like "I've enjoyed meeting you," "I'll look forward to seeing you at future meetings," or "Let's talk further later." Such exit lines also work well to extricate yourself from a conversation with someone who is talking on endlessly. You might simply comment, "Excuse me, I see someone I need to speak with. It's been a pleasure meeting you."

10. Stay at least fifteen minutes after the event. Don't rush off quickly. Exchange cards with anyone you met earlier, and wrap up any previously unfinished conversations. Take a moment to say good-bye to anyone you met for the first time or haven't seen for a long time.

11. Follow up fast with a phone call. If someone you met expressed specific interest in doing business with you, you need to follow up immediately. Call the next day and arrange a meeting. Send selected materials from your publicity kit for perusal before the meeting. (For more information about putting together such a kit, see *Chapter 6.*)

You probably won't be able to make a follow-up appointment with everyone you have met, but if there might be any future business value from these contacts, you can at least call the next day. First meetings make first impressions, but following up by phone cements them. These short calls can also provide you an opportunity to determine whether an appointment will be a worthwhile investment of your time.

12. Put the names of new contacts on your mailing list. Periodically send news clippings, reports, or announcements you think will be of interest to them. Include information about your recent activities.

13. Always send a thank-you note or place a call of thanks to anyone who sends you a referral. When someone has sent you several referrals or one that's particularly profitable, give that person an additional special acknowledgment. Take the person to dinner, send flowers, or give a party to introduce him or her to others.

14. Don't dissipate your energies. Don't try to cram in every event on the calendar; you will get sick of the effort. Keep your networking calendar to a manageable level. Two well-selected events per week are ample for most full-time businesses. You not only want to make contacts; you want to have time to follow them up and enjoy the process. Pace your networking.

If you follow these basic rules of networking, your business will grow. It may not happen overnight, but you will get results that will show up on your bottom line.

Overcoming the Six Major Misgivings About Networking

Despite the fact most successful home-based businesses are built on word-of-mouth marketing, we have found that networking is frequently overlooked and sometimes even consciously avoided. Instead, too often they try to rely on advertising and direct mail. Unfortunately, most popular service businesses like word processing, bookkeeping, and computer consulting don't find that mass mailings and advertising pay for themselves in immediate business. Prospects have little way of knowing how such a business could serve them better than all the other similar services around. Thus they probably won't even read the print ad or mailing. And as a service business, you don't know how you can truly serve a prospective customer until you talk with them to find out how they are being served now and what unmet needs they have.

That is where networking comes in. Networking gives you a chance to demonstrate personal interest in people and in meeting prospective clients' needs. It gives you the opportunity to find out what they need and show how you can serve them better. In the process, prospects also have a chance to discover that they like you, and most people want to do business with someone they like—particularly when they need a service.

So why is there such resistance to this useful marketing method? According to the *Almanac of American People,* going to a party with strangers is the most frequently mentioned source of anxiety in social situations. We suspect misgivings about networking stem from a similar anxiety about being in an unfamiliar social situation. Here are six common misgivings we hear about networking and a fresh way of looking at them.

1. I don't have time to network.   Everyone would prefer simply to answer phone calls from people who eagerly want his or her service. Networking does take more time than answering the phone and setting up an appointment to do business. But if the phone is quiet, networking is an excellent approach to getting it ringing.

Another way to think about the time you invest in networking is that, as a business person, staying current in your field is mandatory. If you make networking part of an ongoing investment to keep up to date with the latest developments in your specialty, you can save time by marketing while attending business and professional activities. Networking also keeps you from feeling alone and isolated when much of your time is spent working alone.

2. I'm too shy to meet people in a large group.   Shyness is an excuse we make when we feel self-conscious. In fact, we're all shy from to time. What makes a successful networker is not a lack of shyness, but the recognition that everyone else in the room is shy too. Recognizing this fact opens the door to stepping away from your own self-consciousness. If you focus your attention away from yourself and onto helping others feel more at ease, you'll become more at ease, yourself.

Think how you feel when someone you've never met comes up to you with a warm smile, hand outstretched, and says, "Hi! I'm so-and-so. What's your name?" If you are honest with yourself, you'll admit that when this happens you are more than pleased. This works exactly the same way when you go up to others and show genuine interest in them—you make them feel good. And you have a new contact. If that contact doesn't need your kind of product or service, at least you've made a new acquaintance.

If you are still uneasy about approaching people in a group, keep in mind that most people don't reject others outright. Rude people usually go somewhere other than to meetings. Furthermore, the feeling you get when people smile in response to your greetings is contagious and addicting. Every time you do it, it gets a little easier.

3. It takes me away from the office. Some people who work on their own do so because they like to work by themselves, and most people who are out on their own have more than enough to do in the office. Networking usually does mean taking the time to go somewhere. Business, however, is a social activity, an interaction between you and others. That means you can network anywhere you go—at the post office, at a family gathering, at a friend's party, over lunch with a colleague, or while doing business with someone else.

4. I don't like to mix business with pleasure. Many people don't. Yet how often does someone at a social activity ask you, "What do you do?" And how often do you ask others what they do? Every such question is an invitation to network. Most people are eager for a chance to talk about themselves and are flattered when someone else takes an interest.

Many of the largest business deals were first discussed or agreed to on golf courses or tennis courts, over drinks at charity events, or even on church steps after services. Think of networking events as business opportunities as much as they are social functions. The purpose of an organized networking party, for example, is business, however enjoyable that business may be.

This is also true of most clubs, organizational events, and charity functions. Without the business community there would be no cause for many of the social events we take for granted. Recognize the value of these events not only to the community at large but also to the business community in general and to your business in particular. It will take you a long way toward both enjoying the activity and utilizing the contacts you make.

5. But I don't want to be a pushy salesperson. Networking is not selling, much less hard selling; it is a means of enhancing your life with new people who are interesting in and of themselves. It is also an opportunity to find out whether or not the people you meet are potential prospects without the pressure of a sales situation.

We never advise selling while networking—doing so gives networking a bad name. Any selling you do comes later. If it turns out that you meet prospective buyers of your products or services, you won't have any of the problems associated with cold calling. You have already opened the door to a sale by establishing a relationship. Simply give potential customers your card and tell them you'd like to talk with them further in the future. Then get their cards and call them during business hours to set up an appointment in person or by phone.

6. I don't like to sell, period.   Outside of the fact that no business can exist long without *some* selling, networking is actually the ideal way for someone who hates to sell to get business. Through networking, by the time you get to the opportunity to sell, you have already established a relationship and determined an interest in your product or service. You are halfway there before you even start. And even when there is no sale, by simply referring back to how much you have enjoyed meeting the potential client and how you look forward to seeing them again at other events, you've already built the foundation for a continuing relationship. Furthermore, if you keep up your networking activities, you will be able to stay in contact with them naturally without having to make those dreaded follow-up sales calls.

While you can't depend on networking to produce immediate prosperity, compared to other business-getting methods, the financial investment required for networking is lower and the return is surer. Annual dues to most organizations cost far less, for example, than running a single print ad. And if you've selected your networking group well, you know the people you're talking with are already in the market for your products or services. So if you want to get more business, start talking and have a good time while you're at it!

Seven Steps to Creating Your Own Networking Group

If you can't find a formal group that is right for you, you can create your own. Here are some steps you can take:

1. Identify four to six other individuals whose businesses are compatible with yours.   They can be your suppliers, customers, individuals you have done joint ventures with, other professionals whom your existing clients and customers rely upon, or colleagues who do different aspects of what you do.

2. Get to know these individuals well.   The better you know them and how they work before you form your group, the better your group will be. You must be sure you can recommend them highly, because making a bad referral can damage your own reputation, not to mention destroy your newly formed group.

3. Build the group one by one. For a personal networking group to work well, each of the members must get along with and respect the others. Getting a mix of professionals who are compatible can be quite a trick, so we suggest that you begin by meeting with one of the key individuals you have in mind to discuss the idea of forming a networking group. Find out in detail what he or she does, what goals and dreams there are for the business, and how you and others could assist in the achievement of those dreams if you formed a group together. If this individual is interested in building a group with you, discuss and agree upon the purpose, process, time, location, and frequency of your regular meetings.

Then ask this individual to meet informally with you and another of the professionals you have in mind. Also offer to meet with any individual whom he or she would like to have as part of the group. The purpose of these meetings is simply for potential group members to meet one another and get acquainted. If, after this exploratory meeting, you mutually decide that a person would be a good addition to your group, invite that person to join you for the next meeting and present him or her with the idea of joining. Continue the process of exploratory meetings, adding one person at a time—three people meeting with a fourth; four with a fifth, and so on—until you have found as many members as you wish with whom everyone would like to network regularly.

Exploratory meetings can in themselves be excellent networking opportunities even if the individuals involved don't fit well into the group.

4. Look for successful colleagues who are team players. Individuals you include should be reasonably successful already so each can make a contribution to others (unless everyone in your group is just starting on their own). Avoid competitive individuals who have to be the center of attention or want to be sure they are one-up on their peers. Select people who believe there is opportunity in the world for everyone to profit and who enjoy sharing their success with others.

5. Decide collectively how the meetings should be conducted. Since you are forming a group of colleagues and peers, you will want it to develop its own rules and procedures. Essentially you have taken the leadership role in forming the group and giving it enough structure to get underway. By building it person by person, you should now have a compatible group of people who share similar goals and objectives. Getting agreement at this point should be easy.

6. Keep administrative decisions to a bare minimum. There is nothing that will kill a networking group of business professionals quicker than long discussions over time, place, rules, and procedures. Having built the group one by one should prevent this, but if disagreements do arise about details, don't use your meeting time to solve them. You are meeting to assist each other's businesses to flourish. Volunteer to invest time before the next meeting to poll everyone's needs and concerns so a satisfactory solution can be reached quickly at that meeting.

7. Serve as a model by making a lot of referrals. If you want to get referrals from the group, begin the process by providing them yourself. The referrals you make do not always have to be for potential clients. Be forthcoming with whatever information, resources, contacts, leads, or ideas you can provide to help everyone in the group succeed beyond their expectations. If you have chosen the right people, they will be grateful and eager to reciprocate. There are several processes you can use during meetings to assist one another:

- Each person can identify the one thing he or she would like assistance in achieving. The group can brainstorm possible ideas and referrals for each.
- Members can describe how they would like their business to be six months from now, and again everyone can offer ideas, leads, and referrals.
- Each person can bring the name of one individual he or she thinks each other member of the group would benefit from contacting and describe why.
- Group members can share "wins," positive, exciting news and developments in their business. Often these wins uncover possible opportunities for other members of the group. For example, when one member of a networking group announced enthusiastically that she was going to be speaking at a special series of seminars for a local department store, other members quickly requested how they too might become involved. Phone numbers were exchanged and ultimately they were all included in this excellent promotional opportunity.

Finding Mentors and Gatekeepers

Networking is not just a great way to get business; it is also a great way to meet people who can help you get business and tap into a wealth of knowledge, expertise, and support. We believe that success in business is almost always a joint venture. And the more support and assistance you have or can create for yourself, the better. That is where mentors and gatekeepers come in. A mentor is a wise and trusted counselor or influential supporter who takes a personal interest in your success. A gatekeeper is an influential individual who is in a position to open the door to resources and contacts. Both are usually authorities in their field and know everyone who's anyone in that field.

When Leslie Nichols began doing fashion and product promotions for television game shows, she knew she was entering a very competitive field. She started cautiously, doing a show here and there. While doing one of her first shows, "The Price is Right," she met Edward Jubert, vice president of what was at the time Goodson Todman Productions, one of the major television game-show producers, now known as Mark Goodson. Jubert was impressed with how every time Nichols was called, she would go the extra mile to come up with whatever prizes they needed. He became her mentor, encouraging her and opening opportunities for her. "He has been and continues to be the kind of person who says, 'All I want from you is your success'," she says. "When I decided to do this as a full-fledged business with letterhead and all, I called and told him what I was about to do. He said, 'Do it! Do it!'" Twelve years later, Leslie Nichols Promotions is a highly successful firm specializing in fashion promotional placements for film and television. Nichols remains grateful for Jubert's ongoing support.

Virginia Cartwright wanted to be a world-renowned potter, but she knew the odds were not in her favor. Few individuals ever attain recognition as a potter, even if their work is good. Virginia especially admired the work of one prominent potter, so she enrolled in courses he offered in order to study his technique. Gradually, her teacher began to see potential in her work and took a professional interest in her success. He provided her with the opportunity to begin assisting and eventually conducting some of his classes. All the while she continued her studies. Under his tutelage, Virginia set up a studio in her home, and she began exhibiting at art fairs and ultimately in galleries across the country. Over the past ten years she has accomplished what she doubted she could actually do—she is a world-class potter.

Running a small business on your own takes you into difficult and unfamiliar territory. A mentor or gatekeeper can ease your way through these tough, competitive waters. Mentors and gatekeepers open doors for you to knowledge, to skills, to referrals, and to contacts you might otherwise need years to access.

If you have such supporters already, you undoubtedly know and appreciate their value to you. If you aren't enjoying the support of gatekeepers or mentors as yet, the following can serve as your guide to discovering and developing such resources for yourself.

They May Already Be in Your Backyard

Many people who could be of invaluable help to you in building your business are right under your nose. You may have overlooked them, taken them for granted, or simply been too shy to call upon them. Think back over your lifetime.

- Who has taken an interest in you in the past?
- For whom have you done a good job at some time?
- Who has encouraged you in your career or business?
- With whom have you accomplished or overcome something difficult?
- Who helped you through a tough time?
- Whom have you helped through a tough time?
- Whom do you know of that has done what you want to do?

Previous employers, co-workers, distant relatives, friends of the family, teachers, scoutmasters, ministers or rabbis, long-lost friends and comrades from your past—all these people are possible mentors or gatekeepers for you—or may be able to introduce you to people who will be.

Most people are flattered and even honored to be helpful to others as long as those requesting their help are courteous and respectful of their time and sensibilities. Sometimes, if you need considerable assistance or you are asking for advice that others provide as part of their own business, you should offer to pay them for consultation or simply offer to take them to lunch in exchange.

A valuable exercise is to make a list of the people you most admire in your or a related field and find out how you can learn from them. They may provide consultations, do workshops or seminars, or have written a book. They may be willing to allow you to observe, apprentice, or assist them.

When Joanne Gregg decided she wanted to do a particular type of psychotherapy called rebirthing, she turned to her own rebirther, Diane Vaughn, who was one of the best in the field. Joanne asked if she could study with Diane, and Diane agreed. Ultimately she allowed Joanne to assist at her workshops, and as Joanne's skills grew, Diane began referring low-fee clients to her. Thus Joanne was able to begin building a practice of her own.

When Janet Greek was an aspiring television and film director looking for her first opportunity to direct, she learned that a well-known television director whom she greatly admired sometimes allowed new directors to come onto his set to observe. She called him and asked if she could be one of them, and he agreed. After she had been on the set for awhile, he offered her an opportunity to direct an episode. That was the break she needed. She has gone on to become a successful director of many popular television programs.

Such mentor arrangements are commonplace. You simply have to have the courage to ask and the willingness to do what it takes to show off your skills by participating in classes, volunteering, assisting, doing grunt work, handling overload, or taking on work the mentor no longer does.

Networking to Find Gatekeepers

While there are many avenues for reaching the key person or persons you need, networking is probably the most powerful one. If you begin putting the word out through your existing network about the kind of person, information, or expertise you need and follow up on every lead you get, you will be amazed at how quickly you can gain access to anything you require.

Whenever you need a key resource to assist you in getting business, we recommend building a *networking tree*. Turning an 8½-by-11-inch sheet of paper sideways, write along the left-hand side the names of all the people you know who might have some information to help you find what you want. Call them one by one. If they can't help you themselves, ask whether they know of anyone who might and write that person's name and telephone number to the right of the person who referred you. Call these people and repeat the process. Soon you will have a whole tree of possibilities that will lead you to precisely what you need.

Case Study: Networking

Imagine you are starting a magazine for the suburban business district where you live, to be funded primarily by advertising and distributed free throughout the area. You have prepared a sample issue and begun soliciting advertising from appropriate businesses. Although you have been able to sell a few small ads, many business owners are hesitant to spend the money, and they want to know whether Nolan Glazier Real Estate will be advertising in your magazine. Obviously Nolan Glazier is a gatekeeper, as other business owners take the lead from him. You proceed to try to contact him immediately, but your phone calls and letters fail to get past the secretary.

If this sounds all too familiar, here is how networking can get you around this roadblock. After building your networking tree, as described above, you discover that:

- A friend in real estate will invite you to the Board of Realtor's Meeting that Glazier attends each week.
- A neighbor offers to take you to a meeting of the Chamber of Commerce, to which Glazier belongs, and introduce you to him. He also gives you the name of the Chamber program chairman and will recommend that you speak to the group on how to create effective advertising.
- A public-relations specialist you meet at the first Chamber meeting you attend suggests that you write a short article on community spirit for the local newspaper and interview Glazier for the article. She gives you the editor's phone number.
- The free-lance designer who helped you do the sample edition of your magazine thinks her best friend knows Glazier's wife. She gives you her friend's name and when you call, the friend just happens to be going to a party in two weeks that is sponsored by the Community Environment Coalition, which Glazier's wife founded.
- The owner of the shop where you do all your printing thinks Glazier is heading up the committee for the local fire-department fundraiser. He thinks they could use some help.

An Emergency Networking Strategy for Getting Business Fast

If you are new to a community or for some other reason starting from scratch and need business fast, try this approach:

Identify people in a position to know who needs what you offer. Make face-to-face contact with these people for the purpose of gathering information about who is buying what you're selling. Ask permission to use the name of any person you talk with. Then make contact with the companies or people you learn about.

For example, if you're a landscaper, a painter, or a carpenter, you can talk with bankers about who is getting construction loans. You can contact lumber yards about who is buying material for new homes or major remodels. Real-estate people, property managers, and city personnel involved with zoning and planning are all apt to know of leads for you to pursue. If you live in a major city, you might use a publication called *Contacts Influential* that lists firms and the names of specific contacts.

From this wealth of leads, how can you miss eventually making contact with Glazier? And, if by some chance none of them pan out, you can always create more.

This case study also introduces several other valuable marketing tools you can use to meet gatekeepers and mentors to bring in more business: community involvement, volunteering, and sponsorships. Consider the possible benefits of these.

Opening Doors with Community Involvement

Community involvement is a powerful networking tool, because in addition to providing opportunities for getting business, it affords you the opportunity to pay back the community that provides you with the means to build your business. The most successful businesses in every community give something back to the community that gave them support.

First and foremost, the value of community involvement to you is visibility. Becoming active in your community provides visibility in the local media, in the community itself, in a particular segment of the community, and in your marketplace.

The second advantage of community involvement is that whatever publicity you receive from it is almost guaranteed to be positive. Since publicity by definition is uncontrolled, the more you can do to insure a positive slant on the exposure you get, the better.

Third, community involvement puts you in touch with the movers and shakers in your marketplace. Meeting and working with the decision makers in various industries is an ideal route to many gatekeepers not otherwise available to you. And again in the competition for customers, support of a known and respected colleague gives you the edge.

Fourth, gaining a reputation for your community participation increases your credibility in the business marketplace. And finally, community involvement doesn't have to cost a lot of money. There are numerous ways to get involved in your community that fit the budget of even the smallest business. Consider these three:

Volunteering Means Business

Volunteering is the least costly and most rewarding form of community involvement. It is rewarding both in a business sense and in a personal sense. In fact, research has shown that volunteering is good for your health. It seems that one's immune system and mood improve when doing good things for others.

You will find many levels of volunteerism in which you can become involved. Charities abound in virtually any community and they need all the help they can get. Your volunteer labors need not be limited to charities per se, however. Working for a political candidate or popular civic or social issues can be just as effective.

If you are beginning your first foray into volunteering, it is wise to learn something about the organization of your choice by working for at least a short time at the lower, get-your-hands-dirty level. Some of the jobs you can seek out at this entry level of volunteering are:

1. envelope stuffing.
2. decorating.
3. grunt work (that requires muscle).
4. typing.
5. working directly with recipients.

In order to maximize the benefit to your business, however, you will also need to volunteer your efforts at a managerial and fundraising level. This is where you have the opportunity to meet associates and network effectively in the process of providing a needed service to your community. Such activities put you shoulder to shoulder and face to face with many valuable contacts you could not make otherwise. Some of the more high-profile jobs you can work toward are:

1. organizing functions.
2. speaking on behalf of the organization.
3. soliciting cash donations.

4. soliciting service/merchandise donations for auctions.
5. training volunteers or other personnel.

In addition to these generic tasks, volunteering also provides an ideal avenue for sampling, which is one of the best start-up marketing strategies available for self-employed individuals. Sampling involves giving away your product or service in such a way as to show off your particular expertise and stimulate new business. For example, if you are a computer consultant, you might convince a hardware manufacturer or dealer in your area to donate a computer to the organization of your choice. Then you could offer to set it up and install the software needed to do the particular tasks the organization needs. A graphic designer could volunteer to design a program guide, a letterhead, or a wall poster for a fundraising event. A public-relations firm might volunteer to do the publicity for the event; a caterer could agree to cater it; a floral designer could do all the floral displays; and a limousine service might contribute a car and driver to pick up award recipients. The list can go on and on. Whatever your expertise, both business and personal, it can be valuable to most volunteer organizations.

Although you may get greater media attention from volunteering for civic and charitable activities, you can also volunteer samples of your work to trade and professional organizations and to other private commercial ventures. For example, an artist might volunteer to display his or her paintings or sculpture at the opening of a new restaurant, an interior decorator might agree to decorate the office suite of an architectural association, or a list broker might volunteer to supply a list of new businesses for a colleague who consults with start-up businesses. All these activities will provide opportunities for valuable exposure as well as for referrals.

When volunteering in any of these ways, it is appropriate to ask that your name and business cards be on display and that your name be listed as a contributor in menus, program guides, announcements, news releases, or newsletters. And, of course, you can send out your own news releases featuring your involvement.

The major limitation most small businesses face in using volunteering to promote their business is scheduling the demands it makes on their time. We suggest that you allow two to four hours per week for your volunteer activities—not too much to take from your week or weekend, yet enough time to be effective in whatever job you tackle. These hours, however, should not be scheduled as a half-hour here and there. Usually to be productive as both a volunteer and a business person you need to dedicate this time in a block.

In any area or phase of community involvement, remember not to get involved in a particular activity for business reasons alone. Your involvement is personal as well as business. Be sure you are committed to the cause as well as to your own benefit.

Donations: Getting from Giving

There are marketing benefits as well from making a simple cash donation to a charity or organization. The only drawback to this is that to get much recognition for a donation, it has to be a rather large one, probably larger than a small business can afford.

One alternative, however, is to contribute to a charity that is less well known and well supported than the mainstream ones. Or you can donate something unusual or unique that will attract media attention. A landscape designer, for example, donated a rare shade tree to a local nursing home. A balloon-bouquet service donated balloons for a charity event for a hospital— the name of the service artfully woven into the design on the balloons. When a large event was canceled at the last minute, a catering service donated the party with all the trimmings to a local shelter for battered women.

Sometimes the best contributions of this nature arise from something you simply want to see changed. Before the homeless had received much media attention, attorney Kenny Kahn of Santa Monica was watching these people wandering through the park below his window during the holiday season. Suddenly he had a great idea: he decided to pay these individuals to clean up the park. This quickly became popular with the homeless, and others in the office building began contributing too. A program called People Helping People grew out of this idea. Kahn's story was featured in several newspaper and radio stories.

Occasionally the sudden abundance of a windfall will provide the opportunity to make a donation. When Michael Colyar won the $100,000 1990 Star Search comedy award, he donated 50 percent of his winnings to organizations serving the homeless in Venice, California, where Colyar had worked as a street performer on the boardwalk for five years before his victory.

Short of such opportunity, however, various businesses in Dallas, Texas, discovered a way to make a reasonable cash donation do far more for their image than the same amount of money in advertising could have produced. They turned to their local public radio station's biannual pledge drive as a way to make a difference. Instead of making a simple donation, these businesses offered a challenge to the listeners: they offered to make donations ranging from $500 to $2,000, depending on the time of day and the program, if the pledges received over a fixed period of time reached a certain level. Such a donation could double the amount of the pledges during that time. Throughout the specified time period, the businesses involved got what amounted to a continuous radio commercial and some even got the opportunity to participate on the air in the pledge drive itself, while the station benefited from greatly increased subscription rates. So everyone wins from a challenge like this.

Of course, this type of donation will not suit every business. A great deal depends on the demographics of your particular marketplace. For instance, in Dallas the public radio station plays an eclectic array of music, whereas in other markets it may be limited to classical music. This changes the listening audience substantially. However, there are programs that are universal to most affiliates of National Public Radio that may pull listeners who fit the demographic profile of your market.

Another avenue for donations that can be of great value to the small-business person is a televised auction, usually designed to benefit the arts. These auctions are always in need of products and services to sell to the highest bidder as part of a fundraiser for local organizations. Items range over all levels of value. Since these programs run for many hours, they generally have three or four boards of ten items each with values ranging from $10 to $200. A board is scanned with descriptions about three times before it is closed to bids and then is refilled with new items. There may be one or two mini-boards of ten items with values ranging from $200 to $500, which are scanned with descriptions about six times before each board is closed and then refilled. Lastly, the maxi-board may have fifteen to twenty-five items ranging from $500 up. This board is rarely closed. Items are closed and replaced from time to time during the course of the auction.

Obviously, there is a spot for almost any product or service. Any service business could offer a few hours of its service as an item for bidding. The computer consultant, for example, could offer a special consultation for home or business of one or two hours, a bed-and-breakfast inn could offer a week-end for two.

Even if there is no televised auction in your area, many charities hold an annual fundraising auction. Donating to these auctions also gets you an invitation to the function at which the auction is held. Such events are excellent routes to meeting gatekeepers or key people in your community.

You can also make a donation offer as part of a special advertising campaign. For example, Les Trois Petit Cochons, a maker of superb patés, terrines, and other delicacies in New York, donates a flat amount on all full loaves of paté or terrine sold during the Christmas season to the Coalition for the Homeless. They simply sent a letter to their current customers and any prospects on their mailing list explaining how a portion of every sale will be donated to the Coalition. You could do something similar in your marketplace for your favorite cause. It might be the one thing that makes a customer decide to buy from you.

Sponsorships

Sponsoring community activities and events need not be as expensive as you might think. It is not necessary to sponsor an entire event such as a golf tournament or a marathon. You can, for example, sponsor one runner in a charity race or a booth at a community health fair or environmental exposition.

Financial planner Gordon Curry from Northern British Columbia prides himself on using innovative marketing strategies. Noticing that the local stock-car races were drawing large crowds but that racers were struggling to get sponsors for their cars, he offered to sponsor a car for one of the races. He paid only $50 and in return had his name and company name printed on the trunk of the car. Because the spectators sit looking down on the track, everyone watching the race saw his name again and again as the car raced around the track. And much to his surprise, the car he sponsored won the race, so his name was also prominently displayed on the victory lap! He picked up three sales from this exposure and netted a total of $935.

There are many such opportunities to sponsor worthy causes. You can sponsor a showing for a struggling artist, fund a trip for the local high-school wrestling team, or support the school's marching band. You can sponsor a local soccer or little-league baseball team. All these events present public-relations opportunities as well, because local newspapers and even TV news programs often do features on this type of community activity.

And you don't have to do these activities alone. Fundraising and other sponsored events offer opportunities for you to approach people who otherwise might be out of your immediate circle or whom you might be uncomfortable approaching on your own behalf.

Chapter 1 discussed how getting business to come to you occurs along a time/money continuum: the more money you have to spend, the less time you personally have to put into marketing. Networking is a high-time, low-money marketing strategy. If you need business right away, it's not your best strategy.

Networking is like planting a garden; you don't get to harvest the crop until you've planted, watered, and nurtured the seeds through the growing season. With networking, however, you never know ahead of time how long the growing season will be. You could get a major client on your first foray, or it could be months before your efforts pay off.

The adage "a watched pot never boils" applies directly to networking. If your attention is always on when you will get your next referral or contact, you may overlook the best opportunities and you'll most certainly find networking a frustrating and unrewarding process. After all, what seedling can grow to maturity if the farmer is always digging it up to see how it's doing?

If you have a good product or service that the people you are networking with need, time is on your side. As long as you are networking with people who need and can afford to buy what you have to offer, you can relax and continue participating wholeheartedly. The investment you make in time and energy will bear fruit, probably more abundantly than you imagined.

CHAPTER
THREE

■ ■

Getting Referrals: Business That Generates Business

Howard L. Shenson, known as the consultant's consultant, claims that the creative professional practitioner should be able to derive 80 percent or more of his or her new business from referrals, follow-up, or add-on business from existing clients.

Once you are able to do this, you have a self-sustaining business. And that is the goal of all people who venture out on their own: to be so well-established that the business they have produces all the business they need. Once your business is self-sustaining, you are free to concentrate your time primarily on developing your craft, whether it involves creating products or services, expanding your business, or launching a new venture. All your networking, promotions, advertising, and direct mail—all of your marketing efforts—should be focused toward ultimately attaining the goal of becoming self-sustaining.

Most of the businesses they polled in a *Venture Magazine* survey relied heavily on word-of-mouth referrals from business associates in purchasing professional business services: 44 percent chose a lawyer by word of mouth; 45 percent, an accountant; 45 percent, an advertising agency; 42 percent, a business consultant; and 42 percent, a marketing firm. And it is a safe bet that this percentage would hold consistently for consultants and most service businesses.

Developing a Self-Sustaining Referral Business

A common misunderstanding about business is that if you do a good job with your product or service the referrals will come automatically. Sometimes this happens, but not usually. Typically a self-sustaining business is the result of a concerted effort to build referral momentum. Essentially this effort is a matter of priming the pump. Pump away at your marketing efforts long enough and hard enough, and the referral business ultimately begins flowing in. Then you can ease up on the pump—at least temporarily.

Referral business doesn't just happen. Even after producing excellent results year after year, you still may get very few referrals unless you are in a high-demand business. If, however, you concentrate specifically on ways to prime the referral pump, you can speed up or even jump-start the referral process. Once free-lancers or small-business owners learn how to develop and generate referrals purposefully, they begin coming in. The product or service is the same; what is changed is how these people go about turning the business they have into more business.

You can never take referrals for granted. Another common myth is that once your business becomes self-sustaining, it will remain so. Occasionally it does, and of course that is what we would all prefer. Many things can interrupt a well-established, steady flow customers, however. The market can change, making what you offer less in demand. Your client base can change, and clients may begin seeking features you don't provide. Technology can change, rendering your service obsolete. Key personnel who purchase from you may leave the company. Your competition may undercut your prices.

Keeping a consistent referral-generating effort underway will enable you to pick up on such changes quickly. By responding to them immediately with necessary adjustments and additional marketing activities, you can often short-circuit any drastic drop in your business. In fact, as a small or home-based business, the relative ease with which you can respond quickly to keep pace with the marketplace is one of your strongest assets. Large businesses usually can't redirect their efforts on a dime, but you probably can—if you attend to your referral network. Well attended, it will do a masterful job of reconnaissance for you.

Three Referral Strategies

1. Getting Clients and Customers to Refer Others to You

Your most reliable source of business is your existing client base. Your clients can speak more effectively than any other medium about why someone else should buy what you have to offer; they know better than anyone what you can do. Approached properly, they can become a walking, talking sales force for you. Here is how you can get them to do that:

Make sure that every experience customers have with your business is positive. Although word-of-mouth marketing is not something you can control directly, what people say about you—positive or negative—results from your customers' contacts with you, your personnel, and your product or service. Thus if you want referrals, "The customer is always right."

On the average, a satisfied customer will tell three people about his or her positive experience over a month period. And on the average, an unhappy customer will tell seven people of a bad experience within one week. So while realistically it may be impossible for everyone to have only positive experiences with you and your business, that should be the goal toward which you strive. Always provide the very best quality you can, and if anything goes wrong on your end, be willing to accept full responsibility and do what it takes to make it right. Stand behind your product or service.

If there is a problem, fix it fast.   Of course, many of the problems that develop in a business are beyond your control. Your child gets sick; a supplier or subcontractor does not deliver on schedule; a file or bill gets lost. These, however, are your problems, not your customers'. If you want customers to make referrals, you must rectify any problem to the customer's satisfaction. The good news is that customers are just like all of us. We all know about Murphy's Law—that if anything can go wrong, it will. Often it is your handling of problems that creates your most loyal and dedicated customers.

You probably can think of times when someone lost your business due to a shortsighted desire to be right or to save a little money. We know of a decorator who lost thousands of dollars in future business and referrals because she wouldn't offer to pay a few hundred dollars to cover the cost when a fabric she recommended cracked after only a few months of wear. A free-lance writer lost thousands of dollars of work and suffered a lot of negative word of mouth when she turned a project back incomplete when a larger project came her way. Worst of all, when the person who referred her the business heard what happened, the free-lancer's name went from the referral list to the *never, never* list.

In the first case, eating the loss and in the second, turning down other work or at least seeing to it that the first project was complete, would have paid for itself over and over again. The same holds true for problems that are clearly caused by your customers. Perhaps they change their mind or forget to tell you something critical to your task. Or maybe they're unhappy about their bill. Think how grateful and appreciative you have been when others have gone out of their way to make a last-minute change or adjustment for you as a result of your own oversight. Such goodwill can't be bought.

So while you can't let customers walk all over you, you must find amicable ways to resolve any misunderstandings or conflicts. When no amicable solution can be found, let a lawyer, business manager, or collection agency be the bad guy for you. Their efforts, however, should always be the last resort, and ideally they will simply open the door for you to enter once again as the good guy who is willing to work things out.

Make customers so happy they want to go out and shout about it. Nothing sells like results. Whenever possible, don't just leave customers feeling positive, leave them feeling ecstatic! A customer who is thrilled can't stop telling others about how great you are. And whenever such customers hear of someone else who has a need for your service or product, they can't wait to suggest you.

Often this involves honing your skills and going the extra mile to exceed your customers' expectations. When editor Sherry Glanville left her job to free-lance, she found business to be frighteningly slow. One small publisher told her they wouldn't hire her themselves but would recommend her to an author who they thought needed editorial help. The author didn't think her book needed editing, so she was willing to pay only a low hourly fee for cursory copy editing. Sherry took the job, but as she got into the project she could see that the book needed major surgery. Instead of trying to back out or talk the author into more money, she decided to do the best job she could and several weeks later turned over a beautifully completed manuscript.

The author was overjoyed! Her book now read like a masterpiece. She was so grateful that her check was double the amount agreed upon. She has gone on to write additional books and always hires Sherry. Of course, she also recommends Sherry to all other authors she meets who are seeking editors, and the publisher has referred Sherry to others as well.

Although every extra effort will not produce such dramatic results, the results are cumulative. In business, it is true that the more you give, the more you get.

Let your clients know you want referrals. Often clients do not realize that they can provide you with valued referrals. And even when they do, according to Howard Shenson, they often won't refer without some sign or gesture from you. Therefore, while you never want to beg, pressure, or imply an obligation to refer, it is important that you convey to your clients that your business is based on referrals by saying something like, "I get most of my business by referrals. It's the best way I know to spread the word about what I do, so your recommendations are important to me."

Fill them in on how and when to refer. Some individuals who are perfectly happy to refer may not do so simply because they don't know when or how to go about it. Some professionals actually prepare a "When to Refer" or "When Someone Needs Me" sheet that spells out how to recognize when someone needs their service.

One way to do this is to write an article for a local newspaper, magazine, or newsletter entitled "How to Know When You Need. . . ." Then have reprints made up of the article and give them away to customers; send them in the mail with bills or have them sitting out in your office for people to read or take while they wait. A public-relations specialist might write an article called "When You Need PR"; a psychologist might write "When Does a Child Need Professional Help through the Trauma of Divorce?"

Be sure to provide easy opportunities for people to provide you with names of potential customers or clients. Use gift certificates or special-offer coupons that they can fill out for you to send to others whom they think might be interested. Such a certificate might have a blank line that you can fill out in longhand, noting that the person who recommended your service thought the recipient might enjoy it. Or you can ask for names to include on your mailing list or let the recipient know you are willing to receive or make calls. Also make sure everyone you work with has your phone number and address. Using an imprinted giveaway can come in handy for this purpose.

Listen for and act on referral flags. Many times clients will actually mention situations that we call referral flags. You have heard them yourself when someone has said, "I have a friend who . . ." or "So-and-so tried something like this but. . . ." Sometimes we let these signals go by or simply assume that a referral is going to follow. Usually, however, nothing will develop unless you pick up on a flag and take the initiative to suggest the next step. Listen carefully for such referral flags and offer to help by saying something like, "Perhaps I could be of help to them" or "I could probably help them with that." Then proceed to suggest a next step such as, "I would be glad to call them," "I would be glad to send them our brochure," or "I would love to invite them to our free introductory session." Since your customers are busy and likely to forget your offer, arrange, when possible, to be the one to make the contact.

Provide an advantage for making referrals. Offer an incentive in the way of discounts, gift certificates, and specials to those who refer new customers to you. This is a common practice among many businesses. A seminar leader could offer discounted enrollments when someone brings a friend or a free second audit of the course with the referral of two other enrollees.

Norm Dominquez has built his Phoenix mobile-communications company by generating referrals. He offers his customers credit on their account for free service when they refer someone who becomes a new customer. He calls this "cheap marketing," and fully 80 percent of his business comes from customer referals.

Optometrist Dr. Michael Levin of Pacific Palisades, California sends his clients a letter (shown on the following page) to inform them of his appealing incentive for referrals.

Get frequent feedback. To make sure you aren't getting negative word of mouth, convey in person, on a sign, or in your written product information, that customer satisfaction is important to you and that you want to know about any complaints. For example, a sign in our local car wash reads, "If you aren't satisfied with the job, we aren't either. Let us know and we'll take your car through again."

Research shows the majority of dissatisfied customers never report their dissatisfaction. They do, however, feel free to express their unhappiness to others. The designer we mentioned earlier who lost thousands of dollars of additional business by not offering to pay for damaged fabric never knew

Sample Referral Request Letter

Dear Mrs. Sarah Edwards,

Since I began recommending ACUVUE Disposable Contact Lenses to my patients, I've discovered that ACUVUE patients are the most enthusiastic contact lens wearers in my practice. And if you love your lenses as much as my other ACUVUE patients, I'm sure you are already recommending them to your family and friends.

In order for you to share the advantages of ACUVUE, I've enclosed three certificates for free ACUVUE lenses that you can pass along to others. Simply fill in your name and theirs and have them call my office for an appointment. If ACUVUE is right for them, I'll give them a free pair to wear for a trial period.

And to thank you, I'll give you a FREE ACUVUE multipack for every person you refer to me who becomes a Contact Lens patient in my practice.

Thank you in advance for sharing your enthusiasm for ACUVUE and confidence in me—with people important to you. You can be assured that I'll provide them with the same quality of service that you have come to expect from me. I look forward to meeting them and introducing them to ACUVUE.

Sincerely,

Dr. Michael I. Levin

---

what she had lost. The person who told us about the incident had been too embarrassed to bring the issue up with the designer.

One way to avoid this is to offer guaranteed satisfaction on your products or service. Another is to use feedback forms or to ask directly whether someone is satisfied. A time-management consultant was doing a two-day program for a large government agency. He felt the project was going well but noticed a less-than-enthusiastic response from the project director. He wisely picked up on this body language and asked the director how she felt the program was going. Although at first she said everything was fine, when the consultant emphasized how much he wanted to meet his clients' specific needs, she told him about several things she felt needed to be changed. He was more than happy to comply. Without such a diligent approach, he would have finished the day, collected his fee, and never known his clients were less than satisfied. By correcting midstream, the project was a success and the consultant was invited back to conduct future programs.

Whenever someone who has been a regular client suddenly stops doing business with you, take the time to contact him or her and find out why. This will give you a chance to repair any broken fences or simply let your clients know you are thinking of them.

2. Networking Through Your Clients' Networks

In addition to getting referrals directly from your clients and customers, you can also tap into their referral networks. For example, if you have a book-keeping service, each of your clients probably uses an attorney who makes referrals from time to time to bookkeepers. Similarly, you occasionally have access to people who need an attorney. Such contacts can be mutually benefi-cial. Here are some ideas for making the most of these opportunities:

Find out the names of professionals and other services your clients recom-mend to others. Professional-practice consultant Gene Call recommends that professionals create a special referral-intake form requesting clients to list the names, addresses, and phone numbers of the other major professionals they use (such as doctors, lawyers, and accountants). While such an approach will not work for everyone, most businesses can find some way to connect with the other professionals, suppliers, and business services their clients rely on. This can be as simple as mentioning that you occasionally have clients who need a certain kind of product or service and asking whether they have someone they recommend.

Build bridges. Call and establish contact with the other businesses whose names you get from clients. Do not ask for business or referrals; this would most likely appear presumptuous or imply that you are desperate for business. Anyone appearing too hungry inadvertently raises the question as to why they don't have more business. Instead, call to find out two things: more information about what the business is and when and how you can refer clients to them. If they are interested in networking with you, they will inquire about your services as well. Unless the person is a crucial gatekeeper, don't waste your time with a contact who isn't responsive to your offer. Look for others who are eager to network.

Always ask how your clients and customers heard about you. Often the referral will be from someone else with whom your client is doing business. Not only does this help you track the results of your marketing efforts, it also enables you to thank those who are sending you business and gives you the opportunity to meet and network further with these new colleagues.

Let your work speak for itself by making sure it's visible. Often referral sources are hesitant to refer to someone they don't know well. If, however, they have heard about you or read about you in local media, they will have more confidence in you, knowing that others have recognized your talents and abilities. Such exposure is one of the primary benefits of a solid public-relations effort. For more information on how to increase the visibility of your product or service, see chapters 5 through 8. Also, any materials you send out should convey an image that engenders confidence in your ability. See Chap-ter 4 for how to create a business image that will help you sell yourself.

Of course, no matter what you offer, if people cannot in good conscience recommend you, your product, or your service, they will not do so. Therefore, again it is your responsibility to make sure that your product or service not only accomplishes the purpose it is designed for, but that it does it better than your competitors. If you cannot do it better, do it cheaper. If you cannot do it better or cheaper, you had better be the only one providing it and it had better be something essential.

Emphasize your niche, your unique expertise. The more generally you describe your business, the more difficult it is for others to know how to refer people to you. Suppose you meet two dentists, one of whom tells you she works with anyone who has teeth and the other, that he specializes in seeing patients who have dental anxieties. To which dentist will you be more likely to go to or refer? Or perhaps you meet two professional speakers, one who says he speaks on any motivational topic and the other, that he talks on how to save money on business travel. Or you meet two chiropractors, one of whom describes himself as holistic practitioner, while the other says she specializes in treating women with PMS-related problems.

In order to make a referral, most people need some hook to hang you on in their minds. Once they get your hook, you will be someone who comes to mind when there is a need for what you do. People have very specific needs; thus they want very specific referrals. A bookkeeper who specializes in serving doctors' offices, for example, and is recognized for having designed special systems for medical-patient tracking will find it easier to get referrals than someone who does general bookkeeping. A psychotherapist who specializes in treating adolescents with drug problems is more likely to get referrals than one who works with children of all ages.

Build an image of yourself as a knowledgeable leader in your field. The more you can do to build your reputation as a leader in a given speciality, the easier it will be for others to turn to you. Establish yourself as a source of the latest information in your specialty, someone who knows the meaning of the latest trends and developments and is advancing the state of your field. Usually this will require that you do more than read your trade journals.

You can, for example, conduct informal surveys or polls, advance your own theories, and write articles or even books on your work. Send copies of relevant news clippings and summaries of survey results to your referral sources. Always be ready and willing to provide key information and act as a clearinghouse for giving excellent referrals. With such a reputation, you will be the one people call when they need any resource in your area of expertise. That means business is just around the corner.

Another way to have influence among your peers is to know people in other fields. Research has shown that professionals take advice from the people in their field who have widespread contacts outside the field. By joining networking and civic organizations, you can become a center of influence.

Be a promoter, mentor, or gatekeeper for others. Those who help others succeed will reap even greater success. Take every opportunity you can to promote those who can be of help to you, and help people who are just starting out in fields related to yours. Often you can even feel comfortable supporting your competitors' success, because, as Howard Shenson reports, between 11 and 21 percent of new business in many fields comes from the competition. They refer business out when they are too busy, need to subcontract, or get calls for areas of business outside their own.

3. Using Letters of Reference and Endorsements

Often satisfied clients and customers will tell you how pleased they are with your product or service, how much it has helped them, or what outstanding results they have had as a result of your business. This is an excellent time to

---

Eight Tips for Boosting Referrals

1. Build your own mailing list of all past and present clients and other referral sources.
2. Send a mailing to everyone on your list monthly or at least quarterly: a newsletter, copies of news clippings or articles, announcements of speeches or TV or radio appearances you will be making, information on new products or services, and special offers.
3. Keep your mailing list up to date with a database management system or professional-contact management software program such as *Act!* by Contact Software International. Be sure to purge outdated names regularly.
4. Be positive and enthusiastic about your business. Your enthusiasm will be contagious and will generate business. People like to do business with others who make them feel confident, positive, and optimistic.
5. Build a glowing reputation. Be prompt, reliable, ethical, polite, and competent. Never accept work you are not qualified to do; refer it to someone else.
6. Include an information-request card on your brochures, newsletters, and other mailings so people can make additional contact with you easily.
7. Always send a thank-you note immediately to everyone who provides you with a referral. Express your gratitude to those who are especially helpful by sending appropriate gifts of appreciation.
8. Follow the 80/20 rule, which states that 20 percent of any effort will usually produce 80 percent of the results. This will undoubtedly be true of your referral base. Invest your time, energy, and money in the 20 percent of individuals, organizations, and activities that provide you with the best response.

---

ask for their help. Ask whether they would be willing to serve as a reference or assist you by putting their thoughts in writing. Usually they will be delighted to do what they can.

Endorsements or thank-you letters build credibility. They offer written proof that what you say in your proposals or brochures is true. In fact, they make excellent additions to a proposal or brochure. There are two examples on the next page of how powerful quotes can be when used in a brochure or direct-mail piece.

When clients are willing to provide such an endorsement (and it is permissible to solicit one), make it easy for them. Don't expect them to take the time to compose it and mail it to you themselves; people tend to get instant writer's block or to delay writing. Instead, ask whether they would be willing to dictate a few comments to you on the phone about what your product or service has done for them. Jot down what they say, edit it for grammar and style, and read it back to them for their approval. Once the brochure is printed, send all people you have quoted a copy along with a note of appreciation. Should you need to have an actual letter of endorsement for a publicity kit or proposal package, another alternative is to mail these people a copy of what they have said on the phone and ask them return it to you on their own stationery.

Often prospective clients will ask for the names of others you have worked with. Satisfied clients can be of enormous help to you by serving as a reference for prospective clients and customers. Start building a list of such references as soon as you can and have their telephone numbers handy to give out as needed. Even when you know that someone will be glad to serve as a reference, however, always call to request permission, and from that point forward, call to let the person know when someone will be calling. No one should ever be surprised to receive a reference call.

Three Referral Taboos

1. **Never focus on your need for business.** Focus on how you benefit others. Present yourself as successful and competent. Build mutually satisfying business relationships in which everyone wins.
2. **Never dump a lot of promotional materials on referral sources.** Do not mail or drop by with a pile of your brochures, cards, or newsletters unless a person requests these resources or there is some particular opportunity for him or her to use them, such as an open house or seminar. This is a waste of your money and time and is aggravating to those who must do something with the materials, which usually end up being thrown away.
3. **Never speak poorly of a competitor or client.** Whoever is listening can only wonder whether they will be next.

The purpose of everything else you will learn in this book is esentially to assist you in reaching the point at which your business can survive and thrive on referrals alone. Public relations can help because it gives you added credibility and visibility; promotions can help because they give people an incentive to buy in the first place; and advertising and direct mail can stimulate or increase awareness of your business. But nothing can substitute for a steady source of reliable referrals, which are as close to the security of a paycheck as you can get when you work for yourself. In fact, tried-and-true referral sources are actually more secure than a paycheck, because every single one of them would have to decide to fire you before you'd be out of a job!

CHAPTER
FOUR

■ ■

Word-of-Mouth Multipliers:
Creating a Business Image That Sells Itself

There is a saying that you don't get a second chance to make a first impression. Nowhere is this adage more true than in your business life. Whether you are writing a letter, sending a direct-mail piece, placing an advertisement, making a simple telephone call, or walking into someone's office, you have mere seconds, if that, to make people want to see or hear more. Therefore, it is up to you to create not only a good product or service, but to make sure that your first impression is a positive one.

Whether your first contact is in person or in print, making a positive first impression begins with having a distinctive business identity. The first thing you hope will register in someone's mind is your name or the name of your service, product, or company. Major mass-market manufacturers spend millions on developing what is called *brand identity* for their products. As a small or home business, your business name is your brand identity.

If the people you meet can't remember your name when they need to call you or refer to you, if you don't have any printed materials to follow up with, or if the ones you have give an amateurish, sleazy, or slipshod impression, all your word-of-mouth efforts go down the drain. On the other hand, if when someone needs to reach you, your name pops quickly to mind, and if that person has your card, brochure, or other follow-up materials on hand and they speak well for you, your word-of-mouth efforts will be magnified and will multiply.

The right choice of a name used effectively on all your marketing materials can go a long way toward helping your business sell itself. For example, a Los

Angeles man hit upon a name that, by itself, brought him all the business he needed. He named his hauling company Grunt and Dump and took out an ad in the yellow pages. Something about that name made his company the first people called when they needed to have something hauled. The Starving Students moving-van company has a similar story. Since the rates a moving company could charge were essentially fixed by the state at the time, Starving Students' rates were not appreciably less than others, but somehow their name hit a note that made sense to people looking for help in moving.

While your business may never stand on its name alone, it can and will stand, or fall, on its image, and in this chapter you will see how you can get your business image working to attract business to you. We will demonstrate how everything from the name you choose to the printed materials you send out can multiply and magnifiy all your other marketing efforts.

Choosing a Business Name That Sells

Once you are self-employed, whether you operate as a free-lancer, home business, or independent contractor, you will be operating under some business name, even if it is simply your own. Your business name appears on your letterhead, cards, and stationery. It is the name you list on your business bank account and place on your business license. From a marketing standpoint, however, the name you choose is anything but a formality.

The choice of your company name is the single most important marketing decision you make—and the one with the lowest cost. The name you choose can be an important sales tool and a crucial factor in developing a positive image, or it can be a source of confusion to prospects and even to customers.

Therefore, before launching a marketing effort to get new customers and make yourself more visible, it is wise to examine your company name to determine whether it is a help or a hindrance to you. If you are interested in getting more business, now is a good time to review the effects of your name, because it is far easier to modify or change a name when you are starting out than when you have become better known.

You can put as little or much into a name as you choose, but the choice you make will have a bearing on how hard or easy it will be for you to market your business. For example, how much easier it is for people to respond to and remember a bookkeeping service called "Accuracy Bookkeeping" than the one called "The John D. Callahan Company?" In such a situation, it is not the person who is providing the service that is the important factor; it is the service itself that you would want to promote.

In contrast, suppose you were a well-known hair stylist like Edward Salazar, who has established his reputation through having his own cable-television show. In such a case you might want to name your salon simply "Salazar," because your name is as important in drawing business as the

Five Choices in Naming Your Business

The Owner's Name

Martin Wallach & Associates
Judith August Company
The Silverman Group
Barabas & Covey
Fleming, Ltd.
G.G. Bean, Inc.

PROS: Useful only when you *are* the business, as in a consulting service, or when your reputation makes you a major asset because you are well known in your field.
CONS: Doesn't tell who you are or what you do or what your business has.

The Owner's Name Along with What the Company Does

C.B. Behrman Photography
Karelson Custom Boats
Susan Block's Match-Nite
Clampitt Paper Company
Cahlin/Williams Communications
Jai Josefs, Songwriter

PROS: Lets people know both who you are and what you do. Often used by professionals.
CONS: Does not allow you to expand into other areas or to be specific about how you are unique.

A Name That Communicates the Primary Benefit

Affordable Word Processing
Rent to Own Computers
One-Hour Messenger Service
Guaranteed Room Mate Finder
Day & Night Pest Control
No Mess Chimney Sweep
Safe & Sound Security Patrol

PROS: Your name is an ad, selling your key benefit. Because it's what people want, it's easy to remember and the eye will be attracted to it.
CONS: You've got to live up to your name, and it can limit expansion possibilities.

A Description of the Company's Main Activity

Class Reunions, Inc.
Law Library Management, Inc.
Computer Rents
Notary on Wheels
The Newsletter Factory
Roof Leak Detector Co., Inc.
In Absentia Pet and Plant Care

PROS: Allows you to convey more specifically what your business does in a way that sets you off from all others. It can become a mini-billboard for your company.
CONS: Can limit expansion into other areas.

A Made-Up Name

The ADD Group
Vericomp
Whiskering Heights
ECM Limited Partnership
Profitivity

PROS: Useful when the company is used as an umbrella for several diverse business activities or product lines.
CONS: Doesn't tell who you are or what you do.

service you provide. Or, just in case some people haven't heard of you, you might call your business "Hair Styles by Salazar."

Your company name can have side effects, either positive or negative, that you may not have considered. For instance, imagine you have a greenhouse in your backyard and are growing plants and flowers for sale to the general public. How much would you expect to pay when you shop at a greenhouse with each of the following names:

The Greenery
Stamens & Pistils
Korn's Plants and Flowers
Kathy's Greenhouse

A lot depends on where each of these businesses is located, of course, but most likely the expectation would be that the first two would be selling plants at substantially higher prices than the latter two. That is fine if it reflects the pricing level you have chosen; it's not fine if your name gives the wrong impression to prospective customers about what they can expect.

Certainly for marketing purposes, the more specific you can be about your business, the more easily it will sell itself. And the more the name conveys the benefits you have to offer, the more you will stand out from the others. Consider, for example, these names for a word-processing service:

Britannia Word Publishing Inc.
While-You-Wait Word Processing
Ward Parkway Executive Secretarial
Constance K. Mallory Business Services
Letter Perfect
MoneySavers Office Services
Suzie's Word Processing

Someone with a low budget might be attracted to MoneySavers or Suzie's. Britannia sounds top-of-the-line. Certainly there is an attraction to "perfect" letters. Someone living near Ward Parkway might find that location convenient. If Constance K. Mallory is well known in the community, her name will be appealing, but it is meaningless if no one knows her. If you are in a hurry, While-You-Wait sounds great. Your choice of name can and will appeal to certain types of clients or customers. Therefore, it is wise to make sure it attracts the types you want.

On the other hand, there are times when you don't want a specific company name. For example, your company may involve the efforts of several individuals, or your product or the service line may be such that an individual's name is not appropriate. Or you simply may not want to use your own name. In such a case, an entirely made-up name can be a solution. For example, The ADD Group was made up to stand for its three partners, Abels, Douglas, and Douglas. The software company Vericomp was composed as a combination of *veri,* meaning "truth," and *comp,* referring to computers. Kathryn Dager created the name "Profitivity" for her customer-service training firm because it combined two important benefits of her training, profits and productivity. Each of these names also makes positive subliminal statements without limiting the scope of the products or services the company provides.

There is one caveat in using a business name other than your own proper name: a name you're considering may already be in use and may also be the name of a product or service that is protected by a *trademark* or *service mark.* There can be serious legal consequences of even inadvertently using a name already in use. You may be forced to change your name and have to start rebuilding your identity and, of course, reprinting all your materials. But whether there would be legal consequences or not, using the same name as someone else can be confusing and dilute your marketing efforts.

In most cases, if your business will operate only in your local area (township, city, or county), you are merely required to make a reasonable check to

---

Steps for Creating Your Business Name

1. **Generate a long list of words that describe what you want your business to reflect.** Think of adjectives, time, place, uses, feelings, features, humorous aspects of what you do, images you have about the business, results you produce, and products you offer.

2. **Piece these words together. Play with them.** Consider phonetically pleasing names and words that together make up an acronym.

3. **Review your creations in relation to what you know about the people who would or do buy from you.** Are they more technologically oriented or more people oriented? Do they turn to you because they want expertise or support? Are they at the top, the bottom, or the middle of their field? It is this kind of soft information that enables you to come up with a name with some pizzazz.

4. **Select the best names you have created.** List them on a sheet of paper; and if you have a laser printer and desktop software, experiment with different type styles. Ask twenty-five existing customers or prospects to look over your list and tell you which company they would be most inclined to contact and why.

5. **Make sure the name you select meets most of the following criteria:**
   Easily identifies what you do
   Stands out from the competition
   Is readily remembered
   Is neither too short nor too long
   Is simple to spell and pronounce

Checking Whether A Business Name Is Available to Use

To find out whether someone else is already using the name you are considering:

1. Check the yellow pages and call information for more recent listings.
2. Contact your county courthouse for fictitious name registrations, also referred to as "dba's"—"doing business as."
3. Write to the state office that handles corporate names, usually the Secretary of State, to determine whether someone has reserved or taken the name for corporate use. ·
4. Search a computer database of company names such as the Electronic Yellow Pages, compiled from all the nation's telephone directories.
5. Conduct a trademark search. A trademarks and patents attorney will advise you whether your name is the type that can be registered and will conduct a trademark search for about two hundred dollars. Trademark searches can also be done on the *Trademarkscan* or Thomson & Thomson computer databases. The attorney will check for legally similar names as well as exact duplicates at the federal level and in all fifty states.

determine whether or not it is in use in your trade area. However, if you plan to do any advertising or other promotion outside of your local area, you may have to take further measures to insure your right to use the name.

Should You Change Your Name?

Before starting your marketing efforts, take a look at your company name to see whether it is an asset or a liability in terms of helping you get more business. Have you been having any of the following problems?

1. Customers can never seem to remember the name of your company. It may be too abstract, complex, or unusual.
2. When you introduce yourself with your company name, it doesn't register, or people repeatedly say, "You do what?"
3. People are surprised when they hear your prices. Your company name may imply higher or lower prices than you charge.
4. Your business is constantly being confused with another company with a similar name.

If you consistently encounter any of these problems, you may want to reevaluate your choice of company name. Unless you have spent years building a reputation and therefore have a high name recognition, it is rarely too late to change it.

Instead of actually changing the name, you might simply add a different name. For example, if you don't wish to change the umbrella name for your company but are expanding your product or service line, you can put the new products or services under a different name either as a sister company of your current name or as a subsidiary, depending on your structure. Or without even changing your name, you can make some substantial changes in its recognition power by simply adding a tag line describing what you do. For example, The Bohle Company adds to all its printed material a line that reads "Corporate and Marketing Public Relations." Dr. Nancy Bonus, whose company name is The Bonus Plan, adds "Non-Diet Weight Loss" immediately following or beneath the name. Helen Trent Designs is clarified by "Glorious Interiors"; Lee James is enhanced by "Graphic Designs." In each case, without the name having been changed, what the business does becomes quite clear. The tag line establishes a definable image.

Using a Graphic Image That Sells

A second thing you can do to help your business sell itself is redesign your graphic identity to make your letterhead, cards, and other collateral materials as visually dynamic as possible. Think of every letter you send and every card you hand out as a mini-billboard for your company. How do the materials you're using now stack up? Do your mini-billboards turn any heads?

Having a powerful graphic image is particularly important to companies who sell their products or services to other companies. But whatever business you're in, don't settle for your company name centered on the page in 16-point Helvetica type with the address and phone number placed directly beneath it in black on white paper. Your graphic image needs to be unique. It needs to stand on its own, because often you will not be there when people receiving it get their first impression of your company.

Spend some time looking at the graphic image other businesses have created for themselves. Look through a printer's sample books, which contain many examples of possible designs. Keep a file of the letterheads you receive that impress you. A highly effective graphic image does not need to be expensive. Feel free to experiment with several ideas until you find one that makes your business stand out in the way you want. Most companies change the design of their letterhead several times before settling on one that fully captures the image they wish to create.

In selecting your visual image, keep in mind who your clients or customers are. What do they expect from a business like yours? The creative and unusual? The tried, true, and trusted? The highly professional and classy? A matter-of-fact and down-to-business attitude?

Good Design on a Shoestring

The elements of your graphic image include the design itself, the colors you use, the paper you select, the way the information is laid out, and the typeface you use.

Color choice. If your budget is extremely tight, consider simply using a colored paper stock for your materials, perhaps with a colored ink. A deep burgundy on ivory or gray paper or a deep blue on light-blue or gray looks much more upscale and successful than plain black on white, and it costs very little more.

If you can spend just a little more, think about using two colors of ink. For example, you could keep the same deep burgundy and add black or gray ink on bright white paper or use brown and blue inks on ivory.

Paper choice. The paper you choose for your collateral materials has a great deal more importance than most people realize. After design choice, the choice of paper is the next most important decision you will make in creating a successful business image.

In most instances, your envelope is the first thing people see with your company name on it; the letterhead is the second. And they will not only see it, they will touch and feel it. There have been studies on the various types of letterheads that make it through a secretary's hands to his or her boss. The better quality the paper choice, the more likely it is to make it to the desk you want to reach.

Keep in mind that the difference in cost between an average letterhead stock (what is called a #1 bond with watermark) and a very expensive letterhead stock (100-percent cotton content) is approximately one penny per sheet! That's only $10 per thousand sheets, but it makes a big difference. Your choice depends on the cost of your product or service. But make sure that you use either a watermarked bond, a 25-percent rag bond, or a good fancy-finish text sheet and that your second sheets are the same as the letterhead itself. Photocopy paper for letterhead or second sheets won't do. Envelopes, too, must match letterhead stock.

Typeface selection. Take time to look at typeface books, too, to choose the face that best suits your particular company name. For a high-tech company a sans-serif typeface is usually more appropriate, and there are many such faces to choose from. A designer of country crafts, however, might choose a more calligraphic typeface.

Layout creation. Your next most important design decision concerns the layout of your cards and stationery: the position on the page of each of the several key pieces of information, including your company's name, address, phone number(s), and, if applicable, facsimile number, and any design aspects such as logos, lines, or squares. The way you arrange each of these items on the paper will make a statement about your business, whether you want it to or not. The layout can detract from or assist in creating a strong business image.

Take a look at the samples on the next page. In each pair the same typeface is used; however, in one the information is used strictly as information, while in the other each piece of information is treated as an essential design element. Which in each pair do you think creates the stronger company statement? Which looks more professional and competent? Which does a better job of selling the company name?

Although each of these examples was professionally designed, it is not necessary to hire a designer. Most printers have sample books showing varieties of layouts, and some have low-cost design services. But do invest as much as you can afford in making your design a good one. The investment you make in designing a dynamic visual image for your business will come back to you in referrals and future business.

Whatever layout you choose, be prepared to live with it for a very long time. A company image takes time to create and even more time to change. Also be prepared to use the basic elements of this layout in every piece of printed material you produce, from business cards to presentations packets, invoices to mailing labels.

Using a Logo

If there is no way to make your company name especially distinctive or memorable, you might consider designing, or having designed, a *logo*, which is short for logotype. A logo is a unique typeface and format or graphic design

---

Eight Money-Saving Design Tips

1. Hire someone who is just beginning in the field of graphic design.
2. Use an artist who can design your artwork and layout on a computer.
3. Design your materials yourself with desktop publishing or presentation software, such as *Ventura Publisher* by Xerox.
4. Go to a college with an art department and arrange for a design class to take on designing your materials as a class project.
5. To keep printing costs down, order cards and stationery in quantities of one thousand or more.
6. Get estimates from several printers, because prices will vary substantially.
7. Buy your paper at a self-help paper house for the same price printers can buy it for. Such stores are listed in the yellow pages under paper dealers.
8. Consider using an out-of-state printer through mail order. To find mail-order sources, pick up a free copy of the *Horsetrader*, a tabloid found at paper houses.

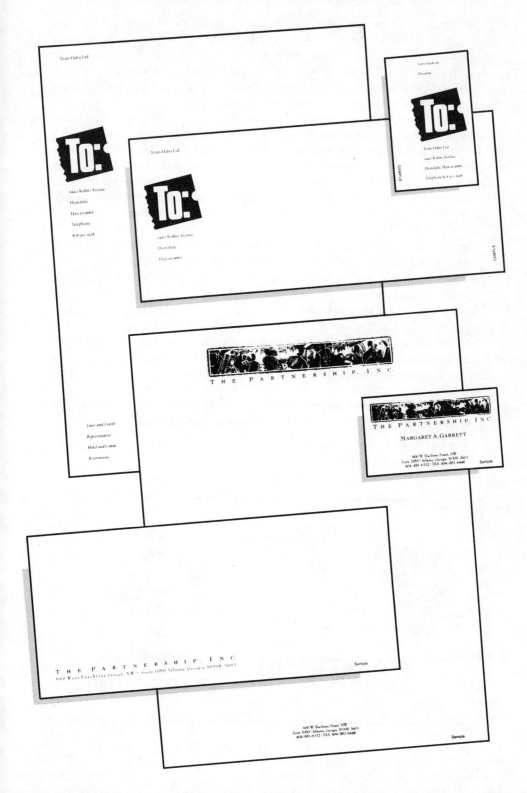

that represents your company or product. It provides an immediate visual identity that distinguishes you from any other business. You can use it in all your advertising and promotion. You can also use it in lieu of or in conjunction with your company name as your proprietary trademark or service mark. As before, however, you must initiate a search, usually through your attorney, to make sure your design is available for use.

If you do intend to use a logo as a central feature of your business image, we suggest that you protect it by registering it with your state, if it provides this protection, or with the United States Patent and Trademark Office so that others cannot use it. Others may want to *borrow* a good logo for their own use. AT&T failed to register their clever yellow pages walking fingers. Now all yellow-pages companies can use the graphic, and many do. Thus people receiving solicitations from these other companies are confused and think they represent AT&T.

In previous years, to secure a trademark or service mark you had to prove to the government that you were already using the mark by submitting examples of labels, tags, and other materials that displayed it. That process made securing a mark an extremely expensive proposition for a new business if ultimately its registration was denied.

Fortunately, the laws were recently changed. All you have to do now is state the intention to use the mark you desire to register. However, because there are other decisions to be made about registration, once again this should be a job for your attorney. You will need to know:

- whether the mark will be used strictly on a local or statewide basis.
- everything involved in maintaining your rights to the registration mark.
- what to do if you choose to register locally now and run into a conflict later when you want to go national.

Securing the advice of an attorney with some expertise in the field of trademarks can save you a lot of grief later on.

Create and Maintain Your Company Identity with Consistency

Once you have made your design choices, follow through with them on your business cards, proposal forms, invoices, and everything else you send out. Keep the same colors, typeface, and layout whenever you print anything to be sent to a prospective or current customer. It is this consistency that reinforces the company image you are working to create. And, since once you have paid for some of these design elements you can use them again and again. Sticking with a consistent graphic can save, instead of cost, you money.

Every piece of advertising, promotional material, or collateral you use should carry your logo, if you have one, or your company name and layout of choice. To facilitate this your printer can prepare what are known as slicks. These special coated sheets have your logo in various sizes printed on them in heavy black ink, which can then be cut out and stripped onto camera-ready art for various advertising and promotional purposes.

Turning Your Business Card Into a Mini-Billboard

A highly effective business card draws a second glance. Then the person receiving it will give you a second look as well. That person may comment on the card itself but more likely will simply be a little more interested in finding out about you and your business. You have risen in his or her esteem. The effective card says, "This is a person of note."

For a home-based business, a business card is far more than a piece of paper with your name, address and phone number on it. It should be thought

---

Your Paper-Based Sales Force

The following is the basic inventory of paper tools you can use for marketing purposes. Not all businesses need every tool.

- Business cards
- Letterhead
- Second sheets
- Envelopes
- Mailing labels
- Invoices
- Flyers and brochures
- Product and price lists
- Newsletters
- Presentation packages
- Product packaging
- Point-of-purchase displays

---

of as one of your most important marketing tools, serving many purposes. It can be a mini-billboard, a brochure, an advertisement, or even an order form. When done well, your card makes an impression, establishes your credibility, and lets you stand out in the memory of those you meet for future business or referrals. On the other hand, when done poorly, it is relegated to a pile of other faceless business cards that ultimately get thrown away. Here are several tips to make your card stand out as a business-generating tool.

1. Keep your card consistent with all your other printed material. Do not be tempted to use one of the standard business-card formats available from your printers; use the same unique graphic image you use for your letterhead. Sometimes a card is simply a letterhead design in miniature. This can save money and yet still be effective.

2. Cover the basics. Any card should contain:

- the name of your business.
- your name and title, if different from the business.
- your logo.
- your address.
- your phone numbers: voice, fax, and modem.

3. Think about the needs of your customers. Arrange the basic elements of your card in accord with what your clients or customers will be looking for. The phone number is what most businesses want their clients to use the card for, so make sure it stands out prominently. We recommend placing it at the bottom right corner in larger type, because we all read from top to bottom and left to right. If for design reasons you choose to place it differently, be sure to make it big enough to spot at a glance.

Include all phone numbers people will be needing. The more types of phone numbers you offer, the more substantial your business appears. Listing your fax is not only a convenience, but also subtly communicates that you are a sophisticated business. You might also list your CompuServe or other online service identification number.

Some home businesses do not want to include their address, and should you work primarily at another site, there may be no need to list an address. (Just be sure it appears prominently on your invoices!) As a general rule, however, we recommend including it if your home is zoned for business and your clients or customers will need to mail anything to you or come to your office. An address communicates respectability, substance, and permanence. If you are hesitant to use your home address or have a zoning problem, consider using a mailing service or the address of your answering service.

When clients must come to your home and the directions are complex, consider printing them on the back of your card. And if your customers are likely to be over forty years old, make sure you select a large enough type size that your card is easy to read.

4. *Go beyond basics.*   Make your card into a mini-brochure by including the key services and benefits of your business. This can be done in the form of a slogan or a series of bullets that highlight your services. If you include a list of services, we find it looks best left-justified with bullets to highlight each item.

Include such information as why someone should patronize you, what you offer, and how your products or services differ from those of the competition. Give people a reason to call you by including special benefits like "calls answered twenty-four hours a day," "same-day service," "no overtime charges," "free estimates," "free consultation," or other features relative to quality and price, ease, comfort, dreams, safety, fun, approval, and status.

If you use your personal name or a business name that doesn't convey

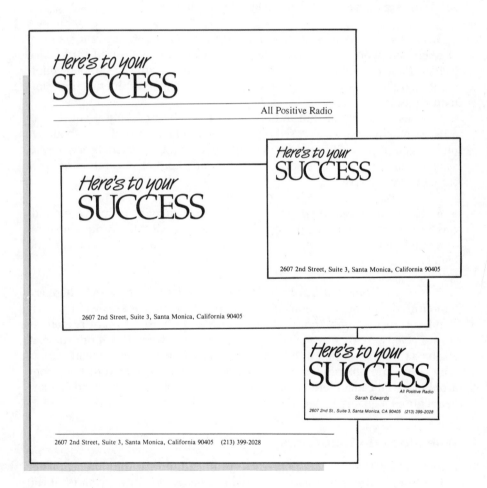

what you do, having a slogan or headline that identifies your field is especially important. Slogans can target your customers and create an image as well as communicate what your business does and its benefits. For example, a slogan could read: "On-site Fax Repair," "Résumé Writing While You Wait," "Catering with Finesse," or "24-hour Emergency Computer Repair Service." Emphasize it with a larger point size and bold lettering.

Incorporating phrases like "In business since 1979" or "11 Years' Experience" communicates substance, as does listing professional certifications or license numbers even if including them is not required by law. When you don't have a logo for your company, consider using the logo of your trade or professional association to enhance your credibility.

An exciting software program for adding your logo or other designs to listings, reports, badges, labels, spreadsheets, or anything else you print is *Dan Brinklin's Page Garden,* published by Bloc Publishing.

5. *Be open to creative alternatives.* Instead of simply using a standard business card, consider a printed Rolodex card or a double-sized card folded in half. Double-sized cards become mini-brochures, with the standard information on the front to be seen at a glance and additional benefits and information inside.

Or consider using an illustration or photograph, especially if you are an artist or photographer or are selling a unique product. A head-and-shoulders photograph of yourself is effective when you're selling a personal service such as counseling or public speaking. Use only one photo or illustration to avoid cluttering your card.

6. *Use a high-quality paper.* Use a minimum 65# (sixty-five-pound) cover stock or .008 (eight-point) card stock, and consider various textures compatible with your staionery such as smooth, textured, fancy finish, and high gloss. Each texture creates a different impression.

7. *Keep it simple and leave plenty of white space.* Even though there is a lot to include on the card, don't clutter it up. White space makes what you say stand out. Include only indispensable words and phrases. Instant readability is your goal, so select a readable typeface that is not complicated or ornate. A business card is too small to mix typefaces, so use two at most; create variety with sizing and boldness of letters and spacing. For most of your body copy avoid using all capital letters, because they make your card less readable and detract from a quality image.

When to Redo Your Cards

If you're not getting a good response to your card, now is the time to change it. If your response is acceptable but could be better, you might wait until you run out of existing cards or need to change a phone number or address. In the meantime, keep a file of the best cards you see. When the times comes to reprint your cards, lay your collection out on a table and select the cards that most attract you. Consider why you like them, and take the opportunity to redesign your cards to incorporate the elements that work best.

Getting Business from Flyers and Brochures

Often potential clients, customers, or referral sources will ask you for some form of written materials. Such materials are almost like a theater ticket: unless you have one, you don't get into the show. Even when using advertising and public-relations efforts that will be described in upcoming sections, you may be asked to send additional written information. Therefore you need to have some written materials describing your background, your company, and your products or services. These materials may take the form of a publicity kit or, more simply, a brochure or flyer.

Although innumerable definitions abound, a flyer or circular is simply a single-page item often printed on only one side with no folds. We are most familiar with flyers geared to the general public and usually distributed en masse, such as on car windshields, on store counters, posted at bus stops and mass-transit stations, and on public bulletin boards. However, flyers and circulars are also used as part of business presentations.

Brochures, on the other hand, are more complex pieces of printed matter. The chief difference between brochures and flyers is that a brochure is usually folded in some way that is intrinsic to the design of the piece. A brochure can be any size and any number of pages printed on both sides and is usually, but not always, printed in two or more colors. A simple brochure might be one 8½" × 11" paper folded in half or thirds, whereas a more informative brochure might have several pages.

Whatever prompts you to produce a brochure or flyer, keep in mind that in addition to the original planned use, once you've gone to the trouble of producing it you will want to leave one at every meeting and every personal call you make. Once you have these materials, you can make them available at every appropriate public place (including the library) and every trade show you attend. You can include one piece in every presentation you make and in every publicity kit you prepare. Both flyers and brochures can also be mailed to prospective clients or customers as a direct-mail piece.

Unfortunately, however, most brochures and flyers get thrown away, often because of poor design. It is better not to have one than to have something that people routinely discard. So if you're going to produce a flyer or brochure, make it worth the effort.

Most of the principles we have discussed in designing a good letterhead and card apply to brochures and flyers as well. Take a look at the example on the next page, produced by Thomas Hudock and his partner, Sean Bickerton, for their company Systemax Computer Graphics. It is a simple, single-page flyer printed in black ink on white paper. In this case the business owners wisely chose to use a coated paper to enhance the crispness of the printed image.

Systemax uses this flyer to generate requests for more information. What Systemax wants is that a reader request a copy of their complete brochure, which, as you see from the copy, is a sample of their work in animated computer graphics. The flyer is sent with a cover letter and reply card, given out at trade shows and again included in the company's customer presentation packet. As you can see, a little imagination and a clear purpose can produce a dynamic piece of collateral for relatively very little money.

Emphasizing benefits in your brochure is crucial. A computer consultant who created a brochure headlined "Custom Applications" was disappointed with the response to it. The problem was that his prospective clients aren't interested in custom applications; they may not even know what the term means. Rather, they are interested in solving their own particular problems.

Knock Their Socks Off!

Dazzle your clients and trounce the competition with the power of television packed into a PC. Shimmering color graphics and eye-catching animation will get your message across and your product seen! Introducing the DiscBrochure™ by Systemax Computer Graphics.

Sock It To'em!

Stand out from the crowd - whatever you're selling, don't blend in with the competition. Flat bar-charts on an overhead projector just don't cut it anymore. Make those bar-charts 3-Dimensional, growing right in front of their eyes with firworks bursting in the background in brilliant color. Animated computer presentations are being used successfully by dozens of the most innovative companies worldwide to win the hearts and minds of new customers.

So, throw out that 20-page proposal and put MOTION in your PROMOTION, PIZZAZZ in your PROSPECTUS, SPARKLE in your SELL...you get the picture and they will too!

See for youself how a custom-designed DiscBrochure™ can help you win clients and TRIPLE the response rate to direct mailings. It's so EASY! Just drop the the postage-paid reply card in the mail and we'll send you a FREE copy of our own Electronic DiscBrochure™.

Make Your Next Presentation a Sockcess!

201 East 87th Street, Suite 24E
New York, NY 10128
(212) 348-8756
CompuServe - 71511,1375

SYSTEMAX
COMPUTER GRAPHICS

The consultant's piece would be much more effective if instead the headline read, "Payroll Driving You Nuts?" or "Inadequate Financial Reports Making You Tear Your Hair Out?" These are problems his potential customers recognize and identify with immediately.

You also need to make sure you know who your customers are so you can address your brochure to their needs. A small software company decided to send out a flyer to dealers and distributors announcing a new product. The owner decided to send a self-mailing card that simply detailed all the functions the program could do on one side and offered a free evaluation copy on the other. Unfortunately, he had given all the important why's for the end user but no reason for the dealer to stock the program. With a little revision, he ended up conveying twice as much information for about the same money using a different focus altogether. Instead of a small postcard, he used a heavyweight paper stock twice the size. The cost for the paper was about the same, as was the press time; even the postage remained the same. This time, however, the headline read "Boost Your Competitive Edge!" giving the dealer something with which to identify—an advantage to him.

The rest of the brochure consisted primarily of two rows of three boxes. The first row was boldly headlined "What Memory Master Can Do for Your Customer," and each of the three boxes contained a major selling point and how the software accomplished it. The second row of boxes was boldly headlined "What Memory Master Can Do for You!" The three boxes beneath that headline read "How You Can Increase Your Sales!," "How You Can Lower Your Costs!," and "How You Can Increase Your Profits!" The balance of the piece gave the necessary information about the package.

The Secret to Business from Brochures and Flyers That Sell

The above stories reveal the secret to creating effective written sales tools. Effective printed materials were created with the customer or client in mind. They open with strong statements, are dynamic and full of excitement, and, most importantly, have one clear purpose—to get prospective customers or clients to take some specific action. The most effective brochures and flyers are designed to elicit one of the following types of actions:

1. an order
2. a request for more information
3. a call for an appointment
4. receptivity to a future contact

Each flyer or brochure should have only one of these purposes as its *raison d'être*. Without making a choice as to which response you want and keeping that goal firmly in mind as you prepare your material, you are simply wasting your money. This does not mean that your printed piece can be used to accomplish only that purpose, but without a clear picture of what you primarily want it to do you will not know how to proceed to make it effective. So here are four ways you can get a flyer or brochure to lead to specific orders, inquiries, appointments, and sales.

1. Tell people how you will solve their problem.   The computer consultant in our case study switched from a weak informational opening to one that hit a potential sore spot. One of the primary reasons an individual chooses to take action is that he or she is in difficulty, facing some sort of problem that you are offering to solve. Don't be afraid of such an approach. Businesses that solve problems succeed; businesses that don't know what the problems are don't get business.

2. Focus on the benefits, not the features, of your product or service. Effective printed material focuses on the customer, not on you or your business. This is often a surprise to people who are new to marketing. The tendency is to elaborate on the features that make your product or service a good one, such as your background, your materials, and your methodology. Effective printed pieces, however, focus on benefits, not features. Benefits are the specific results your product or service provides to your client or customer. They answer the question "What's in it for me?" (WIIFM) The features tell how you accomplish these results. No one is interested in how you get the results until they know what the results are.

For example, people are more interested in knowing that your cookies are low in cholesterol and chemical free than in knowing that they are made with soy oil and purified water. Clients are more interested in the cost savings for using rechargeable laser cartridges than they are in the method of recharging.

3. Make people the offer they can't refuse.   Another primary reason customers choose to take immediate action is because they have been made an offer that is too good to refuse. Many doctors and lawyers who advertise on television these days offer a free consultation. If their service is something you need, how can you turn that down?

The same type of incentive can be offered on a product. When a greeting-card company needed to do something to boost sales during their slowest season, they sent out a brief flyer informing their distributors that for a limited time only they would receive a free dozen cards with every twelve dozen they purchased. Their sales jumped 30 percent during that period each year.

Whatever your business, you can offer something too good to turn down: offer a discount, free sample, free trial period, special guarantee, or special sale for immediate action. Provide a telephone number or even a coupon or reply card on your brochure or flyer. Chapter 9 will go into further detail about how to use such promotions to bring in more business.

4. Show that others value your product or service. Another primary reason people choose to take action is because someone else they trust and admire has done it, too. In other words, they respond to some form of endorsement or testimonial. A caterer, for example, might offer a prospective client a brochure with the prominently displayed statement "As seen on 'AM America,'" or a security consultant might proudly quote a prominent executive who reports that "This program stopped our security leaks!"

Each of these endorsements adds credibility to the statements and offers in the brochure. But if you use endorsements or testimonials, they must be real and they must be specific. No one believes quotes such as "'Great product!'— Mr. B. R., Des Moines, Iowa."

The important thing to remember in preparing a brochure or flyer is that you must know your prospective customers. You must know what motivates them to buy and what motivates them to act. Chapter 14 will discuss in detail how to design materials and write copy that does that.

The Informational Brochure

There is one more purpose for creating a brochure: as reference material. A strictly informational brochure is not appropriate for all businesses; however, it is essential to some. For instance, a bed-and-breakfast inn must have something to mail to those who call requesting information and for guests to take with them and keep as a reference. A custom artisan may wish a general brochure with photographs of some of his or her previous work.

However, even in creating standard reference materials it is important to maintain your company identity—particularly since you do not have the luxury of motivating buyers to take some immediate action. Therefore, you want to be sure your prospects keep your material until they are actually ready to make their decision, so it should be as appealing and as professional as your budget allows.

Printing Product/Service Lists and Price Lists

If you are a single-product or service company, your flyer or brochure can also serve as your product or service list. If, however, you offer several products or services under a single umbrella, a separate service or product list will be useful.

The purpose of a service or product list is purely to inform. It is not a sales piece in the motivational sense, but a sales tool in that it provides your prospective clients with an inventory or listing of what they can buy and, in some cases, at what prices. For example, the computer consultant described earlier who does custom applications could benefit from a service sheet that spells out the variety of applications he is capable of producing, with the appropriate pricing information. A word-processing service that offers a variety of formats will undoubtedly find many uses for a sheet that enumerates these services.

A product or service list can be *static* or *fluid.* A static list is one that remains constant, whereas a fluid list changes regularly due to changes in the nature of your business. If your products or services and your prices change only infrequently, your list is static and should be designed to complement your cards, letterhead, and brochure. It should be typeset and printed on a good-quality paper in matching colors to reinforce your company identity.

If what you offer is sufficiently constant, you may even want to incorporate your product list within your brochure; however, doing so has pros and cons. Within the brochure the list must be done quite simply and provide quick answers to immediate questions, and having only one piece also limits the number of separate contacts you can offer your prospect. Additionally, brochures are less likely to be kept in permanent files than product listings.

When what you offer is subject to frequent changes, your list is a fluid one, such as a caterer's menu, an artist's inventory of current work, an animal breeder's list of current stock for sale, a party planner's current calendar, or a list of special offers. You can print your fluid list using a dot-matrix or laser printer rather than going to the expense of having it typeset. The appropriate business could also have a calligrapher prepare such a list. Typewritten material, unless produced by a good-quality electric machine with no errors or obvious corrections, is not recommended.

No matter how often this list is prepared, it must still reinforce your company identity by following through with color schemes, layout, and the use of your company name and, if you have one, logo. Even the most changeable piece you put out should coordinate with your company identity and enhance your image.

Most important of all, your list must be readable. Of late, copiers have commonly been used to reproduce these pieces. This can be acceptable if the copier's output is better than average; otherwise it is worth a few extra cents to have it run on a small offset press, which will produce clear, readable, and professional-looking materials. Your printer can be very helpful in determining the most cost-effective method of producing each piece of collateral material you need.

Designing Presentation Packets

Whenever you will be sending or handing out several pieces of promotional material at one time, the more professionally these materials are packaged, the more receptive your prospect will be to them. Therefore whether you are sending a proposal, making a sales presentation, simply following up with materials for an interested client, or responding to a request from the media, you may want to place the materials in an attractive folder or envelope of some type. Such a package is referred to as a *presentation packet.*

The goal of packaging your written materials together is to reinforce your company identity. The mailing label needs to match your envelopes, and the cover page of any proposal you submit needs to match your letterhead. Everything should, to the extent possible, be coordinated with your one overriding graphic image. Some rules of thumb for producing these materials—what they should look like and how best to put them together physically—follow.

Designing a Universal Cover Page

A universal cover gives a finished look to any collection of individual pages. Such a page is merely a plain sheet of paper with your company name and logo enlarged as artwork. You can use it for proposals, notebooks, handouts, presentation folders, and so forth, so it is highly versatile and cost effective. Whenever you need to provide information on your products or services, instead of sending an envelope full of single sheets, it is far more professional-looking to present your materials in a binder or folder with a simple cover sheet.

Creating a cover sheet is easy. Cut out one of the larger versions of your company name or logo from a sheet of slicks. You may also include your company address, telephone numbers, fax number, and other information as you see fit. Using a T-square and a ruler, carefully position the type in a graphically interesting spot on a plain piece of white matte board. You can add an optional border from clip-art books or software, or have a printer prepare one. Have the cover sheet printed offset (not photocopied) on a quality paper stock that matches or coordinates with your stationery in texture and color. You now have a cover sheet that can be used for many purposes.

Once it is printed, be sure to get your original artwork back from the printer and keep it scrupulously clean for reuse. Tape a plain piece of paper or acetate to the back of the board and fold it over the front to keep it free of smudges and dust.

Another interesting, though more costly, way of packaging your materials is to create a customized presentation folder. Select a cover stock that matches your letterhead as closely as possible and have your printer create a relatively inexpensive die-cut folder from this stock. Then have your logo or company name printed attractively on the front in an ink that matches all your materials.

In order to make your folder as impressive as possible without exceeding your budget, ask the printer to print a tiny version of your logo or company name all over the inside of your folder using the primary color of your letterhead (other than black). Then have the largest size of your logo printed in reverse on what will be the outside (if you are using an ivory paper stock and a dark red ink, for example, the outside of the folder will be solid red and your logo will be ivory). The result will be a very expensive-looking presentation folder that can be used for brochures, proposals, publicity kits, and other promotional materials. In larger quantities, it will probably cost far less than buying and printing your logo on premade folders.

Packaging and Point-of-Sale Displays for Products

The labels, displays, and packaging on your product will serve as your ultimate sales tool. Whether in a catalog or on the retail shelf, if the package doesn't grab attention in a pleasing way, your product will be overlooked in favor of others nearby that do. Once someone picks up your package, it also must answer any questions they have in making their decision to buy.

Packaging and point-of-sale materials, however, are a very specialized business. If you are involved in a product-based business and your products are geared to the general public, it is wise to consult with professionals on the design and preparation of these materials. Do not leave this to an amateur, even if the amateur is you.

There are, nonetheless, some instances in which you will need to handle aspects of packaging as part of preparing your collateral materials. For example, suppose you have been growing, drying, and supplying herbs and flowers to local craft-supply stores but now are thinking of creating your own potpourris, wreaths, or floral sprays for sale in antique and country-craft stores. You will first need to decide whether your current company identity is appropriate. If it is, much of your task is already complete. You can use your company name as your product name within your local market if your state regulations permit. Then you must decide whether your potpourris will be packaged in cellophane bags, plastic bags, or boxes of some sort. You can approach manufacturers of various boxes and bags to see what stock sizes exist and which size best suits your purposes for both packaging and shipping. The choice of container will dictate the form of closure you will need, such as yarn or ribbon for bags or tape or small stickers for boxes. You will also need to design a simple, pressure-sensitive label with your company name as its framework accompanied by the product name, in this case a specific blend or fragrance. For sprays, wreaths, and the like, you may want a tag with your logo or company name on it.

In the event your company name is not appropriate for your products, you will need to create an entirely new graphic identity for them, following through the same steps discussed previously. For a crafts type of business, the labels and tags for initial samples can be hand lettered. However, you will need to consider printing for most products and higher volumes.

Be sure to investigate and register (as previously discussed) any new product name, company name, brand, or graphic identity to protect yourself and your rights.

Rules of Thumb for Packaging Your Product

Things to keep in mind when working with package designers:

1. *Packaging can make the difference between a sale and a pass-it-by.* Wherever you go, packaging competes for your attention. Most purchase decisions are influenced in some way by packaging.

2. *Big budget isn't essential.* What is essential is knowledge of both your potential customer and the end user. Expensive packages don't necessarily draw; eye-catching, useful, and appropriate packaging does.

3. *Packaging provides a golden sales opportunity.* A good package captivates and educates the buyer. It is one of the best advertising methods available to the manufacturer. When the product inside is more or less indistinguishable from competing products, what will be remembered is the way it was presented.

4. *Packaging can make or break repeat business as well.* A purchasing agent doesn't really care how rolls of facsimile paper are packaged inside the box as long as they are properly protected; however, the machine operator that breaks a fingernail or has to cut away several feet of paper to free a glued edge can and will complain long and loudly.

5. *The packaging on one of your products can affect the purchase of others.* The more your packaging reinforces your company image the more likely a purchaser will associate one product with another, making for additional selling opportunities.

Selecting a Supplier to Produce Your Package

To produce a package that sells, first you need to find a good supplier. If you don't know anyone with a strong recommendation, begin your search with the yellow pages. Package designers or packaging specialists often can be found under their own heading. If none of those listed do what you need, try talking to some printing firms, who should be able to guide you to some other sources. Or try getting referrals from commercial artists to find someone who specializes in package design.

Don't necessarily choose the first supplier you talk to. Ask to see samples of what the suppliers have done, especially if they have worked in your industry. Discuss your ideas and the approach you want to take. Be ready to explain all the tools you plan to use to get your product seen or known by the public including public relations, advertising, or any other selling activity. Be sure to state your package budget clearly and explain that you want a top-notch package within those parameters.

To help the suppliers understand what you need, you can show them some samples of what your competition is using, explaining what you like and dislike about each package. Give them all the important information about your product, including the benefits you want to highlight or explain on the package. Identify your main themes from the general data you need to convey on your package. If you are producing something that people will decide on in the typical five seconds they give an item at the supermarket, limit the points you make to two or three.

Don't settle for a single package idea—request that your supplier come up with several alternative ideas in rough form, and examine each idea in turn without making quick judgments. If you like aspects of more than one concept, work with the designers to see whether there is some way to combine the good aspects of each into a single package. Don't accept a design that looks cluttered. Coming up with a perfect package is a trial-and-error process.

Once you have a couple of designs that work for you, have some prototypes or mock-ups made to test with various distributors or prospective customers. Take them into the field and experiment. If you sell through stores, ask permission from the manager to set up a display with the various designs, and ask passing customers to complete a short questionnaire about the designs they see. This is as much to the benefit of the distributor and retailer as it is to you, as it enables you to provide your outlets with merchandise whose packaging will sell the product.

As soon as your package is finished, have it photographed in both black-and-white and color. These package shots are helpful when sending press information or when applying to be included in a catalog.

Display and point-of-sale materials are an extension of your packaging and are geared primarily toward product sales. Selection of display materials,

---

Rules of Thumb for Designing
Product and Point-of-Sale Displays

In addition to considerations of cost, appearance, and reinforcement of company image, the following are important considerations.

1. *Find out if your outlets utilize display materials.* Not all distributors can or will use special displays.
2. *Display materials must suit the space provided by the outlet.* Not all outlets have the same size or type of display space. A counter display is worthless if an outlet has no counter.
3. *Display materials should be easy to erect and use.* The simpler the setup is, the more likely an outlet will be to use it.
4. *Display materials should be reusable or easy to dispose of.* Keep your outlet's convenience in mind when creating materials.
5. *Display materials should neither compete with nor detract from the packaging of the product itself.* You want to sell product, not a pretty display.

whether free-standing or shelf-oriented, requires a complex analysis of your distribution network.

Display and point-of-sale can also be used to great advantage in service businesses. Ask a current client to permit you to place a small display containing your flyers or brochures at his counter or in his waiting room. Some will be happy to help you out. With others you may pay for the privilege, or you might work out an exchange for some of your services.

For example, if you are a software consultant, you may wish to work out an agreement with several local software stores to provide them with a given number of hours of consulting services in exchange for placing your display or point-of-sale materials in public view in their store. Or, if your business is typesetting or desktop publishing, you might pay a local printer with a great deal of traffic a fee to place a special display of your promotional materials on the counter. A nutritionist might request, trade for, or pay for a display of his or her brochures at the reception desk in a dentist's or doctor's office.

To get materials that will do the best job for you, work with a single designer to prepare all display and packaging materials. If the designer you are working with is employed by the packaging production firm, be sure he or she sees all of your other promotional materials and clearly understands the image and identity you are promoting for your product or service and for your company as a whole. Once you have created a package, the rest of your promotional materials should reinforce the visual image your package creates.

Packaging a Service Business

Packaging isn't limited to product-oriented businesses. Movies are commonly referred to as being packaged, a term used for the process of pulling together the idea, the talent, the scriptwriter, and other crew to sell to a studio for production. Financial news speaks frequently of stock deals being packaged, referring to the combination of several services into a single integrated product or service. Services are just as packageable as products.

Although the package you use for a service is not cardboard, it is just as important as the box you use for a product. It consists of the people and service elements involved, and it includes your appearance, telephone presence, dress, and manner, as well as every other aspect of what you offer. If you are a service business, the more professional you and the people who work with your customers are, the better your package. All of your identity materials—letterhead, business cards, brochures, catalogs, price lists, and any other materials you present to the public—are also part of your package. These materials include your proposal forms, invoices, and statements.

The major advantage to packaging a service is that it doesn't have to cost as much as packaging a product. But, as with all packaging, producing less than the best you can afford will exact an expensive toll in lost sales, even if you cannot see the true cost of that loss.

All the materials we have been discussing in these chapters—your collateral materials—represent you when you're not there. Sometimes they precede you. They create a sense of anticipation about who you are and what you do and how much it's worth, and they may result in your getting or not getting an appointment. At other times collateral materials are what you leave behind to serve as reminders to those you have met or as a means of introducing you to others. With quality collateral materials on hand, you are also prepared to make the most of the other marketing methods that follow.

Marketing Technique Measure-of-Success Probability Chart

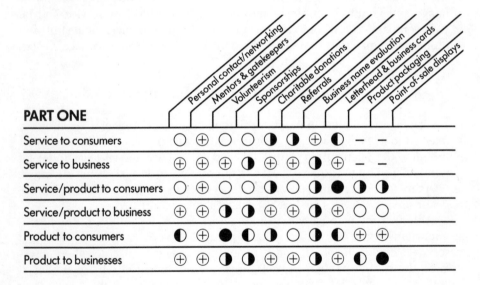

	Greatest probability of success		Less probability of success
⊕	Greatest probability of success	◐	Less probability of success
◑	Good probability of success	●	Least probability of success
○	Medium probability of success	—	Not applicable

PART ONE

	Personal contact/networking	Mentors & gatekeepers	Volunteerism	Sponsorships	Charitable donations	Referrals	Business name evaluation	Letterhead & business cards	Product packaging	Point-of-sale displays
Service to consumers	○	⊕	○	○	◑	◑	⊕	◐	—	—
Service to business	⊕	⊕	⊕	◑	⊕	⊕	◑	⊕	—	—
Service/product to consumers	○	⊕	○	○	◑	○	◑	●	◑	◑
Service/product to business	⊕	⊕	◑	◑	⊕	⊕	◑	⊕	○	○
Product to consumers	◐	⊕	●	◐	◑	○	◑	◐	⊕	⊕
Product to businesses	⊕	⊕	◑	◑	⊕	⊕	◑	⊕	◐	●

*Public Relations: Establishing
a Reputation That Means Business*

CHAPTER
FIVE

■■■■■■■■■■■■■■■■■■■■■■■

Publicity: Your Passport to Recognition

Most people want to do business with someone they know or at least have heard of as having an unblemished reputation. Thus, when you are starting out in a new business, you are confronted with the proverbial chicken-before-the-egg dilemma: you need customers to develop a reputation and you need a reputation to get customers.

So how do you establish the reputation you need? The fastest way out of this dilemma is to give yourself and your business as high a profile as possible. You need to begin making an impression as quickly as you can, so that when people need what you have to offer they will think of you and say, "Oh, yes, I've heard of. . . ."

That's exactly how organizational-development consultant Marilyn Miller was hired to undertake a major citywide project in Malibu, California. As the city began looking for a firm to do the project, person after person suggested Marilyn's name. Then when their representative called her, he said, "You must be the person we need. We keep running into your name wherever we look."

Once you get that kind of presence working for you, getting business can be easy.

How would you like to open the newspaper one morning and find a feature story about you and your company? Or imagine that whenever an article, news feature, or story about your field appears anywhere in print or on radio or television, your views are quoted extensively or your products are mentioned prominently. And suppose that anytime your business undertakes an activity or event that you would like people to know about, the media eagerly announce these happenings?

That's publicity. Next to getting a referral, publicity is the most reliable way to create the reputation necessary to attract business to you. Your reputation is, after all, built on what others say about you. You have undoubtedly read articles featuring businessmen and women in your community and have probably used their services after reading such articles. You also have undoubtedly seen interviews and news stories on television featuring professionals in your community, such as the tax attorney who is interviewed on the local news at tax time, the consultant whose analysis is sought in response to a new technological breakthrough, or the local doctors quoted in the story on advances in plastic surgery. These men and women are enjoying the sweet rewards of publicity. They get so much business from this exposure that many businesses pay thousands of dollars a month to PR firms to make sure that their name gets into these features.

When you read articles or watch news stories such as these, quoting and interviewing experts in your field, you may wonder, as we once did, why you weren't included. After all, aren't you usually just as knowledgeable or interesting as those who were selected? We used to think that when people became good enough at what they do, the media would seek them out. However, even if you are the most outstanding expert or authority or have the best product in the world, if no one knows about it, no one will know to call you to talk about it. So in all but the most unusual of cases, you need to create publicity by your letting the media know about you.

The most direct way to do this is to contact the media yourself, either in person, through your representative, or by mail. A more indirect route is to make sure that the sources to which the media turn for information mention you whenever they are asked for names of people to contact.

In the sense that ultimately publicity generates more publicity, it is a very cost-effective investment over time. Look through the magazine, newsletters, and newspapers you receive each week and notice who is quoted in the many articles you read. Who is featured? Who is interviewed in local newscasts? You will be surprised at all the publicity opportunities that are right under your nose. Here are just a few of examples from a single day's reading:

- Dan Rosenthal, owner of Way-To-Go travel service, was quoted in a *Los Angeles Times* article advising readers how it can pay to carry extra luggage.
- *Inc* magazine did a human-interest blurb on how Jacki Baker, owner of Mother Myricks' ice-cream shop and mail-order candy business, has offered a free ice-cream-and-cake special to encourage children to read more books.
- The *LA Times* announced in its "Save the Date" column that the South Bay Center for Counseling is sponsoring a "Lose Your Blues" benefit.

- "Hot to Shop," another column in the *Times*, responded to a reader inquiry by describing a new product called Wave Webs from Hydro-Fit. Readers were given the 800 number through which they could order these novel gloves for exercising in the water.

- Still another column called "In Brief" announced a nutrition workshop being conducted at a local YWCA by consulting nutritionist Rene Klag.

- A business-section feature on spotting clues to when to sell mutual funds quoted advice from the editors of several different financial newsletters in various parts of the country.

- An *LA Times Magazine* feature called "Rubbed the Right Way" described a variety of massage salons including Nice to Be Kneaded, Massage Masters, and Massage Therapy Center, that specialize in serving executive women.

- The Personal Business section of *Business Week* magazine featured several closet-design firms, such as Hold Everything in California and Perfect Closet in Gross Point Farms, Michigan. They also gave a phone number for requesting a catalog for organizational storage items.

Seemingly simple publicity such as this can produce dramatic results. When Shell and Judy Norris of Chicago opened Class Reunions Inc. to manage college and high-school reunions, they thought it would be a part-time business. But, when the *Wall Street Journal* picked up a story about their service, a flood of calls kept them busy full time almost from the start. Similarly, Dan Cassidy was still in college when he started a computerized

---

Publicity Opportunities

Be quoted or featured in:
Professional and trade papers
Local newspapers
National newspapers
Specialized newsletters
Books in your field
Local, and national magazines

Be interviewed on:
Network television news or
   talk shows
Local and national radio
   news or talk shows
Cable television shows
Public-access television programs
Video text services

Be featured as:
Guest presenter at a special ceremony
Sponsor for civic activities
Contributor to a charitable event
Recipient of a professional or
   civic award

scholarship-matching service. Having few funds for advertising, he arranged for a guest appearance to talk on a local radio station about his new service, and within a week he had received over a hundred calls from eager listeners. Over the years, he has continued to use radio and television talk-show appearances as his primary means of getting business.

Although the response to publicity is not always this dramatic, these stories are illustrative of the benefits to be derived from well-placed public relations.

The Pros and Cons of Publicity

Often such exposure is referred to as free publicity; however, publicity by definition is unpaid, but it usually isn't actually free. Even if you do all such promotion yourself, you must invest considerable time and energy and a certain amount of money to generate publicity. Time and money are involved, for example, in sending materials to the press in the form of a publicity kit, including the cost of printing these materials, paying for the postage, and footing the bill for the mileage involved in traveling to appear for interviews. But recent studies show that small businesses increasingly find that, dollar for dollar, they can have at least as great an impact with PR as with advertising.

However, because publicity is unpaid, you will not have control of exactly what is and is not said about you. The media pride themselves highly on being independent and objective. They will use the segments and comments they choose and will slant them in a the way they choose. Also, sometimes

---

Public Relations

Pros

- Editorial coverage is more highly regarded than advertising.
- Editorial coverage is more credible than advertising.
- Maintaining a high profile within a specialty increases credibility.
- PR can bring you in contact with peers throughout the business community.
- PR activities open doors to mentors and gatekeepers.
- PR coverage is free.
- Whatever you do for and in your community usually comes back to you tenfold.

Cons

- PR can take a considerable investment of time to create.
- PR takes time to produce results.
- You must develop and commit to a long-range plan.
- Because PR is unpaid, it is also out of your control.
- Media will print and broadcast their impression of you, not necessarily the one you want.
- Postage, kits, and materials require financial investment.
- Getting media attention requires skill, knowledge, and creativity.

---

scheduled features or segments are dropped at the last minute when unexpected hard-news events occur. Therefore, when you need to know that specific information will definitely appear or need particular sales-oriented information to be announced, advertising is a better route.

In order to open the door to such valuable publicity opportunities you will need to learn how to use three primary promotional tools: the publicity kit, the news release, and the query letter. This section will provide you with the basics of how to create and use these tools to get your name in the public eye. It will also discuss the public relations advantages of making public appearances, including giving speeches or seminars that attract business.

CHAPTER
SIX

■■■■■■■■■■■■■■■■■■■■■

Building a Publicity Kit to
Introduce Yourself with Fanfare

Whatever stage your business is in, you can benefit from having a basic publicity kit on hand. Even if you don't plan to launch a promotional campaign anytime in the near future, we advise putting together the components for a publicity kit now and maintaining it, because you never know when publicity will tap you on the shoulder unexpectedly, and when it does, you'll want to be ready to respond.

Whenever an opportunity arises to speak before a group, to be interviewed for an article, to appear on radio or television, or to avail yourself of countless other unforeseen chances for exposure, someone will invariably ask quite casually to be sent your publicity kit. And, of course, that person needs it immediately! A publicity kit is like the cover charge you must pay before you can get in to enjoy a popular performer or the password that opens the magic door. The presumption will be that you have one. If you don't, you are likely to be passed over for someone who does.

Whether you use the entire kit or only bits and pieces, a publicity kit is a valuable tool that should be kept up to date and on hand at all times. And the time to build a publicity kit is *now*, not when you need it. It is not something you can easily throw together at the last minute. Done properly, however, the elements of your publicity kit will serve a wide variety of uses in addition to introducing you to the media. Many of the same elements, for example, can be used in presentation folders, sales packets, and correspondence. So creating a kit is a highly cost-effective investment of your time, energy, and money.

The Fundamental Components of a Basic Publicity Kit

1. Your biographical profile
2. A description and history of your business
3. A 5″ × 7″ or 8″ × 10″ black-and-white glossy photo of you
4. A complete description of your service or product (including technical specifications)
5. A sample or black-and-white glossy of your product, if applicable
6. Copies of articles written about you and your company or letters of endorsement from customers or clients
7. A broadcast résumé
8. Feature ideas, story hooks, or a list of questions interviewers can ask that focus on unique aspects of what you do
9. A sample or novelty
10. A newsworthy press release or query letter

Your Biographical Profile

A biographical profile is a brief, thumbnail sketch of your personal résumé with such facts as your accomplishments, career and educational background, and fundamental goals in relation to your company or the particular event you are publicizing. If you can add a pithy or substantive quote, so much the better. And be sure to include reference to previous media attention you have had and any awards or other professional acknowledgment you have received. You should also have a profile of any other key individuals involved in your company or other primary participants in the event you are promoting.

There are several different formats for a profile. You may be advised to use the same format for your profile as you would for a news release, including a headline and date. We advise against this format, however, unless you have a large production budget. We suggest instead that unless you have hired a public relations firm and will therefore be using their logo, you print your profile directly onto your letterhead or on a special abbreviated version of it that includes only your logo. Place your name at the top as the headline or title. This format will allow you to print large quantities of your profile to use for multiple purposes at different times.

Using your letterhead for this and other items in your publicity kit, as we recommend, requires that you have a first-class, professionally designed letterhead, preferably two color. However, since you will be using it for many purposes, you can justify having large quantities printed and keep costs down.

Your profile should not exceed a single page unless there is a compelling reason for it to do so. If it contains more material than you can fit on a single sheet, use the excess material to create ideas for news features.

Company Description and History

Your company description provides a thumbnail sketch of the history of your company. Again use your letterhead, and follow the same one-page format you used for your profile. Your company name should serve as the headline or title. Keep the description simple and to the point; do not overembellish. Stick to the facts, beginning with the year of the company's inception. Cover pertinent data such as the guiding principle behind the business, your primary activities, and general plans for the future. Be sure to include reference to any other publicity the company has received from the media.

Product/Service Description

If you have a narrow or highly technical product line, this sheet will detail your products' specifications. You can title it Fact Sheet or Technical Specifications. Again, you can use your letterhead and follow the same format, using the same design features to match the other pieces in your publicity kit.

If you are promoting a varied product line, this sheet will serve as a sample list of items, each with a few words describing the items as vividly as possible. The amount of detail in the descriptions needs to be enough for a reader to picture what you are talking about without photographs, yet by keeping it short the text will still fit on a single page. However, if it is necessary to use multiple sheets for technical specifications such as benchmark tests on computer hardware, then do so. Here, again, do not use extraneous descriptive adjectives—keep each description as short and to the point as possible.

In describing a broad product line, begin with a short paragraph detailing the focus of your merchandise followed by a sample list of items. For example, Whiskering Heights, a pet gift and supply catalog business based in New York, describes itself as a small company that fully tests each product before including it in its mail-order catalog. Its product listing for a publicity kit might look like the one in the box on page 94. It summarizes a fifty page catalog in a manner sufficient for an editor to determine whether perusal of the catalog itself would be in order.

If your company provides a service, you will need to list or describe each aspect of that service to give the reader a general grasp of what you do and whom you serve. Do not use abbreviations or acronyms with which your reader may be unfamiliar without defining them. If you provide desktop publishing services, for example, your sheet might list: typesetting, layout and design, pasteup, and newsletter preparation. Include any additional services your company provides as well. If, as in this example, you also provide word-processing services or mailing-list management, indicate such services in an equally clear manner.

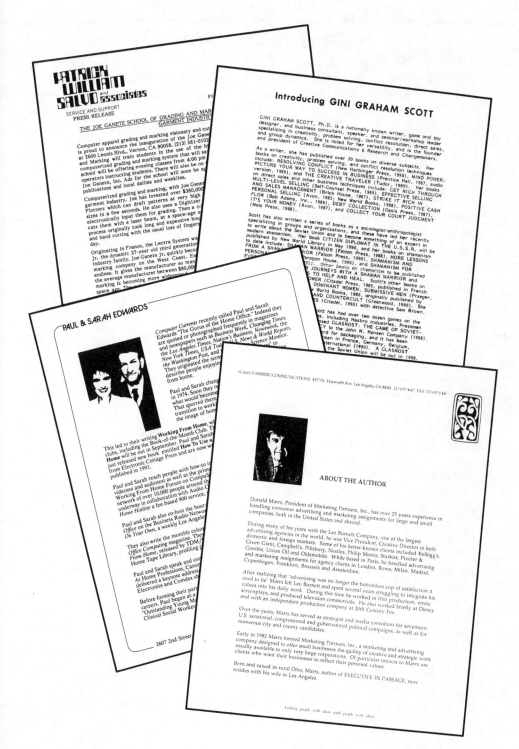

Sample Product Sheet
Whiskering Heights

Whiskering Heights is a small company that provides pet supplies and people products with an animal theme through a specialized mail-order catalog. Our products are personally tested for quality and satisfaction by our experienced and unsurpassed research department: Tori (a golden retriever), Squiggy and Lenny (tabbies of the feline purr-suasion), and our newest addition, Pepsi (a stray cat who adopted us). Our product line includes:

Flea and tick preventives
collars, sprays, and shampoos

Specialty grooming supplies
tearless and conditioning shampoos, brushes, and combs

Puppy training supplies
how-to books, pads, and odor removers

Adult pet supplies
leads, tags, collars, harnesses, and food dishes

Toys
catnip bags, bones, pull toys, squeaky toys, and healthy chews and treats

Owner aids
dental-care kits, pet-food containers, waterers, clean-up aids, and gifts

---

Suppose you provide a single service that is difficult to describe in such a manner. Systemax Computer Graphics based in New York, for example, provides a customized computer animation service. That statement says little or nothing to someone who is not familiar with computer animation, so it is necessary to describe what it is and, if possible, provide either drawings or photographs of sample screen pictures.

Test out your product and service descriptions with a variety of people to be sure your descriptions are understood. After they have read your descriptions, ask these people to tell you what they think you do. You may be amazed to discover that what you thought was clear has left the reader unfamiliar with your field in a fog.

Publicity Photos

We recommend that every publicity kit contain at least one photograph of you or your product. A picture isn't only worth a thousand words; it may be worth thousands of dollars to you. Publicity is one of the most cost-effective marketing methods you can use, and you will increase its effect a hundredfold if it includes a flattering photograph.

People love pictures. Brochures, mailers, newsletters and newspaper articles attract more attention when they include pictures. Think of your own response when you receive a mailer or read an article. Don't you enjoy seeing the writer? Yet unlike entertainers and performers who know all too well the magical power of a photo, businesspeople only rarely have a ready supply of professionally photographed black-and-white glossies on hand.

Suppose you have volunteered to give a speech or workshop for your local trade or professional association and the program director tells you, "If you can send us a picture right away, we'll feature you on the front page of our newsletter." Since you need a minimum of three weeks to have professional photos taken and developed, you have missed a great opportunity unless you have one on hand.

Or you receive a direct-mail solicitation to be listed in a new directory. The offer looks good, so you apply. The listing includes a picture but the application, with photo, must be received within the week. So, since you had no photo handy when the directory came out, instead of having a picture next to your name there is an empty gray square or a stylized directory logo, leaving you wondering whether the listing was really worth the money.

Situations like this used to happen to each of us all too frequently. Not only were we missing these opportunities, it was embarrassing having to apologize for not having a photo. Since it seems that the best publicity opportunities often arise on the spot, have publicity photographs made as soon as possible. Then, when an unexpected publicity opportunity comes along, you will be able to say with confidence, "I'll Fedex you my publicity kit with the photo this afternoon."

The best photograph to include in your kit depends on your particular business and the product or service for which you are trying to gain recognition. We suggest having at least two types of photos on hand: a professional-quality head shot of yourself and either a photo of your product or product line or a candid shot of yourself in action providing your service.

You will actually have many other uses for a head shot. If you speak at a professional association, for example, the program may include pictures of the presenters. If you are receiving an award, the organization will often include a photo in its mailing about the upcoming recipients. If you write a column or article for a publication in your field, you may be asked to send a photo to appear next to your byline. In such cases a formal head shot is expected. (And if it isn't requested, you should ask to have one appear.)

Newsletters, newspapers, and magazines, however, are usually more interested in candid action shots than in a formal head shot, particularly for reviews and feature stories. They may want to see a unique product or capture you engaged in some aspect of what you do. Sometimes they will even send a photographer out to take a picture of you in action. But you will increase the likelihood of a publication using your story or news release by including an intriguing photo.

If your publicity kit is primarily to showcase a single product, a package shot showing off the product is essential. Magazines are likely to require a package shot if they plan to review the product, and it is important for a consumer to be familiar not only with the name of the item but also what it will look like on the shelf. So a software publishing company, for example, should be more interested in showing off its product in publicity shots than in picturing the people who created it. A package shot is also a solution if your product itself does not photograph well, as with a bowl of potpourri or a computer software program.

In the event you are promoting a business with a broad product line, you might consider a group product shot. A photograph of assorted birdhouse designs clearly indicates the breadth of the line. However, don't try to include a sample of every product you make in the photograph. Squeezing everything in will reduce the size of each item substantially, making the photo too busy, and items will be difficult to recognize. Three to five items are probably all you will need to give an idea of the breadth and quality of your product line.

When promoting a service business, the type of photograph to use will depend on the results of the application of your service. For instance, if you design custom wedding gowns, a photograph of a sample gown you've created or a collage of candids showing your gowns is the best way to go. On the other hand, if you are a computer consultant, the important thing to promote is you and your skill. Therefore, you might choose to include a photograph of yourself working with a client and a computer. If you are a landscape designer, you might use a picture of yourself sitting on a forklift with a huge ornamental bush on it or working at a garden bench in front of a beautifully manicured lawn.

Although 4″ × 5″ is an accepted size, most people still prefer 5″ × 7″ or the older standard of 8″ × 10″; the smaller size can get lost in a comprehensive publicity kit. If newspapers and newsletters comprise the bulk of your contacts, black-and-white photos are preferred; magazines, however often require color. It does not cost much more when having your photo taken to ask the photographer to take a roll of color shots, so you can have a supply of both on hand.

Each photograph you send out must be captioned with a brief typed description. This is particularly helpful for product photos and action shots. There are two methods of applying the caption: affix it to the center back of the photograph, which requires the editor to flip the photo over to see the caption, or taped to drop from the bottom of the photo. The former is neater, but some editors find the latter more convenient. It never hurts to check with some of the editors to whom you will be sending photos to see which caption style they prefer. Another alternative is to have the caption printed on the photo, although this adds to your cost.

We have used our pictures for every one of these activities at one time or another, although when we had them taken we never dreamed so many photo opportunities would arise. Here are a few tips for making the most of such opportunities:

Fifteen Uses for a Publicity Photo

To determine whether having publicity photos taken is truly worth the time, energy, and money, we consulted Los Angeles photographer Charles Behrman and discovered at least fifteen reasons why you should have a photo on hand:

1. To accompany an article you have written
2. To accompany articles written about you
3. To include on brochures and other promotional pieces
4. As part of your advertising
5. To send out with a news release
6. To accompany your listing in professional- and trade-association membership directories
7. To use on cards, letterhead, or postcards
8. To accompany announcements about you or your business in club and organizational newsletters
9. As part of direct-mail pieces about your product or service
10. To include on invitations to open houses or promotional events you hold
11. To use on a book cover or jacket
12. To mount on an easel to promote your speeches, workshops, or booths at trade shows or conferences
13. To use as a portfolio of your work or to show you in action working with clients
14. To include in a scrapbook on your company's history
15. To be included in a program guide with a description of workshops or speeches you give

1. Have your photographs professionally done. It costs more but is worth it. The muddy, fuzzy pictures frequently found in directories and newsletters are often from snapshots someone submitted because they didn't have a professional picture.

2. Select a photographer with an excellent track record. Get referrals from satisfied colleagues in your field. Always review the photographers' portfolios and decide whether they shoot the type of look you want for yourself and your business. Since you can expect to invest several hundred dollars in your pictures, you don't want to have to do them over again. Worse than having to select between the lesser of two evils is having to select among a proof sheet of fifty evils. Good photographers provide proof sheets with a variety of great shots among which you may choose.

ROBERT FULGHUM
Author of ALL I REALLY NEED TO KNOW I
LEARNED IN KINDERGARTEN; Uncommon Thoughts
on Common Things (Villard Books, October 1988)

Photo Credit: Dan Lamont, 1987

SANDRA McKNIGHT

Publicity photos can be 4″ × 5″, 5″ × 7″, or 8″ × 10″ headshots, package shots, or informal shots. Including your name on the photo is desirable.

3. Have your hair and make-up done professionally. It is worth the investment for both men and women. Some photographers provide these services themselves or make other professionals available to you; alternatively you can hire your own. The best photos may look as though they were snapped at an impromptu moment, but they weren't. Every detail of hair, clothing, make-up, lighting, and shading was attended to before the spontaneous moment was captured. When deciding on your hair and make-up styles, avoid trendy looks that will be dated quickly.

4. Expect to spend several hours with your photographer. Having a good photograph taken is like going to your accountant at tax time: it always takes longer than you expect. Don't expect to be in and out in an hour—set aside a morning or afternoon.

5. Order a decent supply of black-and-white glossies to have on hand. Don't think twenty-five or more is too many. You don't want to have to wait to order prints when a publicity opportunity arises, and ordering in quantity is cheaper. Glossies need to be crisp and clear with a high contrast between the background and your image.

6. When including your photo on printed publicity materials, always have a quality screen made. A photograph has continuous tones that blend into one another, but printing processes can reproduce only discrete lines or dots. Therefore anytime you print your photo on a brochure, bio, product sheet, or any other printed material, you need to have it screened into a halftone prior to printing so that it will reproduce properly. The halftone needs to match the type of paper and printing process you will be using so that the photos don't look grainy or fuzzy. Behrman recommends a 65-dots-per-inch screen for newsprint quality, a 135-dots-per-inch screen for magazine quality, and a 150-dots-per-inch screen for brochure quality. The printer you choose will make a big difference too. As a rule, he says, "Print houses can provide 50-percent higher resolution than instant print shops."

7. Keep your photo up to date. You want people to recognize that you are the person in the photo, so take new photos to account for major changes in your appearance: hairstyle and color, clothing style, and age.

Once you have good photographs on hand, not only can you respond to publicity opportunities more readily, but you also are apt to create more opportunities for their use.

Copies of Articles, Testimonials, or Endorsements

As soon as possible, your publicity kit should include clippings of recent articles that have been written about you. These clippings are evidence to the media that there is in fact already an interest in you, your work, and your company. This is an example of how publicity begets more publicity. You can build a collection of media coverage by starting with articles from whatever small publications you can get to write about you and advancing toward coverage in the most influential publications in your field or community.

Until you have built a history of news articles for your kit, you can include letters of endorsement from clients and colleagues who have had dramatic results or experiences related to your product or service.

A collection of good articles may take you some time to build, but if you keep at it, you will eventually have an excellent set. You might begin your efforts by agreeing to speak for free to a local civic group and requesting that they do an article about you in their newsletter to promote the program. Or you might send a news release to your small community newspaper, as such papers are often looking for newsworthy articles about local residents.

Once some articles have been written about you, we recommend photocopying them on a high-quality paper such as Hammermill Laser Print, Mead Moistrite X02, or Union Camp's York Town. If you have a copy shop do your printing, ask them to show you a test copy before proceeding with your order. You can get great-looking copies from newsprint (even with pictures) from top-notch, well-maintained machines. Find a copy shop that produces the quality you seek. Initially use one sheet for each article. As your print portfolio grows, however, copy news clippings on both the back and front. If you are printing on both sides of the page, investigate some of the #1 offset sheets.

Your Broadcast Resumé

Just as the print media wants to see what has been written about you, the broadcast media wants to know what radio and television shows you have appeared on as evidence that you can handle a broadcast situation without freezing up. Therefore you will want to begin building a similar history for these appearances.

Again, it may take you a while to build this résumé. Should you not yet have any broadcast experience, listing your public-appearance experience might be equally acceptable. You can include any professional presentations you have made, courses or seminars you have offered, or speeches or other public appearances where you in essence held the spotlight.

Your broadcast résumé should include a listing with dates, times, and sources of all such events, programs, and stations where you have appeared.

Feature Ideas, Story Hooks, and Interview Questions

The purpose of each of these sheets is to spark the imagination of the writers, editors, and producers with a list of ideas for intriguing in-depth feature stories or tantalizing interview questions that will motivate them to include you in upcoming articles or programming.

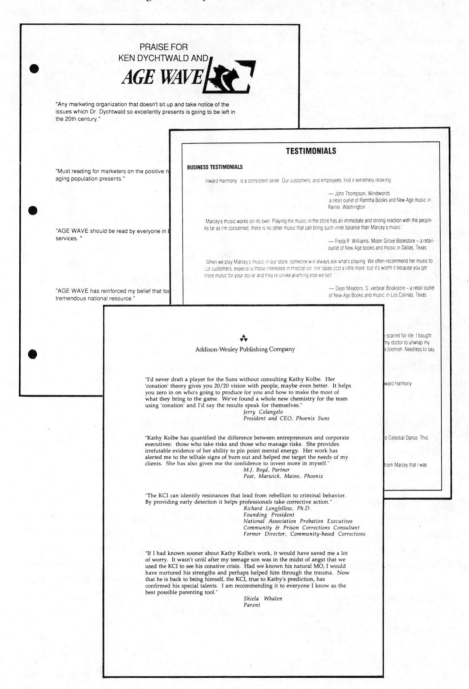

Letters of endorsement or testimonials like these from clients, customers, and colleagues dramatize the results from your product or service.

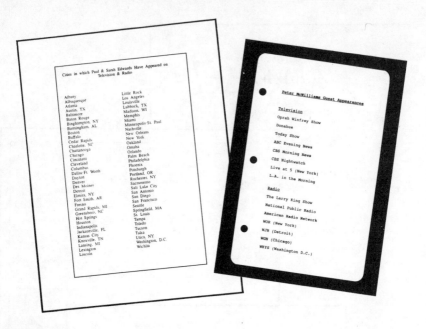

Sample Broadcast Résumés. One of these broadcast résumés lists cities appeared in; the other mentions specific shows. Notice how Peter McWilliams's résumé is done on notebook paper to tie in with the back-to-school theme of his media kit.

For example, perhaps a custom wedding-gown designer creates his gowns from combining modern fabrics with antique laces. His travels around the world acquiring rare laces might be of interest to a newspaper travel section, a travel magazine, or an antiques publication that does features on unusual collections. Another publication might be interested in a feature story on the history of lace. Or what about a wild story on what people wore to the world's wackiest wedding? All of these are possible items to include on this sheet.

A professional organizer might suggest ideas for an article or interview on how to bring order to a teenager's room, organizing the closet no one dares to open, or reclaiming your attic, basement, or garage. A financial consultant might propose articles on how couples who budget argue less about money, the one investment that can set your children up financially for life, or the last remaining tax shelter for the middle class.

Boil your ideas down to simple eye-catching headlines or a list of attention-grabbing questions. Be sure these ideas are of true potential interest to the readers, listeners, or viewers of the media to whom you will be sending your kit, not just of interest to you. If possible, include a photograph that complements the headline. For example, make-up artist Sally Van Swearington, who specializes in doing make-up for bridal parties, might create a sheet listing headlines and descriptions such as these:

SPECIAL FACES FOR SPECIAL OCCASIONS

An eye-catching photo layout of brides-to-be with before and after shots that show the different looks make-up can achieve.

PUTTING YOUR BEST FACE FORWARD

A step-by-step guide on make-up application for brides, indicating how much is too much, what the camera will show, and how to bring out the most of one's features.

THE SPRING BRIDE BLOSSOMS

A detailed discussion of the new colors being used this season for weddings, from attendants' gowns to flowers and accessories, and how to coordinate the bride's make-up to match her choice of colors and enhance her natural beauty.

A Sample or Novelty

Whenever possible, include some type of sample or novelty in your kit to further attract attention and create a fascination with your message. The lacemaker might include a small swatch of inexpensive but attractive and unusual lace. The wedding-dress designer could include a small booklet of tips for a memorable wedding or on how to select a dress style that suits you. The professional organizer could enclose a brightly colored button that says "I'm Organized for Success!" (This would be especially effective if the name of her business were Organized for Success and the button colors matched her logo.)

One of the most clever publicity kits we have received was from author Peter McWilliams and seminar leader John Roger. In promoting their book *Life 101,* in which they write about "everything you wish you'd learned about life in school but didn't," McWilliams and Roger filled their publicity kit with crayons and such other timeless elementary-school supplies as wide-margin paper and flash cards. Similarly, when Michael Cahlin created The Chocolate Software Company, he included a real chocolate disk that editors and writers could snack on while reading the news release about his new computer software that features hundreds of recipes for chocolate lovers. Of course, he sent it out right before the Christmas holidays.

To stimulate ideas for clever novelties, flip through a catalog from one or more of the advertising premium companies like Stucker Specialty Advertising of Chatsworth, California. Although an actual sample of what you do is best, it is not always possible or cost effective to provide one. Be sure that any novelty you use instead creates interest in you and your work. (See Chapter 9 for more information about selecting and using novelty giveaways.)

Packaging Your Publicity Kit

Once you have assembled all the elements for your kit, you need to decide how to package them. Even when someone has requested your kit or you have notified someone that you are sending one, you still need to make sure

QUESTIONS FOR DR. DYCHTWALD

author of

1) What exactly is the "age wave?"

2) What is causing this major demographic shift?

3) How does the age wave differ from other trends one reads about?

4) How will this age wave affect our lives?

5) What about marriage and family? How will the age wave affect traditional family structure?

SUSAN FASSBERG COMMUNICATIONS 431½ N. Hayworth Ave. Los Angeles, CA 90048 213 655 3647 FAX 213 655 1060

SAMPLE QUESTIONS for DONALD MARRS

1. You had achieved the "American dream" — money, success, power... You were at the top of your career, had a lovely family, an active social calendar... What was wrong?

2. What does "EXECUTIVE IN PASSAGE" mean? Why did you write this book?

3. Is the personal crisis you describe only an "executive disease"?

4. Isn't EXECUTIVE IN PASSAGE about a mid-life crisis? Or is there something significantly different about your experience?

5. Does trying to align one's values with one's work always result in such difficulties? You went through some very trying times...

6. Why does it seem so difficult for so many people to find a career that brings true contentment? What is the greatest obstacle to building a life based on one's inner dream?

7. How would you advise people who are experiencing the kind of dilemma you're talking about? And what about helping a friend or loved-one who's having trouble?

Sample Question Sheets. Having a list of sample questions like these in your publicity kit provides editors and programmers with ideas for ways to include you in their features or programs and makes interviews easier for feature writers and hosts.

your publicity materials get the attention of the editor, writer, producer, or meeting planner once they arrive. Can you imagine receiving up to 2,000 pieces of mail across your desk every day, all asking you to consider them and take action? That's what many of the people who will be receiving your kit are faced with, so how you present your publicity kit is just as important as what is in it.

In order to get attention for their clients, major public relations firms have been known to use every tactic in the book and more to make sure they stand out from the crowd. From sending a release in a gift-wrapped box to having pop-up art that jumps out when the kit is opened to announcing the arrival of the release with the sound of trumpets, there isn't much that hasn't been tried. One of the most notorious (and least popular with the editors who receive them) is the release that is folded with glitter that sprinkles everywhere when the package is opened.

As a small or home-based business you probably don't have the budget to use such tactics, which in any event are not necessary, and can backfire. What is necessary, instead, is a professional look and a personal touch.

The Presentation Folder

A professional look can be achieved by using an attractive presentation folder to enclose all the materials in your kit. There are at least three options for creating such a folder; you can have your logo, picture, or slogan printed onto a folder; you can have your logo printed on adhesive labels and place them on standard die-cut folders, which are available in most office-supply stores or mail-order catalogs; or, if you have written a book, workbook, or other published work with a title similar to what you are featuring in your kit, you can have extra copies of the cover made at the time of printing and affix these to the covers of standard die-cut folders.

Make sure that the folders you select are color coordinated to complement and enhance the color of your logo and stationery. Carry out your color scheme throughout the entire kit, and make sure you have plenty of copies of all materials on hand.

Opportunities for media exposure often require immediate action, because reporters and writers are working on deadlines—they may need your material "yesterday." Have multiple copies of your publicity materials made up and collated so when an opportunity for publicity arises, you will not have to drop everything and rush out to pull them together. Make up enough copies to cover a three-month period. Somewhere between ten and fifty sets should be adequate. Each time you have additional sets duplicated, add copies of your most recent articles or testimonials and drop less current ones unless they are from very prominent publications.

We advise against actually assembling the kits, however, until you need them, because those elements of the kit to include depend on the person to whom and the purpose for which you are sending each kit. In assembling

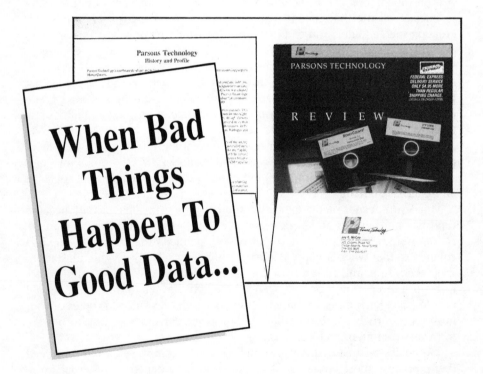

Examples of presentation folders.

your kit, simply insert the appropriate elements in the right-hand pocket of the folder with a cover letter, news release, or query letter on top, including your business card in the pre-cut slot. Place any photographs and articles about you in the left-hand pocket. Then place the folder, news release, and cover or query letter in a large envelope imprinted or clearly marked with your company logo or other identification. A printed mailing label is perfectly acceptable. Then, type the name and address of the person or organization to whom you are sending the kit.

Now that you have all the publicity materials you need on hand, do not wait passively for someone to request them. As you will discover in the next chapter, with a well-conceived news release or query letter you can take the initiative to generate publicity for yourself.

CHAPTER
SEVEN

■■■■■■■■■■■■■■■■■■■■■■■

Getting Media Attention

With the above elements of your publicity kit on hand, you are fully prepared to respond effectively to any media opportunity. However, chances are, that no such opportunity will simply happen along at first. In the beginning you have to prime the pump to get the publicity flowing. Then, the more visible you and your business become, the more likely people are to call you for media opportunities.

Begin by approaching the media yourself. There are two primary ways to let them know about you: a news release or a query letter. A news release enables you to announce something you and your company are doing that is newsworthy; a query letter is a means for introducing ideas for stories or interviews about you, your field, or your business.

A news release must be newsworthy. Whether you are sending an entire publicity kit or just a single-sheet news release, keep in mind that an editor of any publication or program receives dozens, if not hundreds, of news releases and publicity kits every day. Begin by identifying what you are doing that will grab the editor's attention because it speaks to his or her audience, and write a news release about it. That is what newsworthy means: of sufficient interest to the public or special audience to warrant coverage. Your news release needs to show editors why people need and want to know about your product or service.

Keep in mind that with any type of news, what will command extensive coverage in a weekly rural newspaper might not even warrant consideration in the *Kansas City Star*, much less the *New York Times*, so you must tailor your news releases and query letters to the particular publication or program you want to approach. A local community newspaper, for example, might do a story about the opening of an aerobic dance studio if it is the first such service in the community, because before this studio opened people from the community who wanted to attend an aerobics class had to drive out of town. The *New York Times* wouldn't do such an article, however, because there are hundreds of aerobics classes in New York. However, they might do a story on how attending aerobics classes can affect one's sex life!

In fact, that is exactly how psychologist Dr. Linda De Villars got national coverage for herself and her Loveskills Seminars. Her national survey of how exercise affects sexuality was first reported in *USA Today* and then appeared in numerous national magazines and other media, including the *New York Times,* and the evening television show *USA Today* contacted her for stories. Over a year and a half later she is still getting media calls as a consequence of the publicity that came from announcing her survey results.

So the secret to newsworthiness is relating what is unique about what you are doing to something that people want or need to know. If you have clients and customers who buy your product or service, you must be doing something uniquely valuable. All you have to do is recognize it and find the hook that makes it newsworthy.

Making Yourself Newsworthy

The most important part of your press release is that hook, the angle with which you stimulate the interest of your reader. This hook needs to be contained in the first few words you write. You have only a few seconds to arouse an editor's interest—about the time it takes to read a headline and the first sentence of your release.

To find the hook that will make you and your business newsworthy, be alert to the issues, events, fads, problems, and concerns being addressed by the media to which your clients and customers tune in, be they trade journals, newspapers, newsletters, radio, or television. Do you have a new product or service that addresses one of your clients' major concerns? Do you offer an improvement to products or services currently being discussed? Have you discovered a new way to do something your competitors have touted already? Are you doing something that hasn't been done before? Have you responded to a community crisis or need? Could you hold an event or sponsor an activity that would call positive attention to your work? Could you do a survey or mini-study related to your work that would provide enlightening, surprising, or intriguing insights? Jump at any opportunity to send a news release about each such development.

Speech and diction coach Sandy McKnight, for example, has found a way for people to reduce or eliminate an unwanted accent. Part-time computer programmer and full-time free-lance clown Alan Macy has created a new software program featuring 504 jokes suitable for use in business presentations. Free-lance make-up artist Sally Van Swearington has found that today's brides want to have a magazine-cover-perfect look. Chellie Campbell's bookkeeping service has developed a system for taking the stress out of budgeting.

There are opportunities for innovation in almost any field. A desktop-publishing company or word-processing service might sponsor a free workshop for local merchants on how the latest technology can give their printed materials a Fortune 500 look without increasing expenses. A landscape designer could donate a magnificent rare tree to a local nursing home.

Each of these examples has the material for a terrific news release. Where business-related news releases too often fall down, however, (and therefore get ignored by the media), is by focusing on technical facts instead of practical or interesting applications to the readers' lives. Announcing a new line of imported lace wedding gowns, for example, is much less newsworthy than announcing that women are choosing more formal wedding attire this spring than at any time in the past thirty years. The new lace gowns, of course, become examples of what today's bride is wearing.

Hairstylist and colorist Gina Furth found an angle that garnered ample attention for her specialty. She made a study of the variations in blond hair-color preferences from coast to coast and compared the regional choices to the looks of Ivana Trump, Madonna, and Candice Bergen. The result was a *Los Angeles Times* feature story entitled "Battle of the Blonds," which included her picture as well as those of the three stars whose looks she was comparing. The name and location of her salon were mentioned as well.

Here are the basics for writing a release that will grab and hold the reader's attention.

The Standard News-Release Format

Editors expect to see news releases that follow a specific format. A news release should be double-spaced with margins of at least one inch. (It is preferable to use even wider margins to allow for an editor's copymarks.) Use standard typefaces even when you are using a word processor; fancy fonts should be restricted to any accompanying artwork, such as charts and graphs, or other elements of your publicity kit. You may, however, use a slightly larger and/or bold typeface for the headline. Your news release should include the following elements.

Contact person. In the upper left-hand corner of the front page, indicate the contact person and his or her phone number. If you are doing all your own public relations, use your name. If you have a secretary, administrative assistant, or spouse helping you, use his or her name because most editors expect the media contact to be someone other than the business owner. An outside firm handling your public relations will use their letterhead, address, and phone number.

Date. The date of the release should appear either in the upper right-hand corner or on the first line of the first paragraph. In addition to the date you should give some indication of when the information is to be considered available for use; in most instances that will read "FOR IMMEDIATE RELEASE." However, in some cases, such as for appointments and openings, you may want to indicate a particular date as of which the information will be most appropriate; for example, "FOR RELEASE: OCTOBER 31, 1991."

Headline. Next comes the headline, which is in all caps and centered. The headline should be no more than two lines long. There are two philosophies for writing news release headlines. The classic approach is to have a simple one-line grabber that, although you don't necessarily expect the publication to use as is, gives the editor an idea of the impact the headline can have. The alternative is to use a two-line headline consisting of two or three clauses or sentences that encapsulate the release, allowing the editor to determine quickly whether to consider it further or discard it. The latter is particularly useful when you must send your release to a large group of varied publications.

Body. The body of the release begins immediately below the headline. If you are using "FOR IMMEDIATE RELEASE" and the location of the event you are announcing is different from that of the contact, you will need to begin the body with the actual location and date of the event; for instance, "Laceyville, PA—October 31, 1991—)."

Keep your news release to a maximum of two pages. One page is preferable, but two pages are acceptable as long as the information truly warrants them. If you must include more than will fit on two pages, split any additional information or backup data, such as technical specifications, into a second document that is appropriately labeled, such as a "Fact Sheet." If it is necessary to use more than one page, be sure to indicate subsequent pages with the word *more* at the bottom of each sheet. Ensuing pages should be headed with the first two or three words of the headline of the first page, followed by the page number. Indicate the conclusion of your release with either the symbol -30-, the word *End,* or three ### symbols centered at the bottom of the page.

Include at least one good quote from yourself or from someone else involved in whatever you are doing. For example, the landscape designer who is donating a tree could use a quote such as "Nancy Jones, director of the Summerville Nursing Home, stated, "This generous donation and magnificent tree given by Lawrence Landscaping will not only provide a beautiful addition to our garden but will also provide a cheery new view from our public rooms."

If you are sending out a single release without your publicity kit and with no photograph, as for a hot news flash, fold it so that the headline is visible and place it in one of your letterhead envelopes. If it is exceptionally important or time-limited, be sure to write "FLASH" on the envelope itself. You might consider having a stamp made that says "FLASH" and using a bright ink that coordinates with your logo if you do this type of release frequently.

Writing a Release That Gets Results

In writing the release, keep in mind that you are not writing an ad; you are imparting information to an editor. You must, however, impart it in such a way that the editor immediately sees its potential value to his or her readers. Therefore you must state it as briefly and in as exciting a manner as possible. Omit most adjectives, use action verbs, and eliminate nonessential descriptions. Nowhere are these instructions more important than in your headline writing.

Attention-grabbing headlines. Whenever possible, your headline should match the style of the publication to which you are submitting your release. A small staid newspaper in New England might respond positively to a headline such as "EXERCISE IMPROVES MARITAL RELATIONS," while a hip health-and-fitness magazine might prefer something more sensational, like "EXERCISE MAKES YOU SEXY!"

The primary goal of the headline should be to arouse curiosity and stimulate at least one primary question in the mind of the reader, and the first sentence of your release should answer that question.

The headline of each of the sample releases on the following page prompts a question that is then answered in the first sentence of text. As you read the headlines, don't you find yourself wondering how exercise could improve someone's sex life, why fall colors create demands on today's brides, and what the original EDOS package is?

The first sentence should not only answer this initial question; it should raise still further questions like "What kind of exercise classes are these?" "What kind of special demands?" and "How did the software get better?" And the rest of that first paragraph should fill the reader in with what the now inquiring mind wants to know.

By the time the editor reads those first few lines he or she has a good idea whether or not the material will be applicable to his or her program or publication. The balance of the release should fill in the details with all the additional information an editor needs for further consideration.

The following are sample press-release ideas for a variety of businesses and the type of publications for which each might be most applicable.

BED & BREAKFAST HOSTS RECEPTION FOR CELEBRITY

This is an ideal publicity opportunity. As the owner of the inn, you could work out the details for media coverage of the reception with the guest's agent and send out a news release announcing the reception along with your publicity kit to all local publications and the local television news. If you follow up your release with a phone call to the editors, you may well be able to line up both print interviews and local television news coverage at the event itself.

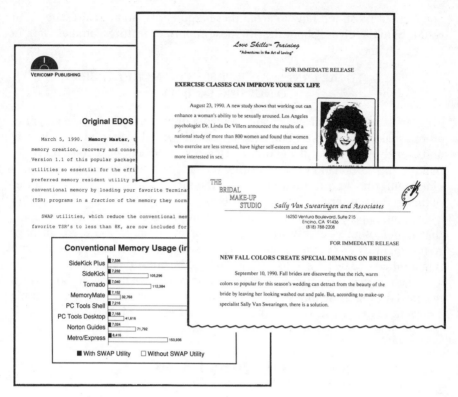

Sample News Releases.

After the event is held, you might send a query letter to local or regional television or radio talk shows about their doing a feature on the growing popularity of bed and breakfast inns, being sure to include information about the news coverage you have just enjoyed.

MOST FREQUENTLY OVERLOOKED TAX TRAPS FOR NEW BUSINESSES AND WAYS TO AVOID THEM BY NOTED LOCAL ACCOUNTANT

If, like this accountant, your business has a seasonal element, you can send a timely news release to the local daily paper and appropriate local business publications. This type of release can be adapted to serve a wide variety of businesses. A dog trainer or veterinarian could send a similar release on the onset of flea season and what to do about it; a floral arranger could send a release on novel gift ideas for valentines; a computer tutor could send a release about how using a computer can be a useful tool for kids starting school in the fall.

Such releases lend themselves to interesting feature stories and need not be limited to seasonal events. Some subjects have year-round appeal. A marriage and family counselor, for example, could send a release on what couples argue about most and how to avoid these arguments, and a real-estate agent could submit a release about the five most important features families want in buying a home.

LOCAL LANDSCAPER PRESENTS "MONEY TREE"
TO NURSING FACILITY

This landscape designer has created a media opportunity by making a gift of an unusual species of tree. The release would be suitable to send to local daily and weekly papers, local radio and television, and feature publications. By making such a donation or sponsoring a charity or civic event, you are provided with the opportunity to talk with the media about the unique features of the product or service you are contributing.

Such an approach is a particularly good way to get exposure for a business that is not otherwise easy to publicize. For example, if you are a medical transcriptionist or operate a mailing-list service, stories featuring your work might otherwise be limited to very specialized business publications.

Creating such media opportunities is also an excellent way to boost your business during those times of the year when it is routinely slow. By planning sufficiently ahead you can arrange to sponsor events or make donations at just the times when you need a little extra business.

Using Query Letters

There are many opportunities to send out a news release, but suppose you don't have anything to announce or don't have the time to create an event or activity that would be suitably newsworthy? Another way in which you can approach the media is to send a query letter, along with your publicity kit, introducing ideas for features or interviews they could do about you, your field, or your business.

A query letter is printed on your stationery and serves as a cover letter for your publicity kit. Addressed to the editor or producer, it simply but effectively makes a case for doing a story on the ideas enclosed in your kit.

In the second example, the query letter and kit were being sent as a follow-up to an initial phone call. We find this to be a cost-effective approach to getting publicity. If an editor or producer expresses initial interest on the phone, he or she is more likely to look over your material when it arrives.

Whom to Send Your Publicity Materials to

Considering the time and money involved in producing your publicity kit, you want to make sure you are sending it to the right person at the right place. We suggest building what we call a Preferred Media Mailing List that includes the newspapers, magazines, newsletters, and radio and television

Sample Query Letters

Dear Editor/Producer:

The most serious issue we face in the 1990s is the state of the environment. Many species face extinction; wilderness areas are in danger of disappearing. But we as individuals can make a big difference.

I am an environmental interior designer. Please look at the enclosed information and consider a story or interview on how each and every one of us can help to improve our environment simply by changing the products with which we decorate our homes.

After years of research I know how to find paint, wall coverings, carpeting, and even appliances that can help save the environment. My clients not only enjoy a healthier environment for themselves and their children; they know they are making a difference for us all.

Thank you for your consideration.

Dear Sarah:

It was great talking with you today about your show and the possibility of my talking about networking and the POWER OF SCHMOOZING on the air in early August.

Enclosed is my publicity kit, which describes how I help people further their careers through networking. You'll find information on the seminar I do and on my company, which I began five years ago. I've also included a list of ideas for subjects we can cover.

Please call if you'd like more information. I look forward to talking further with you soon.

Best regards

---

shows that serve your particular business market. Whatever your potential clients and customers read, watch, or listen to should be on your list.

You probably know what some of these outlets are already. To expand your list, consult directories that list all the major publications and other media along with the names of specific personnel in each position. These directories, found in most libraries, are usually updated on an annual basis. They are especially valuable tools when your promotional plans include national coverage. A sampling of directories is in Resources at the end of the book. The reference librarian at your community library can help you in locating and using the best ones for your business.

The newsstand is another source for good ideas. Look through all the

Sample news clippings. Articles like these can result from your public-relations efforts.

national, regional, and local publications displayed there and select those you think your potential clients and customers read. Inside these publications will be the names of the editors, columnists, and writers, along with the phone number and address of the publication.

Also make a point to read local radio and television listings on a regular basis. Notice the shows that do interviews and news features and what topics they discuss, and watch or listen to those that have topics of interest to your clients or customers. Knowing the format and slant of these shows will be helpful in writing both your news releases and query letters as well as in talking to the person who books the shows.

You will probably need the library to find the editors of all the trade publications for your target market. If the target market for your product or service is, for example, advertising agencies, accountants, or building contractors, you will want to send your materials to any local, regional, or national trade papers and magazines that serve these fields. *Ad Week* and *Advertising Age* are examples of the publications ad agencies read routinely. Major national trade publications like these often have regional editions as well, in which case you will need to get the names of the editors who deal with your region.

Don't waste your time or your materials by mailing publicity kits to editors who would have no interest in them. A complete kit may cost fifteen dollars or more. Although that is a small investment when properly placed, it is far too much money to waste on editors or producers for whom there is no possible interest. For example, the city editors of large urban papers are usually interested only in spot news of general interest, so unless you have a flash release concerned with an event that in your community would warrant front-page or near-front-page coverage, sending him or her your information is the quickest way for it to end up in the circular file. On the other hand, the business or lifestyle editor might be interested in your material for features, product reviews, or events listings.

There are companies and products whose stories would be better suited for other editors. A software company, a custom wedding-gown designer, a landscape consultant, or a building contractor, for example, might send their materials to the technical editor, the fashion editor, the lifestyle editor, or the real-estate editor, respectively.

If you are having difficulty finding the time to do the research involved in compiling your Preferred Media Mailing List, there is a cost-effective shortcut: instead of hiring a public-relations consultant or publicist to handle all of your publicity, hire one simply to select the best media and ask that he or she provide you with such a list, complete with all the pertinent information and mailing labels.

Delivering Your Package

All materials should be sent to editors or producers by name. If you want to increase your chances of avoiding their mail slush pile, call in advance or deliver your kit by hand instead of by mail. If you take the time to deliver it yourself, you might make an invaluable personal contact with key personnel.

When sending material to the broadcast media, put both the interviewer's name and the names of the producers and editors of the program on your mailing list, and send your material to all of them. Usually the host will pass along the material to the producer, netting you double exposure.

The Crucial Follow-Up Phone Call

All media materials should be followed up within a week by a telephone call. Even if your materials were hand delivered, they may just have been placed on the top of the pile, and there is no guarantee they will be read or considered. A simple phone call helps remind an editor of your materials and brings you to his or her attention more personally. This is not a suggestion to pester any editor; one friendly call to check that the materials were received and whether there is any further information that might be helpful should do the trick, and it will enable you to begin to establish rapport with your contacts.

As you talk to editors, you may discover how to pitch your idea more closely to their specific interests and concerns, and as they get to know you better, they may see opportunities that you had never thought of. Even if they don't use your material immediately, your relationship can open doors for the placement of future materials.

We continue to be amazed at how many media packages we throw away only to have someone call later and provide us with information that convinces us to do an interview. There are at least two lessons here: that following up can pay off, and that if your materials are often tossed out, you aren't using the most effective hooks. Follow-up calls can help teach you what your hooks should be.

If Your News Is Not Picked Up

If you have sent out all this material and no one has chosen to use it, don't despair. Even unused releases bring your name before the media, so consider making the most of your effort by doing one of the following.

1. Just because an idea is not picked up by one medium does not eliminate its possibilities. It may be used with a different approach or at a later date by another medium. So if your subject remains timely, you can reissue it to another publication or broadcast medium at a later date.
2. If the personnel at a particular medium change, you can and should resend all materials that weren't used.
3. As long as material remains timely, it may be re-sent to the same people after a reasonable time has passed. However, if some of the material has

been given broad coverage elsewhere, it would be wise to eliminate it from the reissue.

Making the Most of Your Interview

It is important that you make the most of the opportunity to be interviewed by the media, because the more engaging the interview, the more likely it is to lead to business and future publicity opportunities. Here are some tips for making sure your interview sparkles.

Prepare. Write out the key points or message you want to convey to the audience. What do you want people to know about you and your business? It is important to be clear about this and to keep it foremost in your mind during the interview. No matter what the interviewer asks, you should find a way to include your message in your answers. Here are several questions to help you prepare:

1. What is your specialty?
2. How would you describe your specialty in fifteen seconds or less, including whom you provide it to and what it does for them?
3. What problem or problems do you solve?
4. What tips would you give someone facing this problem?
5. What unique solutions do you provide?
6. What examples can you give in which you provided such a solution?
7. What upbeat, encouraging, or funny message can you leave people with?
8. What offer can you make that people can't refuse?

Then write out the most likely questions you will be asked. Think of how you will respond to them in ways that will highlight your unique background, skills, and experience. Include all potentially embarrassing, controversial, or negative questions, and have a good answer even for the things you hope no one will ever ask. However, don't memorize your answers—you want your interview to be lively, spontaneous, and conversational. Practice by having someone else ask you the possible questions you have developed and answering them extemporaneously based on the key points you want to make.

Keep the audience in mind. In answering questions, remember that while you are looking at and speaking to the interviewer, you are simultaneously addressing the audience. In fact, communicating with the audience is your primary goal. When you have succeeded at this, you have done a good job for the interviewer. So find out as much as you can about who will be reading, watching, or listening to your interview.

Don't try to sell yourself or your business. Guest appearances and other interviews are not commercials, and the media is very sensitive to this distinction. Be equally sensitive to the reasons they have chosen to interview you. Usually, your job in an interview is to be informative and to do so in an entertaining way. The more informative and appealing you are, the more likely you are to be quoted in an article and invited back on radio or television. The more unusual and valuable the information you provide, the more interested the audience will be in your product or service. Guests who try to mention their business name repeatedly and urge people to buy their product or service will alienate both the audience and the interviewer.

The best way to make sure you get a good plug is to provide a lot of useful information that is rich with colorful examples from your experiences in a forthright and moving way. As a caterer, for example, you will get more business from a television guest appearance if your food demonstration looks dramatic and tastes delicious to the host than from trying to make a direct plug for your company. Or, as a tax advisor, you will get a better response from an article that quotes your suggestions for several highly useful tax strategies than you would from going over your credentials. Watch media guests, such as Richard Simmons or Dr. Ruth Westheimer, who are invited to appear again and again. They are masters at providing a wealth of both practical and entertaining messages.

Arrange in advance for the audience to be able to contact you. If appropriate, ask before the interview whether the interviewer would be willing to let people know how they can contact you for more information. Such a plug will be far more valuable to you than self-promotion. Often the interviewer will agree to include your address or phone number in an article or at least will make people know where you are located so they can contact you through the phone directory. Radio and television interviewers will often give out a phone number or address where their guests can be reached at the close of the interview. If the interviewer agrees to give out this information but then doesn't do so, it is perfectly acceptable to volunteer the information at the close of the interview. You should always find out in advance how long the interview will be. Then keep a clock in view so you can provide this information right before the end. Don't, however, get caught checking your watch on camera.

One way to increase your chances of getting a good plug is to make sure the interviewer has been able to see or use your product or service sometime before the interview. Be sure to send or bring samples, and offer to do a free demonstration.

To help assure that your address and phone number will appear, offer to give away something free to everyone who calls in response to the article or show. For example, the caterer could give away recipes for the dishes she demonstrates, and the tax adviser could give away a list of frequently overlooked deductions.

In general, we have found that, if you respect the interviewer's desire to avoid commercialism, they will be cooperative about releasing information about you.

Make sure your title and business name are included and are accurate.
Interviewers are notorious for mispronouncing names and for confusing titles, so make sure they have accurate spelling information on both your name and your business. Check to see what title will be appearing on the caption below your image on the TV screen and how you will be introduced. Make sure you are described in a way that will promote your business. For example, being introduced as "Janice Jennings, Cajun Food Chef" is not very helpful, since it doesn't indicate where you cook; "Janice Jennings, Cajun Caterer" is better, and still better would be "Janice Jennings, Chef and Owner of Hot Cajun Catering Service." Should the interviewer give out wrong information, you can correct it as you begin answering your first question.

Restate the question in beginning your answer.   This is particularly important for pretaped radio or television interviews, where your answers will be edited. But it also helps orient a live audience, and it gives you a chance to focus your thoughts and time to formulate your answer regardless of the type of interview. For example:

QUESTION: "What is the most common cause of fatigue?"
ANSWER: "The most common cause of fatigue is . . ."

Reframe the question when necessary.   You do not have to answer a question as it has been posed. Your goal is to convey your message in a way that doesn't alienate the audience or the interviewer, so feel free to reframe a question in such a way as to provide the most effective answer. This is true even if you are live on the air. If someone asks you a question that casts you in an unfavorable light or introduces material with which you are not familiar or that is too complex or obscure to answer briefly, reframe the question. Even in a print interview in which the reporter is simply taking intermittent handwritten notes, never say anything you don't want to be quoted as saying. For example:

QUESTION: "But it takes a lot of money to put on a wedding like that, doesn't it?"

AVOID: "Yes, a wedding does cost a lot of money but . . ."

ANSWER: "A wedding is something people want to cherish for a lifetime. So they will invest as much as they can to make it really special. No matter what the budget, there's always a way to do that. For example, we did a beautiful wedding where . . ."

Keep your answers brief and to the point. Radio and television interviews are a conversation, not a monologue, so if your response to a question lasts longer than 30 to 60 seconds you are probably over-answering. For a print interview you can give somewhat longer answers, but since you want to be quoted, one or two short, clear points in response to each question is preferable. When an answer requires considerable information, summarize it. For example, if asked how you decided to get into your field, instead of reviewing your entire work history you might focus on one pivotal element such as a customer's suggestion that you go into business on your own.

Short anecdotes told with a twinkle and a smile can be effective. For example, when asked why she started her first business, Peggy Glenn often grins and replies, "Because I got mad!" She then tells how, after years of being underpaid and underappreciated, she walked out on her job in a fit of frustration. With three teenage children and a new husband who had not expected to be the sole support of a family of five, she needed to make some money fast before anyone missed her paycheck. So she started a typing service.

Elaborate beyond "yes" or "no." Make specific points, and use examples that will bring home each point. For instance, when a career consultant is asked whether people have to settle for boring, dead-end jobs, she might respond: "I find there is always some way you can earn a good living doing something you enjoy. For example, I counseled a forty-five-year-old secretary who hated her job but loved to sew. Through our work, she decided to start a business doing free-lance custom tailoring for local dry cleaners."

Demostrate that you are an authority. To build your credibility, use dramatic and startling facts, statistics, and findings to make your point throughout an interview. Enumerate points and call attention to them. For example, you might say, "Here's a startling fact! Ninety-seven percent of what we say to ourselves is negative!" or "Now here's a frightening thought: Only 5 percent of the population are financially independent at age sixty-five!"

Give reasons for the points you make. For example, a personal trainer who is asked about how he helps people lose weight might say, "Many times you don't even need to lose weight; you simply need to tone up your body to look great at your present weight," adding, "Tightening sagging muscles shapes the body and eliminates inches even if you haven't lost a pound."

Talk personally, concretely, and colorfully. Avoid academic, theoretical, abstract, and clinical language. For example, say, "I talked with a young woman who feared her chance of finding a husband was about as good as winning the lottery," rather than, "I treated a depressed client who was suffering from the illusion she was destined to spinsterhood."

Always look directly at the interviewer when you talk, using his or her name. When answering a live call-in on a radio or TV talk show, address the caller by name, too.

Be positive and speak with enthusiasm and conviction. Don't dwell on the negative aspects of your message. Provide solutions that inspire hope, encouragement, and confidence, and end each segment with an upbeat, summarizing benefit. For example, a drug counselor might talk about the negative effects of drugs but hold out the promise of rehabilitation, closing with an inspiring story of someone who has succeeded in beating the odds and is now living drug free.

Keep using your best answers. When being interviewed on more than one show or by more than one publication, continue to use the same answers you have taken the time to prepare. You will quickly learn which ones produce positive reactions. You will do better with a clearly thought-out response that works well than by trying to be innovative each time you are interviewed.

Making Sure Your Publicity Leads to More Publicity

After you are interviewed, always get the cards, or at least names, of the writers, editors, producers, and talk show hosts you have met. Send these people thank-you notes immediately after your interview. To save time, you can handwrite your thank-you notes on notecards, preferably imprinted with your logo, name, address, and telephone number. Continue to keep in touch with these media contacts by sending newsletters, pertinent information, and, of course, further news releases about yourself and your business.

Make sure you get a copy of each article and radio or television segment in which you are featured. Although you can hire a news service to obtain such copies for you, you can do this more cost-effectively yourself. Ask writers how to get a copy of the newspapers, magazines, or newsletters in which you appear; they may offer to send you one. Once you have a copy of an article, add it to your publicity kit. For radio and TV appearances, take a blank cassette to the station and before going on the air, politely ask the producer or other appropriate person to dub a copy for you. Usually there will be a charge for this, but it is worth the investment, because you never know when someone will ask you for a sample tape.

The more prestigious the media, the more likely they will be to want to see or hear you on a previous show. Before meeting planners invite you to speak at a conference or other program, they will ask to review an audio or videotape of you in action. Publicity appearances are a relatively easy and inexpensive way to get such demo tapes.

Other Uses for Publicity Press Kits and Press Materials

Once you have developed your media materials, it would be a tremendous waste of your precious sales and marketing time to make only a few limited uses of them. There are several additional ways to maximize the same media materials.

First, you can reprint any or all of the elements of your kit (including the release, profiles, and history) without obvious media flags such as FOR IMMEDIATE RELEASE or dates and send your kit, complete with photographs, to business prospects in lieu of a brochure. Or, you can use the materials, reprinted as above, as part of your initial presentation to a business prospect. If you have been given the opportunity to make a proposal, you can use the reprinted materials and photographs as part of the total proposal package. And finally, you can use the kit to elicit invitations to speak or conduct seminars at civic organizations or professional or trade associations.

Other Media Avenues

Newspaper and broadcast editorials. If you are in an exceptionally large urban area where your press materials are routinely ignored despite being brilliantly written and thoroughly followed up, there are alternative methods of communicating your message. For example, you might think about writing a letter to the editor of a leading newspaper.

No matter what your company does, there is probably some related issue—business or political—that warrants expressing your opinion. An editor who is presented with a well-written, cogent letter, especially in reply to either a story or a previous editorial, will most likely print it or offer you an opportunity to voice your comment.

To get an idea of what is of particular interest to the editor of your local paper, read the Letters to the Editor section for a period of time and keep up with the editorials themselves. Make note of broadcast editorials, too, as many radio and television stations provide opportunities for citizens to express opinions over the air.

Newspapers also invite citizens to write editorials from time to time. The main criteria for both media are a good writing style and having something important to say. If an editor has samples of your writing from your letters, your chances of receiving such an invitation are increased. Some sample general topics you might consider for discussion in a letter to the editor are:

1. local government restrictions on your type of business.
2. the advantages of your type of business to the community at large.
3. the positive impact of your type of business on the environment.

Also consider writing to discuss industry-specific topics. For example, a music teacher might decry the decrease in music education in public schools, enumerating the subsequent disadvantages for students. A security consultant might write on the frightening increase in white-collar crime in all businesses and the effect this has on prices to the consumer. Any repair business can write about the waste generated by our disposable society. Any business might write on the problems of junk facsimile transmissions.

The more creative you are—and the more responsive to what is currently being written and said in the relevant print and broadcast media—the more likely an editor or producer is to select your letter or commentary for use. For example, Albert Moulton, President and CEO of CADworks, Inc., a software company in Cambridge, Massachusetts, wrote a letter to the editor of *Inc* Magazine in response to an article that dubbed Cambridge as the most entrepreneurial place on earth. He opened his letter with "We are one of the firms that has profited from being in East Cambridge: in fact our software was used to design and/or manage two of the buildings shown in the article's opening photographs." Moulton then proceeded to make his comments.

Similarly, designer Caryl Gorski wrote a letter to the editor of *Publish*, a magazine for graphic communicators, commenting on the design changes in the magazine's layout. Computer consultant James L. Daigle wrote the editor of *PC Magazine* describing how one of the software packages reviewed in the magazine had been helpful to one of his clients. Michael Murphy, publisher of the California Technology Stock Letter, wrote to the editor of *Business Week* offering additional alternatives to the electric car described in the Science and Technology section of the magazine.

Articles or a column. If your community has smaller local papers as well as the major dailies, you might consider preparing a complete article for them. Such an article should not be on your business per se but rather on a subject of which your business is an element. If you like to write and are good at it, you might even offer your services as a contributing columnist. Financial planner Gordon Curry suggested several ideas to his local paper for feature articles on investing. The editor liked the ideas and commissioned stories. Ultimately, Gordon was asked to write a regular column.

Almost any business can become a vehicle for a series of articles or a column. A computer consultant might write a series of short articles on the fundamentals of computing. Their particular focus would depend on the readers of the publication and the consultant's specialty. The same consultant might do a column called "Computer Updates" that covers the newest practical breakthroughs in computer technology for home and office. A music teacher might offer to review new classical compact disks; an executive search-and-recruiting firm might do a series on job hunting in a bear market; and a professional organizer might do a series on how to reduce home or office clutter.

Additional outlets for both individual articles and series include company newsletters and trade publications, which do not have to be limited to your own trade. For example, if your mailing-list-maintenance firm primarily serves churches, you might consider offering your series "Using the Mail to Stay in Touch" to church newsletters and regional ecclesiastical publications.

Often, even when an article is not used for a publication, the writer is utilized as an authority to be quoted and thus acquires immediate status as an expert, as occurred when Laura wrote an article for the AT&T newsletter for home offices. Instead of using her article, AT&T quoted her liberally in an article of their own. She was then free to use her original article for other publications.

Before sending anything to a trade publication, be sure to read three or four issues to be sure the article you are proposing is appropriate. If you send in something that is way off base, the editor will likely eliminate you from future consideration even when you produce something that would be of interest. Editors have long memories; be sure their memory of you is positive.

Sometimes calling or sending a query letter before you write an article will increase your chances of having the article published, because you can tailor what you write to the precise interests of the editor. Many people, however, do have one or two boilerplate articles that they tailor to publications in different industries. For example, a time-management consultant has a generic article on how to save time on the job, which she tailors on her word processor to produce such variations as "How Secretaries Can Save Time on the Job," "Saving Time for the Sales Professional," and "How Hairstylists Can Make Time When There Is None."

Again, once you have had something published—whether a story, a feature, a letter or editorial, or a column or series of articles—be sure to ask for tear sheets, then photocopy them and add the copies to your presentation materials and future press kits. Keep the tear sheets handy in a file of all your published materials, ready for making future copies. Remember, the more coverage you get, the more likely you are to get additional coverage.

Helping the Media Find You

Since you never know when a key magazine or newspaper may be doing a feature story and need a comment from someone in your field, sometimes the easiest way to get publicity is to position yourself so that the media can always find you. When the media needs an expert or a story idea, they will turn to their favorite sources. They will talk to other reporters, and to friends and colleagues, will look through professional and business directories, and may even scout the yellow pages.

Psychologist Dr. Linda De Villars has a one-inch ad running in the yellow pages under "Psychologists," featuring her as a specialist in sex and relationship counseling and emphasizing her credentials. A free-lance writer seeking an expert to interview for an article he was doing for *Men's Fitness* saw the ad and called her. Not only did Dr. De Villars appear in that article, but he was so pleased with their interview that he decided to pitch additional stories featuring her on related topics to several other national magazines. Based on these magazine articles, she received requests from two literary agents to write a book on the topic.

So don't overlook the yellow pages. Also list yourself in targeted directories, and join select professional and trade organizations in order to be included in their membership rosters. Appear on panels, attend meetings, and when possible give presentations at conferences and other gatherings that the press will attend. You know you are doing good public relations when members of the press begin to refer you to one another.

CHAPTER
EIGHT
■■■■■■■■■■■■■■■■■■■■■■

Giving Speeches and Seminars That Attract Business

Speaking or presenting a seminar on the right topic before the right audience can not only be an excellent source of publicity, it can also lead directly to new business. This is particularly true if your business is service- or information-related.

You may be able to turn the expertise that makes you effective in your work into a speech that will bring you valued credibility, exposure, and business. On any given day there are an estimated nine thousand speaking opportunities in this country. According to the International Association of Convention and Visitors Bureaus, the 231 largest cities in the United States held 204,829 major meetings in 1988! The American Society of Association Executives reports that 63.7 million people attended large association conventions in 1987 and predicts this number will grow by almost 10 percent every year. And these figures don't even include local meetings and con- ferences or private and church-sponsored events.

Every day, clubs, organizations, and groups in your community, as well as professional and trade associations, are looking for speakers and workshop leaders to give presentations on topics of interest to their members at break- fast and lunch meetings, annual meetings, special events, in-house training programs, conferences, symposiums, and conventions. Informative, entertain- ing speakers—especially free ones—are in great demand.

Although some of these events may pay their presenters a speaking fee, most such opportunities will either involve no fee or a very low honorarium to cover the speaker's expenses. Unless you intend to develop a full or side business from your speaking, however, that should not be considered a draw- back. The opportunity to present your expertise before the right groups is well worth the investment of your time and energy in terms of exposure, credibility, and potential business.

For example, when actress Sandy McKnight decided to create a new business for herself offering speech and diction classes, she built her business almost entirely at first by giving free speeches on how to improve a telephone image to local chambers of commerce and other professional business groups. Mike Anderson, creator of Mad Mike's Burger Spread, has used speeches and public appearances to boost sales of his hamburger spread, and Heidi Miller of Heidi's Frozen Yogurt used public appearances extensively to propel her first yogurt shop in Orange County, California into a national franchise. Mike speaks forcefully on anti-drug topics; his theme is "get high on life." Heidi spoke first on health and fitness topics and later on business opportunities, especially for women.

Finding a Topic

You can begin to take advantage of these opportunities by selecting a topic that will both appeal to your potential clientele and show off your unique expertise and experience. Dottie and Lilly Walters, co-authors of the book *Speak and Grow Rich*, recommend beginning by considering who you are and what you know and then surveying your potential audience to find out "what hurts." In other words, they suggest identifying the major problems your audience faces and applying your expertise to solving those problems. Here are a few examples:

- A psychologist who specializes in counseling singles speaks to singles groups about topics related to finding a mate, such as dealing with rejection and understanding the differences between the ways men and women think.
- The owner of an indoor-and-outdoor plant service speaks to business groups about using plants to boost office morale and productivity.
- An accountant speaks to corporations about new changes in the tax law that will affect the corporate bottom line.
- The owner of a gymnastics school for children speaks to parent groups on the positive and negative effects of sports on a child's self-esteem.
- A sales trainer offers a free seminar on how to work a booth for the exhibitors at local trade shows.
- A literary agent speaks to writer's groups on how to get a publisher.
- An information broker speaks to business groups about how to find information on one's competitors through public sources.

One way to test your topics is to present several related ones to meeting planners and let them select the one most appealing to their audience. Your most effective topics will be those that meeting planners choose again and again. And, of course, you will continually need to develop new topics that are current and relevant to the issues facing your customers and clients.

If you have trouble identifying a unique topic, experiment with standard ones such as "How to Select a . . . ," "When You Need a . . . ," or "What You Should Know About . . . ," filling in your particular field of expertise.

Finding an Audience

Once you have your topic, the next step is to identify the groups, organizations, and associations to whom you want to speak. The goal is to speak to groups that include large numbers of your prospective clients. One easy way to find these groups would be to ask current or prospective clients and customers to what organizations they belong.

Another way to locate groups to speak before is to consult the *Encyclopedia of Associations*, published by Gale Research. This directory lists national professional and trade associations, and a second volume includes local and state chapters. Another valuable library resource is *The Directory of United States Trade Shows, Expositions and Conventions*, published by the U.S. Travel Service of the U.S. Department of Commerce, which lists when and where the major shows are scheduled throughout the country.

Usually you do not need to be a member of these organizations or groups in order to speak before them. They are looking for speakers or presenters who have information their members need to know. Of course, you will also want to consider speaking before the civic, trade, and professional organizations to which you do belong. Speaking to local, state, regional, and national organizations of which you are a member will facilitate fellow members learning more about what you do and make your networking efforts easier.

Most major urban areas have a variety of continuing education programs that provide additional opportunities for speaking. Some such programs are affiliated with local colleges and universities. In addition, independent companies such as The Learning Annex provide a catalog of one-to-four-session seminars on a wide variety of topics.

Teaching in these programs positions you as an expert and gives those present a chance to sample your skills and approaches. You also begin building a relationship with your students. If you have selected a course title that attracts the right audience, some of your students will become clients based upon what they learn and experience from the classes you teach.

Teaching such courses was the sole source of business for computer programmer James Milburn, who taught evening computer-programming classes for small-business owners at a local trade school. Once they found out how difficult programming is, some of his students either hired him to do their programming or to consult with them on customizing off-the-shelf software. Two literary agents in Los Angeles regularly get clients from the class they co-teach on how to get published—so many that they have had to turn away business. And many of the people who attend psychotherapist Dr. Deborah Cooper's classes on relationships sign up for private counseling.

In fact, if your speech or seminar consistently does not result in any business for you, you need to rethink either the topic or the audiences to whom you are presenting. When you talk about something your audience needs and present yourself effectively as someone who has it, at least a few people will want to engage you to provide it.

Here are some sample topics for adult-education seminars and people who might offer them:

- *IBM or Macintosh—Which is Right for You?*, offered by a computer consultant
- *The New Look of Success in the '90s*, presented by an image/wardrobe consultant
- *How to Use Your Mouth to Get More Business: Networking Do's and Don'ts*, taught by a business networking organizer
- *How a Newsletter Can Increase Your Business*, offered by the owner of a desktop publishing service
- *Collecting on Bad Debts*, presented by the head of a collections service
- *How to Get Rid of Clutter*, taught by a professional organizer
- *Getting Anything You Need without Cash*, offered by a business barter service
- *Protect Your Ideas: Patents, Trademarks, and Copyrights*, conducted by a lawyer who specializes in intellectual properties

Once you have your topic and have located the organizations before which you want to speak, find out the names of their meeting planners or program directors and introduce yourself to these people by phone. Tell them about your background and topic, and if they show some interest, send a copy of your publicity kit. Follow up with a second phone call to discuss setting up a speaking date.

Getting Business from Your Speech

Once your speech is booked, do everything you can to make sure your presentation will actually lead to future business. Before the presentation, for example, find out as much as you can about your audience so you can tailor your speech to their interests. The more your speech addresses their needs, the more likely they are to want to do business with you.

Also try to arrange to have the organization announce your upcoming speech in a newsletter article that will provide your background, including your business name and your picture. Find out whether they will be sending a news release to local media as well. If they aren't, do so yourself. Such pre-publicity helps establish you as an authority to the audience and also assists in attracting to the presentation those individuals who have the most interest in your topic, and thus in your business.

Do not leave the content of your introduction up to the whim of someone who has been asked to introduce you. Often this person is a volunteer who knows little about you and may have had limited experience speaking before a group. Instead, using your bio, write a brief introduction and give it to the meeting planner. A well-written introduction will establish your credibility, set you up as an expert, and predispose your audience to welcome you and your message enthusiastically.

In your introduction, describe your business, your background, and perhaps even a glowing quote about yourself. For example, Paul and Sarah Edwards' introduction includes the fact that *The Christian Science Monitor* has called them "the gurus of the home office." Laura Douglas is often introduced with the assertion that her clients call her "*the* source for creative marketing solutions." Do not be modest in writing your introduction. While you should not overstate your case, it is important to make a strong statement of your qualifications and accomplishments.

If there is no one available to introduce you, don't just launch into your speech. Take the time to welcome the audience and cover the points from your introduction so that people know to whom they will be listening.

As with radio or television appearances, in giving your speech you are not giving a sales pitch; even the hint of one will alienate your audience and embarrass and antagonize the program director or meeting planner who booked you to speak—a person who, when pleased with your appearance, becomes a referral source and can write a glowing letter of endorsement to add to your publicity kit.

Structuring Your Speech for Sales

There are several ways in which you can use your speech to get business without giving a sales pitch. The first involves the way you structure your speech. Your speech should focus initially on real-life problems your audience faces relative to your topic. Address the reason these problems occur; let your audience know you understand their situation. Second, you need to provide realistic solutions that demonstrate your expertise.

For example, in her speech on how a business can improve its telephone image, speech-and-diction coach Sandy McKnight outlines the most common mistakes personnel make on the phone and demonstrates the bad image these poor phone skills create. By role-playing scenarios involving such mistakes, she gets her audience laughing and relating to these problems. She then outlines realistic solutions any company can use to train its personnel to speak effectively on the phone. Since few companies have the expertise to conduct this training themselves, however, many are immediately interested in having her give a seminar for their personnel or sending their personnel to attend her public seminars.

PAUL & SARAH EDWARDS

What meeting planners say about Paul & Sarah Edwards

"It was a delight! This presentation was reflective of the high quality ... Paul and Sarah bring to ... sessions. They consistently brings a breath of fresh air -- fresh air in terms of timely subjects, solid and useful subject matter, novel and interesting presentation style and an approach that guarantees the audience walks away thinking about and remembering what they learned."

Interchange, *American Society of Training & Development*

"I thought you should know that our January sales meetings were very successful and the techniques we learned from you at the Bermuda management meeting played a very large part in their success.

Larry Ray, National Sales Manager, Fissons Corporation

"Thank you for your excellent presentation at the NAHD conference this Spring in San Diego. I found the workshop to be useful and engergizing."

Sylvia M. Walker, Conference Director, National Association of Hospital Developers

"We would like to express a tremendous thank you for a job well done at the All-Iowa Home-Based Business Conference. You were quite literally a "keynote" of our day."

Jan De Young, Small Business Development Center, Iowa State University

"Thank you for speaking at our Annual Conference. Your talk, instruction and humor were excellent. Feedback of others in attendance has been totally positive. As we all know, the quality of our speakers make an event."

Elizabeth Byam, Program Chairman, Association of Women in Computing

"Your presentation was a great way to bring our conference to a close. I personally was inspired, challenged and entertained."

Sandy Bucknell, Conference Coordinator, California State Home Economists

Sample of endorsements for speaking engagements. Including testimonials like these in publicity kits you send to meeting planners helps them feel more confident about booking you to speak at upcoming meetings, conferences, and other events.

Similarly, in her speeches for singles groups, psychologist Dr. Deborah Cooper introduces the most common problems singles have in developing lasting, rewarding relationships. She presents these from both the male and the female perspective, with which the audience readily identifies themselves and their dates. She then outlines and demonstrates new behaviors that men and women can learn to overcome these problems and describes many success stories about clients who have mastered these new dating skills. Dr. Cooper invites the audience to try out some of these skills in sample mini-exercises. Once they experience how well her ideas work, they feel excited about learning more and many sign up for one of her seminars, make an appointment for a private consultation, or hire her to present a longer seminar to their company.

Getting Names, Addresses, and Phone Numbers for Follow-up

Another important way to make sure you get business from your speeches is to get the name, phone number, and address of everyone in your audience. There are several ways to do this. One is to offer a free drawing in which you have all participants place their business cards in a bowl and give away something of value to the lucky winner whose card is drawn; another is to give a special prize to everyone who fills out a questionnaire of some kind. Or you can announce that all who wish to receive further information can leave their cards with you at the close of the program.

Before you close your speech, you can offer to answer remaining questions personally at the back of the room. This is an ideal name- or card-getting opportunity. Many times those who approach you will express interest in your product or service that can be turned immediately into an appointment for a follow-up phone call or meeting. To make the best use of the time you have after a speech, do not get into a drawn-out conversation with any individual; others will become impatient and leave before talking with you. Make contacts with as many people as you can and get their names and phone numbers. Then, of course, you must follow-up by phone or mail as soon as possible on all the names or cards that you have collected.

Finally, a prerequisite for getting business from your speeches is to deliver them in a professional, informative, and entertaining way. If people have thoroughly enjoyed hearing you and are eager for more, they are more likely to become customers.

Delivering a Winning Speech

If you have no experience at speaking, we recommend taking a course in public speaking or presentation skills. Such courses are available from private seminar companies and at many local colleges or universities. In selecting such a course, make sure that it will include the opportunity to deliver several speeches. Learning to speak is like learning to drive a car; you can't learn by reading about it or hearing how to do it. So the more speeches you give in the course, the better. We also recommend choosing a course that provides video-tape playback so you can review the speeches you have given. As you watch yourself improve, you will develop an increasingly positive image of yourself as a speaker. Here are a few tips to help you make your presentations sizzle:

1. Do not read any speech. Work from an outline or from note cards with key words that trigger your memory.
2. Be sure to keep within the time limit given to you. Time your talk to leave you some leeway for questions if they are applicable.
3. If you approach your time limit before you reach the end of your speech, skip immediately to your closing statement and end with an upbeat summary.

4. Keep in touch with your audience. If you see eyes starting to glaze over, hear a lot of feet shuffling, or notice people heading for the door, try something different—fast! Ask some engaging questions, invite the audience to share their experiences, or do something dramatic or startling. Even a prolonged pause can bring people's attention back to you.

5. Neither talk over the heads of your audience, using jargon, nor talk down to them. Respect their intelligence.

Even if a speech does not produce any immediate business, keep in mind that by addressing a group of potential clients or customers you have increased your visibility and your credibility. And you have opened the doors to new contacts with whom you can develop long-term relationships.

Marketing Technique Measure-of-Success Probability Chart

⊕ Greatest probability of success   ◐ Less probability of success

◑ Good probability of success   ● Least probability of success

○ Medium probability of success   — Not applicable

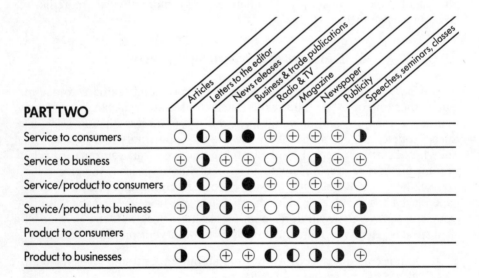

PART TWO	Articles	Letters to the editor	News releases	Business & trade publications	Radio & TV	Magazine	Newspaper	Publicity	Speeches, seminars, classes
Service to consumers	○	◐	◑	●	⊕	⊕	⊕	⊕	◑
Service to business	⊕	◑	⊕	⊕	○	○	◑	⊕	⊕
Service/product to consumers	◑	◐	◑	●	⊕	⊕	⊕	⊕	○
Service/product to business	⊕	◑	◑	⊕	○	○	◑	⊕	◑
Product to consumers	◑	◐	◑	●	◑	◑	◑	◑	◐
Product to businesses	◑	○	⊕	⊕	◐	◐	◑	◑	⊕

PART THREE

Direct Marketing:
Getting Your Message Across One-on-One

C H A P T E R
N I N E

■ ■ ■ ■ ■ ■ ■ ■ ■ ■ ■ ■ ■ ■ ■ ■ ■ ■ ■ ■

Promotional Techniques:
Showing Off What You've Got

Sometimes people are interested in what you have to offer but need an incentive to spur them toward the decision to buy. Without an added motivation of some type their interest may never turn into a sale. Potential customers need a catalyst to move from interest to commitment. Direct marketing can provide that catalyst.

Direct marketing is a term that covers all the various methods successful marketeers use to get their message across directly to people in a way that stimulates them to buy right then and there. It includes such methods as providing samples of what you do; providing giveaways; offering incentives, discounts, and other pricing strategies; attending trade shows; and holding seminars. It also includes the area of direct mail. In this section, we will introduce the creative ways successful small and home-based businesses are using these methods to attract business.

P romotional techniques take your marketing efforts a step beyond word of mouth. They make what you have to say more appealing and turn up the heat to stimulate and entice sales. They are literally what the name implies: techniques that promote sales.

While personal networking and follow-up with top-notch collateral materials help you create a consistently positive image and build ongoing relationships that can turn into business *at some time,* sales promotions are used to provide a compelling reason for those you contact to do business with you *immediately*. They can stand on their own, or they can dovetail to boost any other marketing activity you undertake.

There are a variety of promotional techniques that you can use as building blocks to attract more clients and customers, to be considered in the following sections.

Sampling

The use of free samples is one of the oldest methods of sales promotion in existence and one of the most effective. Until recent years, the concept was relegated primarily to mass-market consumer items such as cigarettes, feminine-hygiene products, and soap and other household maintenance goods. In larger manufacturing businesses it was also a common practice to take a couple of product samples to purchasing agents.

Recently, however—although you rarely read or hear about it—there has been a resurgence of using sampling as a primary marketing method for business of all types and sizes. This is especially true for small and home-based businesses. Our research with successful home-based businesses showed that sampling is an effective business technique in this area.

The premise of sampling is simple: if you try a product or service, you'll like it, and once you like it, you will buy it. We have been amazed at the creative and ingenious ways people have used sampling to start or expand their businesses. Television and radio spots advertising free consultations by law firms, free examinations by doctors and dentists, and complimentary initial visits by weight-loss counselors and health specialists are but one way small businesses are using sampling to break into their marketplaces.

After years of experimenting to perfect her recipe, nutrition counselor J. B. Morningstaar created a line of healthy gourmet chocolates. Her chocolates contain no sugar, butter, or eggs, and some are actually made with oat bran. She uses them as a calling card for her business, offering a taste to everyone who expresses an interest. To launch the line, however, J. B. took sampling a step further. She sent attractively decorated sample boxes of the chocolates to influential health practitioners, health-food stores, and members of the media. Tucked in each box was a sheet describing the philosophy and content of her healthy candies and a request to complete a short feedback form commenting on the taste, texture, and appearance of the chocolates for market research. Those who received these delightful treats were intrigued and flattered. Most loved the chocolates, and orders began coming in.

James Spanos of Nancy's Specialties in Memphis, Tennessee, aroused interest in his "Heaven Scent" bread by giving samples to friends to take to their office lunchrooms. Before long he had orders for dozens of loaves from those who got a taste!

Another person who used sampling effectively is Marie Moreno. When she

Seven Promotional Business-Getting Tools

1. Sampling
2. Offering pricing incentives
3. Providing giveaways
4. Creating your own newsletter
5. Using circulars and flyers
6. Exhibiting at trade shows and exhibitions
7. Holding seminars and demonstrations

began her business doing presentation skills training for corporate executives, she knew she was entering a highly competitive field. Although her background as a performer provided her with the expertise to assist others in presenting themselves effectively, she was unknown in the world of corporate training. To establish herself, she decided to launch her business by offering a by-invitation-only one-day sample seminar to a carefully selected group of CEOs, management consultants, and individuals from corporate training and development departments. They were invited to attend as her guest. She held the event at an exclusive hotel and had an elegant luncheon served. The seminar was a rousing success. The first company to become Marie's client from the guest seminar more than paid all costs of the seminar. In just one day she had created a track record with influential corporate personnel and had her foot in the door with an exclusive clientele.

These are just three examples of the many business owners who have recognized the value of displaying their wares or services in the most exciting manner possible to potential promoters and users.

Case Study: Sampling

Ellen Federico and her partner, David Skovron, started The Event Group in 1986 after the events they planned for the New Amsterdam Brewery became so successful that the brewery management suggested they go out on their own. Since then they have become well known for their highly creative food displays and inventive gatherings. As a full-service caterer and event planner for both private and corporate gatherings, the Event Group assumes complete responsibility for all aspects of their events: the theme; food and liquor; decorations, including tables, chairs, linens, and dinnerware; entertainment; favors; and even the program.

To promote this service, Ellen and David carefully selected seventy members of the media and a scattering of high-profile individuals to receive a specially designed, hand-delivered free sample. This sample was housed in an elaborately floral-patterned handmade hatbox. Inside, nestled in pastel tissue paper was a rose, a media kit with menus, and a free lunch: *crudités* in a pepper cup, cold chicken *au poivre,* "oven-fresh *petit pain,"* and various other delectable items. Recipients' offices were contacted ahead of time to make sure they would be in on the scheduled day, and David himself made most of the deliveries in hopes of making some direct personal contacts.

The response was overwhelming. Fully one-third of the seventy agreed to accept their lunches from David personally and follow-up phone calls resulted in contacts with nearly 75 percent of the recipients. Within weeks of the free lunch, two of New York's top newspapers, the *Times* and the *Daily News,* had both run information on The Event Group and their new idea, and more than one-third of the original seventy recipients had requested further information.

Not only did the promotion net excellent coverage throughout the metropolitan area and in several national publications, but within the first week the approximately $2,500 investment in the free-lunch promotion netted a booking for a hatbox luncheon for five hundred. This one job not only paid the tab for the entire promotion, but according to Federico, it covered the promotion budget of *Fete de Cuisine* and the entire Event Group for a full year. "When you have a small budget, he states, "you are forced to be creative." *Fete de Cuisine* succeeded not only in promoting The Event Group, but in launching an entirely new aspect of their business.

Whatever your business, consider ways to show it off with strategic use of sampling. How might you cost-effectively give people a taste of what you offer? Whose opinion, referral, or endorsement will lead you to more business? How can you creatively enable them to try out what you do? You may well find that giving away samples of your product or service will pay off.

Offering Incentives

Incentives are special offers made to give buyers the extra nudge they need. They are also one of the oldest known methods of promotion. So it's not surprising that using various incentives is another of the most popular ways for successful home-based businesses to start up their customer or client base.

The word *incentive* is derived from the word *incite,* and an incentive can be any means used to arouse a customer to action. The most popular incentives are sales and discounts, giveaways, and contests, each of which can fit nicely into a variety of other marketing activities. In fact, you can use any incentive you choose to boost the results from networking, public relations, advertising, and direct mail.

Using Sales and Discount Pricing

Retail stores and mail-order catalogs have always used the sale as a way to stimulate business, especially in slow times and off season. Unless you are in retail sales, you can't have a traditional sale, but you can induce more business with pricing incentives. These incentives can be used anytime you need to give your business a boost.

Pricing incentives provide you with a way to attract the kind of customers you want at the particular times you want them. Special offers accomplish two purposes: they give you an opportunity to thank your current customers for their business by doing something special for them, and they provide an incentive to new customers to try out your product or service in order to make the decision to become a long-term customer.

There are as many possibilities for special offers as there are products and services. Many professionals offer a free introductory consultation. Print shops often offer a special on business cards or free design services with a printing order; photographers may offer holiday discounts in December, graduation discounts in May, and bridal discounts in June; a lawn-maintenance service might offer a free lawn fertilization for new contract customers. Almost anyone can offer a baker's dozen—one item free with an order of twelve. For example, even a word-processing service can run a special offering each thirteenth page free.

Borland Software used an especially clever incentive to grab spreadsheet customers away from the market leader, Lotus: they offered a special ninety-nine-dollar introductory price on their own highly rated spreadsheet package Quattro Pro to customers of their principal competitors. We bought it, as did tens of thousands of others. A home-based weight-loss counselor is considering a similar special discount on her services to people who enroll in a competing weight-loss program and weren't satisfied with their results.

There are few products or services that cannot be discounted in some way, perhaps indirectly. For example, the creator of Bountiful Baskets, which produces gourmet food baskets, could include a free split of champagne in any basket sent to a new customer for a limited period of time. This would be an ideal means of offering a special incentive to new customers during times when sales tend to be slow. An alternative might be a special mini-basket for the new purchaser of two or more baskets. Prices are not actually discounted in either case, but there is incentive for new customers to try the service.

One way to offer your products or services on a larger scale than you might be able to afford yourself is to tie in with incentives being done by organizations, charities, radio stations, or manufacturers. Select companies, organizations, projects, or events that would complement your product or service and talk with their marketing departments about how you might do such a tie-in. For example, a coupon for a catered meal for two could be bundled with renewals during the local paper's annual subscription drive, an answering service could tie in with a commercial real-estate agency to offer a special to all the tenants of a newly opened office building, and discount coupons for virtually any product or service can be given away with the purchase of a ticket to an upcoming community or civic event. Such tie-ins, where everyone involved wins, work well.

Providing Giveaways

Recent research by Dr. Avraham Shama and Jack K. Thompson of the University of New Mexico demonstrates the business-getting power of giveaways. They found that giving business gifts at the close of sales presentations produces a stronger likelihood that those present will become customers and will recommend the product or service. Their research also shows that a pen worth less than two dollars was as effective as a sports bag worth $10.

There is an entire industry, referred to as *advertising specialties,* or *premiums,* that is built around the concept of adding value by giving something away free. While not all advertising specialty catalogs are particularly creative or unique, specialties can be of great benefit if properly used.

Your giveaway should be selected with the intention of accomplishing a specific purpose that ties in with your overall marketing effort. It should enhance your sales instead of simply spreading goodwill that, however desirable, drains your pocketbook. As a transportation planning consultant, for example, you might give away mini-clipboards that attach to car visors imprinted with your company name, phone number, and slogan—"Put Commute Time on a Diet! Reduce Congestion, Pollution, and Stress." Or someone who goes into homes and companies to care for ailing plants might give away sets of gardening gloves.

Creating Your Own Newsletter

Your own company newsletter can be among the most cost-effective methods of promotion. It permits you to keep in touch with your customers, give them good news, and announce special products or services. It is also a good way to offer incentives, to alert customers to important trends in the industry, and, above all, to give them an opportunity to know you better. A newsletter is a great devise for conveying information you might otherwise find difficult—or even impossible—to report to your customers and prospects, such as news of an award you have received or some outstanding facts about your company.

A newsletter provides you with a chance to sell some of the intangibles about doing business with you. For example, if there is someone at your office with whom your customers or clients talk by phone on a regular basis, you can ask that individual to write a special column and include his or her photo. There is nothing like being able to put a face with a name and voice.

Almost any information of value to your customers and clients can be grist for newsletter's mill: anecdotes, recipes, industry news, organizational hints, jokes, cartoons, vacation-spot information, and information specific to your business, including warnings about unscrupulous or cut-rate competitors (though with no specific names mentioned). However, the fundamental purpose of sending out a newsletter is for it to be read, so it is imperative that your newsletter be more than another piece of junk mail. Limit your first efforts to the length you can fill with compelling, practical information that

What Makes a Good Specialty Gift?

1. **The item should be related to your business in some way.**
   - A plant-maintenance firm could give away small plants.
   - A caterer could offer tea mugs with biscuits or coffee mugs.
   - An interior designer could give away clipboards.
   - An editor could give away marking pens or pencils.
2. **There should be some means of imprinting your company name or logo on the item.**
   - Items should be a solid color, or have a pattern that relates to your logo.
   - If there is no space for a logo to be imprinted, used preprinted self-adhesive labels with your logo, name, address, and phone number.
3. **Items should be functional and usable on a regular basis.**
   - Pens, mugs, calculators, pads, reference books, flashlights, pen knives, calendars, desktop accessories, and tote bags are all functional.
   - Don't purchase any novelty or giveaway until you have a good idea of how your customers work and what they might be able to use.
   - Consider choosing several different novelties to be used for clients with differing needs or to give in sequence to especially important clients.
4. **Items should be designed for use at the location where someone is likely to need your product or service.**
   - A clipboard for an auto visor would be great for a telecommuting consultant; but not for someone selling graphic-design supplies.
   - Marking pens or custom Post It Notes would work well for designers.
   - A copy holder would be great for someone doing in-house computer training for secretaries but useless for sales training.
5. **Items should be durable.**
   - Cheap pens leak, cheap mugs crack, and cheap calculators stop working in the middle of an important calculation.
   - Cheap novelties create a negative image; it is better to get fewer high-quality items than a mass order of cheap ones.
   - Remember, your name will be on your items. You want them to last, to work well, and to reflect well on you and your business.
6. **Items should be easy to integrate into your sales efforts.**
   - Take mugs with coffee or tea and a snack on a morning business call.
   - Give a copy holder while the client is sitting at the computer.
   - Give a designer marking pens at the drafting table.
   - Use a knife to open a carton, then hand it to the customer.
   - Use a bonsai in a demonstration and then give it to the client.

will be of high interest to your existing and prospective clients or customers. To find such compelling information, try reading the trade journals in your industry for interesting tidbits you can pass along to your clients. You may also include governmental activity or industry controversies that might affect your readers, accompanied by appropriate comments from your perspective.

Two areas that can be especially well handled via newsletter are price increases and product or service problems. Your newsletter provides the opportunity to explain the cause of a price increase and use subtle selling techniques to make such an increase more palatable. It is also a forum in which you can make apologies and explain what a customer can do if he or she encounters any problems. Since such notices can be surrounded by short articles that provide valuable information or positive news about your company, the impact of negatives can be softened.

Newsletters are also the ideal way to tell customers about specialized products or services you offer that may not apply to all or may not be mentioned in the normal course of business selling. Furthermore, they can be used to offer special promotions, such as baker's-dozen sales or close-outs, or to promote products or services that haven't moved as quickly as you would like.

Newsletters don't have to be expensive to produce, particularly if you create them using desktop publishing software. Such software packages as *Publish It, Pagemaker,* and *Ventura* for MS-DOS computers and *QuarkXPress* and *Pagemaker* for Macintosh can produce top-notch newsletters, and some word-processing packages, including *Ami Professional, Microsoft Word, WordPerfect,* and *Wordstar*, also have rudimentary desktop publishing features that enable you to create a newsletter.

To produce your newsletter, you first need to create a name for your publication. If feasible, the name should be some sort of play on your company name or business, such as Maxwell Paper's *MaxFacts.* Always incorporate your company's name into the newsletter name, as telecommuting consultant Gil Gordon has done with his newsletter, *Telecommuting Review: The Gordon Report.*

Next, create a flag that consists of your publication name and other important publishing information. Unless you are a top-flight designer, it is wise to hire someone to design your flag, or to use a software package, such as *Bannermania* by Broderbund, to help you design your own. Your flag should be distinctive but not cutesy. The goal is to make your newsletter's flag recognizable by customers and prospects on your mailing list.

You also need an overall design concept for the newsletter itself, with a format and layout that is both readable and distinctive. The pages should be divided into two or three columns for easy reading. In their book *Style Sheets for Newsletters,* Polly Pattison and Martha Lubow have templates for a variety of newsletter formats that can be used with *Ventura Publishing* desktop publishing software.

If you can only afford to print one color, consider using an ink color other than black on a paper stock other than white. Consider matching the colors of your newsletter with those on your letterhead.

NL4-AD1 (page 1)

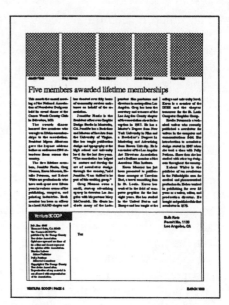

NL4-AD1 (page 4)

NL4-AD2 (page 1)

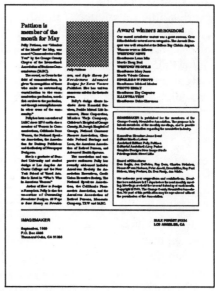

NL4-AD2 (page 4)

Sample Layouts. From *Style Sheets for Newsletters* (New Rider, 1988). Reprinted with permission of Martha Lubow and Polly Pattison.

In order to keep the newsletter easy to read and interesting, use line art, photos, or cartoons. Software packages such as *Newsletter Maker* by ImageBase provide clip art that can be used with most desktop publishing software, and local art-supply stores carry books of clip art and cartoons. There are also companies that specialize in stocking photographs of almost any subject, which you can rent.

Your newsletter may be any size from 5″ × 8″ (folded and trimmed from 8-1/2″ × 11″) to 18″ × 24″ (tabloid size). However, the most well-read newsletters tend to use standard sizes such as 8-1/2″ × 11″ trimmed. You can start with a two-page newsletter, with front and back of one sheet, or if you have enough material, you can begin with a four-page version. An 11″ × 17″ sheet folded in half provides four 8-1/2″ × 11″ pages. If you plan your newsletter to be a self-mailer, you will need to leave a section on the back page for return address, mailing label, and postage information.

If, as your newsletter grows and develops, you find it necessary to expand, you can do so in increments of two pages. When using more than one sheet of paper, do not staple or paper-clip the pages together at the corner, simply insert an additional single page, or, if you use multiple 11″ × 17″ sheets folded in half, have them saddle stitched (stapled) together along the fold.

Permitting your suppliers to advertise can help cover the costs of producing your newsletter. If you decide to do this, be sure that all your suppliers have an equal opportunity and that they advertise without pressure, and don't overload the newsletter with advertising. The point is to promote your company, not your suppliers. Also, be sure you retain final say on the acceptability of ads. You don't want advertising that detracts from the readability of the newsletter or negates the message you want to convey. Finally, don't get caught up in trying to sell a lot of ads, or you will cut into time you need for providing your product or service.

Using Circulars and Flyers

As mentioned previously, circulars and flyers have not been utilized as much in recent years as in the past and should be considered by more small businesses as a valuable tool for many purposes. For example, a contractor who wisely courts real-estate brokers for referrals should consider placing a stack of well-produced flyers or circulars in the hands of every broker in the area, and suppliers of lawn and garden services might distribute a professional-looking flyer to potential customers by stacking them by an unmowed lawn or near a bush in need of pruning in areas where the service operates.

The measure of a successful flyer campaign is the extent to which the flyers reach the people who can and will buy your product or service. So seek locations where people will be interested—not annoyed—to receive them. Some professional, trade, and civic organizations provide tables at their meetings for members and guests to place their advertising flyers. You can also hand out flyers at your booth during a trade show or distribute them with your handouts at any speeches and seminars you give.

Flyers can be accompanied by samples and given away to individuals in controlled circumstances. You might attach gift samples to your flyer as door prizes at a civic event attended by people in your market.

The only limitation to distributing such promotions is your imagination. As a low-cost method of reaching a consumer market in a limited geographic area, circulars and flyers are hard to beat.

Exhibiting at Trade Shows and Exhibitions

Trade shows and exhibitions can be a boon to finding and exploring potential marketplaces. A recent study for the Trade Show Bureau found that seven out of ten firms make purchases as a result of attending trade shows. But exhibiting at trade shows can also be a big waste of money for small businesses.

If that sounds confusing, it can be. Years ago each industry had one or two major shows, usually produced by the principal trade organization, and every buyer or user of products and services within that industry showed up. Nowadays, however, there is a trade show for many industries in some city practically every week. Some of these shows are for retail customers; others are for vendors. Depending on your business, either kind of show—or both—may be worth considering. Unfortunately, the vast majority of these shows are not worth attending. But the right one at the right time can make your year.

The owners of two computer-accessory businesses, for example, made trade shows work for them. Both were women starting their first business. One was producing computer-related greeting cards; the other, manufacturing a foam-rubber novelty bat she developed for safely clobbering computers in moments of frustration. They decided to share a booth at the fall Comdex, where both companies got enough orders to launch their fledgling enterprises. Another person who regularly makes trade shows work for her business is Penny Edwards, who distributes health and beauty products. She exhibits whenever possible at local health and fitness shows, where she always has a crowd at her booth and often sells out of the products she brings.

Trade shows are ideal for businesses that are highly visual in nature or for those that require demonstration, illustration, or explanation. They are a great way to gain immediate access to and feedback from potential end users, retailers, suppliers, manufacturers, or reps you might otherwise have difficulty meeting. Some state governments have trade offices that will advise you on trade shows and sublease booth space rented by the state for shows that are relevant to the state's economy. This could be an economical way to exhibit. Contact your information office to find out about such opportunities.

Six Types of Booth Displays

If you can't afford to buy or create an appealing booth, you are better off simply attending the show. An amateurish, slipshod booth will not only draw a limited crowd but will also create a negative image. Here are six basic types of displays you can use at trade shows in order of increasing expense.

1. A created booth. This is the simplest, least expensive booth decor. Most shows provide a curtained booth, one or two tables, and chairs, and will rent you standard matching table skirtings. On this basic background you can mount photographs or promotional materials. An easel or two with framed blow-ups or a collage of your work can make an attractive display. Plants and flower arrangements can add an elegant touch. Videos, shown with a VCR and monitor, are another effective way to show your work. However, an electrical hookup will cost extra.

The primary drawback to do-it-yourself decor is the fact that other exhibitors could have professionally produced displays that make your booth appear somewhat amateurish in comparison.

Questions to Ask in Deciding Whether to Exhibit at a Trade Show

In deciding whether you should rent space at a trade show, ask yourself the following questions:

1. What do you want to accomplish by taking space? Do you want to make sales, get leads, or boost your visibility?
2. How likely are you to accomplish this goal? Have others like you done it? What is the track record of the show(s) you are considering? Who attends? What are the attendance figures? Do people buy the type of product or service you offer on impulse at such events? Can you follow up effectively on the leads you will gather? What do you need to accomplish to make the exhibit cost effective?
3. How much will exhibiting actually cost you? Do you have the funds not only to rent the space, but to design, furnish, and staff the booth?
4. How can you pull the right people into your booth so that you have the opportunity to talk to them or demonstrate what you do? If you aren't able to hook people's interest in three seconds, they will walk on. How will you get them to stop at your booth?
5. How do you plan to handle logistically the people who come to your booth? Research by Incomm International shows people won't wait long at a booth: 6 percent won't wait at all; 11 percent wait only thirty seconds; 41 percent wait one minute; 38 percent three minutes; and 14 percent five minutes.
6. What displays you will use and what materials or samples do you plan to give visitors to take away for later review?

---

2. Prefab displays.   The least expensive professional displays you can purchase are prefabricated units, consisting of corrugated board that has been integrated with peg board. They come in pieces that must be hooked together somewhat awkwardly and are not flexible. Once you order your unit, you are restricted to that one size and the single arrangement it provides.

3. Stock displays.   A stock display is similar to a prefab but is much stronger and more easily adaptable to various show formats. You can assemble special sections such as shelves, enclosed cabinets, and/or pegboard for mounting displays. Most display houses can rent you a stock display, paint it the color you want, and even add your company name and logo to the header.

4. Modular displays.   Modular units consist of several sections that can be combined in a variety of sizes and conformations to suit the available space and your display needs. Although many shows have standard booth sizes, the configurations are not always the same, and you can easily find yourself with a beautiful display that is too large or too small for your space. If you decide to participate in multiple shows, you probably will want to consider a modular display.

5. Crated displays.   The crated unit is among the more versatile packaged displays. It is custom manufactured and can consist of almost any material and design your budget allows. The unit is contained in a huge crate, however, and must be shipped, emptied, and stored for the duration of the show, brought back to the booth, packed, and reshipped. Transporting and storing the crate can become a problem and you may have less control over when it arrives at the show.

6. Self-contained displays.   A self contained unit solves the problems of the crate display by folding up to form its own crate. These units are more expensive than crated displays at the onset, but the savings in shipping, tips, time, and aggravation fully justify the additional cost.

Laying Out Your Booth

In addition to your display, whether created, rented, or custom manufactured, you will need to arrange your work space to accommodate whatever demonstrations or sales activities you plan for the time you are there. You can use tables as counters, islands, demonstration spaces, and sales areas.

Try to avoid the standard U-shaped space resulting from putting tables around the perimeter of the booth. You can divide your booth space into various work areas by placing tables in T-formations or triangles or by creating islands. For example, you can create areas for the key tasks you want people to engage in while at your booth: browsing, viewing, talking, meeting, and watching demonstrations. Such tasks areas will make your space more visually interesting and inviting to prospects. It will increase your efficiency and maximize traffic patterns so that your staff and prospects won't be stumbling over one another.

Tailor your booth to the needs of those you want to attract. For example, don't try to be too cute and cozy unless such an atmosphere reflects the nature of your business. Including large lounge couches and easy chairs is not an incentive for busy business buyers who are pressed to accomplish their job while at the show. The more efficient you are at helping them do so, the more likely they are to visit your booth. On the other hand, if you are selling stress-reduction courses at a health-and-fitness show, cozy chairs that vibrate with free neck and shoulder massages might prompt lines to form at your booth.

Twelve Trade Show Rules of Thumb

We have spent many hours observing traffic patterns at trade shows in order to determine why some booths seem to attract a steady stream of visitors while others remain mostly deserted. We have also talked with many exhibitors to determine who are pleased with their results and who are disappointed. In addition to selecting a good show and having an attractive booth, there appear to be certain rules of thumb that produce better results.

1. Have some visual element or activity that serves as a magnet to catch the attention of everyone walking by. This magnet can be an interesting sign, a photo, a video, or even music. Studies show that a photograph will work 26 percent better than artwork. Your attention-grabber can also be a demonstration, something you say to people who are passing, or an inexpensive giveaway such as candy, buttons, consultations, or items. If you give away something like a button or a bag people can wear or carry, people who have seen someone else wearing it will be drawn to your booth. Be sure, however, that any giveaway you use is sufficiently related to your business that it attracts people who are in your market. You don't want just a crowd, you want people who need and will pay for what you offer.

2. The exhibit should have one central theme. The decor, banners, materials, layout, and design should support one theme and what you offer should be unmistakable. People give a booth only a three-second glance, and buyers don't stop to figure out a confusing booth.

3. Have others available to help work your booth, even if yours is a one-person company. You will need a break from time to time, and having several people working a booth seems to draw people to it. Also, there are at least two key functions that you must be ready to carry out at all times, and you can't always do them both: to be available to engage people who are walking by and interact with browsers, and to be free to engage in more protracted conversations with serious customers or contacts. So have at least two people present most of the time, and never leave the booth unattended.

4. Make sure all the staff of your booth are sufficiently familiar with your product or service that they can answer most questions. Experts say that what showgoers hate most are overly aggressive salespeople and personnel who aren't knowledgeable about what is being exhibited.

5. Don't waste expensive advertising specialties, four-color flyers, brochures, or complete catalogs on trade shows. Prepare a special, relatively inexpensive brochure or flyer to give to those who request information. Or, even better, respond to the request by cheerfully offering to send information to those who fill out a card with their name and address. Have a limited supply of your best materials available out of sight for the media or for individuals who become serious prospects.

6. Never let a prospect leave the booth without your getting his or her business card or at least a name, company, and location. Then be sure to follow up by phone or mail immediately after the show. Running a drawing for a prize is a good way to get people to leave their business cards. To restrict the contestants to serious prospects, make the prize something only people in your market would want to win.

7. Remain standing and interact with people who pass. People who sit passively at their booths generally have empty booths and get fewer sales. You will miss a lot of prospects if you wait for people to stop and ask questions. Instead, reach out to those who slow down in front of your booth or appear to be looking for something. Ask whether you can demonstrate something or whether they have seen or used what you are offering. Avoid judging prospects based on how they are dressed; people may wear anything to a trade show. Instead, qualify buyers by asking open-ended one-line questions about what product or services they have been using.

Trade shows are hard work, but studies show that 80 percent of qualified trade show leads become orders.

8. Prepare several specials to add incentive for buyers to make an immediate purchase. You can offer a discount or other incentives to those who buy at the show only.

9. Always have plenty of order forms, cards, brochures, flyers, and pens available. Never keep prospects waiting while you dig out something for them to write on. Your name, address, and phone number should appear on every piece of paper you give out.

10. To save set-up time, prepare yourself with a diagram of your booth layout, a checklist of items you will need for display and for use, and a thorough personnel plan. In advance of the show, go over your goals and plans for working the booth with everyone who will be helping you. Goals should be quantified in terms of numbers of leads and sales so everyone knows the target you are aiming for. By spending three to five minutes with each potential customer, you can each plan to talk with ten to fifteen people per hour.

Let the people working in the booth know how you would like them to dress. Grooming, posture, and appearance of personnel are all part of the exhibit. Also review how you expect them to handle various circumstances that might arise.

11. Keep a collection of permanent samples attached to the display. Mount them in such a fashion that they can be used or shown, but not removed.

12. Make sure every staff person in your booth is engaging with the passersby instead of chatting among themselves.   And be sure no one eats, smokes, or drinks at the booth.

Guaranteeing a Productive Show

Nine out of ten exhibitors at every trade show spend a great deal of money on the off chance that someone interested in their product or service will be attracted to their booth. But there is no need to rely on chance.

To ensure that at least those on your current mailing list will look for you and stop by, send a special mailing no less than three to four weeks before the show. This mailing should contain a gift certificate redeemable only in person at the show. Add to the list key prospective clients or customers you would like to have visit your booth. A simple mailing like this should almost double the traffic at your booth, and the gift certificate will increase that number by another 50 percent. But if you want to keep a steady stream of people coming by, make the certificate redeemable for a gift item for the attendee's spouse or child.

Another method often used at trade shows to increase booth traffic is to have a raffle or drawing for a prize related to your product or service. Other ideas for generating traffic at your booth include advertising in trade magazines, business publications, and the show program guide; making up sandwich boards and hiring someone to walk around promoting your exhibit; and donating napkins imprinted with your company name and booth number to exhibit-hall restaurants, receptions, dinners, and other such events.

Use your participation in the show as a media opportunity as well. Most shows have open registration for press. Take a stack of publicity kits to the press room, and watch for people with press badges walking by. They are looking for stories, news, and features to report.

Working a Show Without Exhibiting

There are three primary reasons to take space at a trade show or exhibition: you are there to meet specific customers and take their orders, you want to find new outlets for your product or service, or you have to be there because your competitors are. Any one or combination of the three is a valid reason if your budget can withstand the expense.

However, there is another way to make use of trade shows that is substantially less expensive: attending the shows to find and talk to prospects who themselves have booths. Simply change the focus of the shows you select. For example, as a wholesaler, instead of taking a booth at a wholesale show, you can attend the booths at a retail show. In this case you will not actually make sales, but you will get a good idea of the selling potential of your product or service from the sales reps and managers at the booths. The information you gather can be helpful when you approach buyers of your product or service in person at a later time.

Still another way of using trade shows is to get yourself booked as a speaker. You may not be able to arrange to receive a fee or to have your expenses paid, but you can negotiate for either or both, as well as for space in lieu of your fee. As a speaker at the event, you not only can show off your stuff, but also get the advantage of all the pre-show publicity, increasing your visibility and positioning you as an expert in the field. To find out whom to approach to get booked as a speaker at a trade show, contact the show management and ask for the program director.

Holding Seminars and Demonstration Meetings

Holding seminars or demonstrations for prospective clients or customers is another valuable promotional tool. Promotional seminars are an increasingly popular tactic in today's marketing wars, and they are well suited to small businesses offering either products or services.

Unlike seminars offered through other organizations and groups, promotional seminars are those you put on yourself, inviting a select audience for the sole purpose of previewing and selling what you offer. While the cost of doing this is somewhat greater, these seminars do not have to be done on a large or expensive scale. Under the right circumstances they offer the small-business owner an avenue of credibility that few other techniques can achieve.

Seminars can take the form of anything from a meeting with various people from a client company held in their conference room to a full-scale meeting or conference covering several days in a hotel. The primary difference between a seminar and a sales call or sales presentation is the overt purpose: a seminar is essentially to educate on some level rather than to sell per se. Though in effect you will be selling all the time you are conducting a seminar, your approach should be an indirect one.

For example, a financial consultant used seminars to make contacts and establish his credibility. He offered a free one-hour seminar for successful, upwardly mobile professionals entitled "Investment Opportunities for Professionals," which he promoted through his chamber of commerce and the civic organizations to which he belongs. By limiting each such seminar to ten people, he had ample time to personalize the evening to each person who attended. The moment the consultant offers such a seminar he becomes the expert for those who come. When they have questions about investments, he is the first person many of them call for advice. Thus the seminar opens doors for him. And as there is nothing better than recommendations from the top down, the more prestigious individuals from your market you can attract to your seminars, the better.

A woman who grows and sells wild flowers for use in making craft items tried a different approach: she offered to teach classes on flower arranging in her clients' stores. The stores pay the freight on the initial supplies to be used in the class, do the promotion, and provide the classroom space. The woman's classes bring customers into the store, and if they enjoy the class, they purchase her product and may become regular customers.

Maxwell Paper puts on a free customer-education seminar once a year and always has a waiting list for participants. Reservations for this seminar are limited, and attendees include purchasing agents from some of the largest companies in the country, among them banks, huge retail companies, brokerage firms, and the transportation industry. Although the company picks up the tab each year for some fifty people for hotel, food, supplies, and amenities, the president says that each seminar has more than paid for itself in business contracts within two months of the event. After twelve years, it is a masterpiece in organization and substance.

If you are introducing a new product, you might consider inviting the media and key individuals to an event or party designed to display or demonstrate your product. Personal invitations followed by a personal phone call will increase attendance, as will serving food or providing entertainment.

Dr. Stuart Garber, Director of the Westside Health Institute in Los Angeles, uses a variation on the business-getting event. He collaborates with local artists to host periodic art showings at his clinic for past, present, and potential patients. The art show provides an excuse to show off clinic facilities; clinic staff are available to meet and talk with those who attend, and materials announcing new programs and services are available for guests as they tour the clinic and enjoy refreshments.

Even if your business does not lend itself to any of these formats, most major urban areas have adult extension courses available from local colleges

Three Reasons to Use Promotional Seminars

1. Seminars allow you to show off your expertise.
2. They provide a stage that can open other doors for you.
3. They often are one of the best ways to bring in new customers or develop current ones.

or companies, such as Network For Learning and The Learning Annex, which are valuable arenas for seminars. It is worth investigating these and other possible outlets for educating your potential customers about your field. Assuming a leadership role to educate your market is what gives you the aura of being an expert to whom they can turn when they have a question or problem, and that call enables you to turn them into clients or customers.

Of course, the success of any seminar or event is grounded in careful planning. The more thought you put into details and the more thoroughly you prepare, the more successful your result will be. You cannot simply decide to hold an event, send a letter, and expect results. Before deciding to hold a seminar or demonstration of your own, attend as many others as you can to observe what works and what doesn't. Then plan your own carefully, using that knowledge and experience to guide you.

Many of the promotional methods discussed in this chapter can be the basis for a special direct-mail effort. For example, you can mail circulars and flyers to announce special discounts and giveaways, and send mailings to attract people to trade shows, demonstrations, and seminars. As you will see in the next chapter, using the mail in these ways can make direct mail effective and affordable for small and home-based businesses.

CHAPTER
TEN

■■■■■■■■■■■■■■■■■■■■■■

Direct Mail: Using the Mail to Sell for You

Direct-mail refers to sending sales materials of all types to potential customers. Generally the purpose of doing such a mailing—be it a catalog, a brochure, a coupon, a sales letter, or other specially designed sales materials—is to get the recipient either to place an order or request additional information. In addition to generating inquiries and sales, direct-mail is used to create awareness of a business or product, to build credibility, and to reinforce one's position in the marketplace.

To achieve these varied purposes, any of the promotional materials discussed in this book can be sent through the mail. Newsletters sent regularly to potential and past customers, flyers and announcements of special offers mailed to a targeted group, introductory letters, and even news releases sent through the mail can become an element of a direct-mail marketing campaign. For purposes of this chapter, however, we will be addressing the use of direct-mail for the purpose of actually getting new business.

In theory, reaching potential clients through the mail is an ideal way to free you from having to spend your time getting business so you can go about doing business. In fact, it is often the one marketing tool small and home-based businesses expect will solve all their sales problems. And we do know of businesses for whom direct-mail has proven a primary and steady source of business. For some, it is the only or best way to reach potential clients.

Judi Wunderlich of Schaumburg, Illinois launched her temporary graphic-design service using direct-mail. She sent out 250 letters to local businesses that netted her enough customers to keep her busy for three years, and people actually kept and filed her letter for future use. Two years later, she was still getting calls from the mailing.

Heidi Waldmann of Minneapolis also used direct-mail to launch her desktop publishing business. She sent double postcards to five hundred businesses she thought could use her service, carefully selecting the list herself from the yellow pages and other advertising. She provided a tear-off return postcard and got a 14 percent response. The entire mailing cost her only 150 dollars, but produced several thousand dollars of business.

Tim Mullen of Loveland, Ohio built a successful business publishing catalogs of public domain and shareware software. He sent out twenty thousand pieces of direct-mail every other month. Mailings to past buyers got a 20 to 30 percent response, while first-time lists drew a 4 to 7 percent response for him. In comparing his direct-mail costs to the cost of advertising, he found direct-mail does 20 percent better.

These results show what direct-mail can do and why it entices so many small and home-based businesses to view the mail box as the answer to their business problems. Unfortunately, however, for far too many small and home-based businesses direct-mail fails miserably. Why does mail work so well for some and fail so grandly for others?

The Hybrid of Direct Mail That Works

First, most of those who are using direct-mail successfully are not doing it in a conventional manner. Traditionally, direct-mail has come to mean blanketing large categories of people or geographical areas with hundreds of thousands of mass-mailed advertisements. The cost of buying lists and preparing printed pieces for so many names alone is beyond the budget of most small and home-based businesses, not to mention the cost of postage, telephone lines, and personnel to take calls, sort mail, and distribute goods and services. Even when funds for these expenses are available, such mass mailings usually are a waste of time and a major loss of money for most home-based businesses, when you consider that the overall average of direct-mail response rate is only one-tenth of a percent.

Experience shows that small and home-based businesses that are using direct-mail successfully as a regular source of business are doing what could be called a hybrid of direct-mail. What seems to work best for them is using the mail on a much smaller scale in more customized, specialized, and personalized fashion. In fact, they redefined the concept of direct-mail by devising simple, innovative means of reaching those they wish to reach with small personalized mailings that feature their unique products or services.

As Miami-based David Groves of Groves Financial Services says of his direct-mail efforts, "With the database/mail-merge facilities of my personal computer and a laser printer that prints directly onto the envelope, I can put out one hundred to four hundred 'personalized' letters a month and turn 7 percent of those names into business. That's where the cottage business has it over the 'bulk mailer.' I can put whole sentences specific to the individuals on my list and change them from one form letter to the next."

And that is exactly what those who are able to use this hybrid version of direct-mail are doing: sending out mailings to small, highly targeted lists of people who they know buy the type of product or service they offer. Their mailings are highly personalized to the individuals involved and the needs they have. Often the mailings are followed up with a phone call.

Essentially, home-based businesses that are able to use direct mail to bring in business using this personalized approach tend to meet four prerequisites that seem to be the key to their success.

This chapter will discuss each of these prerequisites and provide you with some basic guidelines for adapting a tailored, customized approach to direct-mail that can free your time and bring you more business. If you decide to use direct-mail, be sure also to read Chapter 14, because the basic principles outlined there apply to any effective direct-mail campaign.

Free-lance copywriter Gregg M. Siegel of Wilmington, Delaware developed an eight-month direct-mail campaign using the postcards on the next page. A new card was sent each month to creative directors or principals at advertising agencies throughout Delaware, Pennsylvania, New Jersey, and Maryland using a list he has personally developed from agency, club, and organization directories, periodicals, and personal contacts. He did all the copywriting, conceptual work, typesetting, and layout himself. Artwork was prepared based on his instructions by a local free-lance artist.

"The purpose of the campaign," he told us, "was to maximize the exposure of my name and services to prospects without incurring the costs of more formal mailing. I wanted each card to be fun, funny, and/or interesting."

Total cost: under $175 per mailing (not including his time).

Results: He has added twelve new clients since initiating the mailing, many of them providing projects on a regular basis.

Four Prerequisites for Positive Direct-Mail Results

1. The business is one that is well-suited to direct-mail. Not all businesses are.
2. The direct-mail piece itself is well written and designed so it won't be thrown out with all the other unsolicited mail. Instead it will get read and acted on immediately.
3. The mailing is sent to enough of the right people to get a profitable response. The more specialized the list, the better.
4. The expectations for what direct-mail can produce are realistic. Many people go into direct-mail expecting the moon and the stars, and when all they get are foothills and valleys, they decide it doesn't work.

Which Businesses Do Well with Direct Mail?

Direct-mail is clearly not for every type of business. Sometimes, eager to find a simple way to get business fast, business owners will turn to direct-mail when some other method of promotion would be more effective. Businesses that do well with direct-mail tend to meet the following criteria. Check off each criterion that describes your business.

The more of these criteria your business meets, the more likely direct-mail will work for you. If you meet very few of these criteria, you should look to other methods.

Is Your Business Suited to Direct-Mail?

_____ 1. Is your market easily definable using finite demographic parameters?

_____ 2. Can you actually reach your potential market through a third-party delivery system, such as the U.S. Postal Service, UPS, or Federal Express?

_____ 3. Is your prospect likely to have purchased a similar product or service as a result of direct-mail in the past?

_____ 4. Is your product or service one that can be sold without discussion or demonstration?

_____ 5. Is your product or service sufficiently visually oriented for the prospect to understand its value clearly from a mailing?

_____ 6. Is your product or service one that is conducive to impulse buying?

_____ 7. Is your product or service highly discounted from those of your competitors?

_____ 8. Is your product or service one wherein a mistake in purchase will NOT affect the buyer or his company in an especially negative way?

_____ 9. Is your product or service one that lends itself to on-the-spot decisions?

_____ 10. Can you afford what it takes to produce a sufficiently impressive package to get your prospect to purchase?

_____ 11. Can you afford either the money to buy appropriate lists or the time to create one sufficient to make any mailing worthwhile?

_____ 12. If you are selling to consumers, can you afford to send your package to enough prospects that a 1-percent return would be profitable?

_____ 13. If you are selling to businesses, are you willing to do the follow-up telephone calls needed to make sure your mailing was received and to discover potential interest?

Designing Direct Mail That Sells

To get results, your direct-mail piece must stand out among all the mail your prospective clients and customers receive. How many of the direct-mail pieces you receive each day do you give more than a cursory glance? How many of them manage to escape your wastebasket? Your prospective customers and clients receive pounds of direct-mail too, and most of this mail ends up being thrown away. In fact, the average person gets seventeen more pounds of direct-mail per year now than ten years ago.

Virtually nobody routinely reads third-class mail anymore. Often someone is screening the mail for your prospective clients or customers, so your piece must get past that person and into the hands of those you want to read it. Then it must entice them to read it, and once they do, they must be moved to make a response immediately by phone or mail. Therefore, your goal is two-fold: you must grab attention and arouse interest even before your direct-mail piece is opened, and then you must elicit immediate action. There are a few guidelines on the following page for designing direct-mail pieces so that they will arouse interest and spur immediate action.

Grabbing Attention

A direct-mail piece is able to grab attention in one of two ways: either it promotes a product or service that is so vital to the particular individual or organization that it grabs a reader like a reflex, or its design is such that the recipient is compelled to look at it more closely, upon which interest can be developed. Even in the first case, the design has to be good enough to convey immediately to the reader what is being represented. Readers will not plow through a printed piece to find out what it is selling unless the design is intriguing enough to draw them into it.

While Howard Shenson claims that only a small percentage of consultants find that direct-mail works for them in analyzing the direct-mail promotions of thirteen consultants and the sales they made, he found those who used different, provocative, risk-taking copy profitably generated business from direct-mail. This does not always mean you have to spend a fortune on design services, four-color printing, intricate folds or expensive binding, special elaborate envelopes, or any of the other things that direct-mail specialists advise. It does mean, however, that you do have to spend time and effort working out exactly what you want your mailing piece to accomplish and how you expect it to do so. You can't afford to waste precious printing costs, list-rental fees, and postage on a slapdash design and lackluster copy.

Essentially you use one of two basic approaches to pique your readers' interest: flash or substance.

Using flash. If you are selling a product to a consumer group, you are generally more likely to appeal to them with drama or glitz. There are all

THE MARKETING MANAGER

ELEMENTS OF A DIRECT MAIL PIECE

Cherry Valley Press
P.O. Box 836
South Pasadena,
CA 91030

> Today's computer revolution opens
> a rare 'window-in-time' opportunity to make
> your dreams for personal and financial independence
> come true....

Dear Computer Owner:

Sitting right there on your desk at home may be your passport to freedom ...fulfillment...financial independence.

Your Personal Computer.

This electronic dream machine can give you freedom from the complexities of today's industrialized world and hassles and frustrations of corporate life, and, best of all, let you reap the rewards of your productivity and enjoy your life and family to the fullest.

"THE TIME MANAGER" is an indispensable one-page planner for work at home that helps you become well organized and totally productive every day.

The "COMPUTER HELPERS" section contains The File Finder, The Electronic Mail Minder and The Database Search Planner -- three important tools you need as you work with your computer.

"THE MONEY MANAGER" is a tested, easy-to-use system for financial records and tax planning, so you'll have everything in one place and you'll know where to find it. It's all here... everything you need to know to turn your home into a fully operable money-making "electronic cottage."

Free 14-Day Trial! Satisfaction guaranteed or your money back!

We're so sure you'll be delighted with your Start-Up Kit that if you're not fully satisfied, we'll gladly refund your money in full within 14 days.

So you have nothing to lose...and everything to gain; your freedom... personal and monetary rewards of untold measure...and the opportunity to run your own business right from home.

You've got half of what it takes now...your personal computer. The other half is ready and waiting for you. Why not get started today? Send for your complete Start-Up Kit now.

Sincerely,

Ben Lizardi
Publisher

P.S. Free Special Bonus! 107+ Ways To Make Money With A Computer! When you order your Start-Up Kit within 14 days, you'll receive FREE 17" x 22" full-color wall poster listing 107+ ways with your computer. Even if ...

INTRODUCING THE COMPLETE MANUAL ON MAKING MONEY AT HOME WITH YOUR COMPUTER.
It's all here...eve... ...ed to know to start and operate a h...

BUSINESS REPLY MAIL
FIRST CLASS   PERMIT NO. 246

No
Postage Stamp
Necessary
If Mailed in the
United States

YES!

CHERRY VALLEY PRESS
P.O. BOX 836, SO. PASADENA, CA 91030

RICHARD VANROY
1524 GOLDEN GATE DRIVE
SAN DIEGO, CA   92116

Direct Mail

FOUR PART FORMULA FOR SUCCESS

1.

ENVELOPE

PLAIN
GRABBER

2.

LETTER

SHORT OR LONG - COPY
GUARANTEE
SIGNED (in blue ink)
P.S. (always get read)

3.

FOLDER

ILLUSTRATION
ACTION
GUARANTEE (put on everything)
COPY

4.

RETURN

ENVELOPE
ORDER FORM
TOLL FREE PHONE NUMBER
   50¢/Call (800) 10-20% increase
CREDIT CARDS Increase 10-15%
GUARANTEE Right near signature
STICKER OR PUNCH OUT
ACTION PIECE
   Something they have to do.

sorts of methods you can use to help create drama in your piece. You can use a special size, a special fold, a unique texture of paper, or even fabric instead of paper. You can use something altogether familiar but out of context, such as a paper bag or a box instead of an envelope. Your printed piece can look like a parking ticket, a newspaper bulletin, a T-square, a giant Rolodex card, a railroad timetable, a roll of paper towels, or anything else you can think of. Your headline can be provocative, asking a daring or frank question or promising a surprising benefit. The only requirement is that your method in some way tie in to your selling message.

Case Study: When Drama Sells

Some years ago a community theater in Dallas began producing special performances of Shakespearean plays for public school children throughout the state. The first year they sent a hurried mailing to every teacher and principal in the state. Their mailer was simple—a simple 17″ × 22″ page of old black-and-white photographs of an earlier run of the play they were performing—*Macbeth*—printed with a 20-percent red screen. The reverse side gave information about the performances, reservations, and prices, and a tear-off return blank for orders. Both sides were two-color: black and red. The sheet was folded twice to create a 5½″ × 8½″ self-mailer. Because each response usually represented fifteen to twenty tickets, the 1.5-percent response rate they got was quite good.

The following year their play was *Julius Caesar,* and they had more time to plan for their mailing. The woman in charge of group sales for the school program decided to have a special poster created just for the mailing. The poster consisted of the same 17″ × 22″ sheet, but this time it was reverse printed in solid black; about one-third down from the top of the sheet was a white laurel wreath to one side of which appeared to drip a small amount of red blood. The name of the play was also in white at the bottom. Some more timid individuals, however, claimed that poster was too dramatic, and since they had the authority to make the final design decision, they vetoed the new poster and decided instead to use the same black-and-white photos they had used the previous year, this time with a blue screen.

The disgruntled group-sales coordinator surreptitiously had half the mailing printed as instructed and the other half printed with the design she had commissioned. The response rate of the old design stood pat at 1.5 percent. The response rate of her new poster design was a whopping 5.2 percent, and the two-week run was fully sold out.

What made the difference? Since the information on both posters was identical, the dynamic selling power of the new design was the only possible explanation. The new poster had such an impact that some school officials asked for additional copies to post on all school bulletin boards. It worked so well because the design took something the students thought of as boring and conveyed it in a way that gave them a better idea of what it really is—a great piece of drama.

You can create an exciting, dynamic mailing piece without incurring extraordinary printing costs. But to do so you have to capture the essence of what you are trying to sell and encapsulate it in an attention-grabbing form.

Conveying substance. If you are selling to business professionals, the flashy and dramatic approach alone most likely won't make it past the secretary. Here you have to approach buyers on their own turf, using their own language and showing that you have an intimate knowledge of their business needs and problems.

Despite many comments to the contrary, the best approach in business-to-business direct-mail is usually the simplest. A letter that clearly shows you understand the reader's business problems and that offers the benefits of your product or service as a solution is the most effective tactic you can find. Even here, though, a hint of flash in the body copy is helpful to maintain interest.

What makes such a letter truly effective is a personalized approach. Each letter should be customized to the individual who is to receive it. However, this does not mean you have to write many individual letters, as you can now easily customize form letters with word-processing software. The letter should be printed on your own letterhead and should be accompanied by any other materials, such as a flyer, brochure, pamphlet, article, reprint, or audiotape, that fortify the benefits of doing business with you.

The key to successful substance mailings is the crucial blending of a well-targeted letter, a touch of flash, and, most important, the right list.

Case Study: When Substance Sells

Thomas Hudock of Systemax Computer Graphics created a superb two page personal letter to send with his flyer "Knock Their Socks Off" (see page 74) along with a response card for requesting further information or a proposal. His first mailing went to five hundred marketing directors of large companies. Although the response rate was a whopping 18 percent, not a single sale was made to those responding. It was evident that, although the marketing directors were sold on the idea, they were not the decision-makers.

The next mailing of the same letter, flyer, and response card was sent to presidents and CEOs of computer-related companies. This time the response rate was much smaller—8 percent—but more than 60 percent of the responses were converted into actual projects and, as of this writing, response cards are still trickling in. The combination of an informative, benefit-oriented letter with a dynamic flyer was intriguing enough to these individuals that they put the information aside for the time when such a resource might be important to them.

Most presidents and CEOs don't have time to read advertising offers that come to them in the mail, but they do make time to read things that might help them do their jobs better. Tom's letter provided all the essential information and showed Systemax's knowledge and competence.

There are several other aspects of getting attention whether you are using flash or substance as your primary orientation. First, be sure to send your mailer to a specific person, not to a title or company name. The extra time spent with the right directories to get people's names reflects the care with which you conduct all your business. There are only two reasons for not sending your mailing to a specific person: when there is no directory that will give you the actual names or the available directory is more than a year old, and when your mailing is so large that telephone calls to find out the name of the right person would not be cost effective. In such cases, be as personal as possible by addressing the person by his or her role, as with "Dear Financial Officer" or "Dear Training Buyer."

The two most important parts of any direct-mail letter are the first sentence and the postscript (P.S.). These are the only two parts you can be sure will be read. The direct-mail letter should begin by focusing on a prospect's single most important need, countered with the single most important benefit your product or service offers. Follow that with the two, three, and four next-most-important needs and their corresponding benefits. End the letter quickly, and offer additional information upon request. The P.S. should state a special offer or a surefire argument.

Also, because it is often the only piece someone will save from a direct-mail package, it is important to include a response card that encapsulates your offer and its chief benefits.

Getting Immediate Action

The trick to a letter mailing is making it appear as close to an introductory sales letter that would lead to a personal appointment as possible without promising the call. Instead, you give the recipients whatever strong motive is necessary to get them to call or send in their order. Offering a guarantee of personal satisfaction will increase your sales.

In a pure direct-mail approach you are not seeking further requests for information or striving for coverage in the local paper. You don't want to announce or inform; you want hard dollar orders. Whatever your design, whatever benefits you are claiming, the single purpose of your mailing is to get the recipient to take immediate action, so make that as easy as possible. Provide anything necessary to facilitate that action. Use postage-paid business-reply cards or envelopes, a toll-free number, a fax number, a toll-free fax number, or whatever is needed. The customer should never have to find or write out an envelope. *Time* magazine even enclosed a tiny pencil to make filling out their subscription order form easier.

Dr. George Allen learned this lesson the hard way. He sent an attractive mailing announcing his new stress-management workshop to all his past clients. He got so few enrollments from the mailer that he had an assistant call recipients to find out why. Dr. Allen discovered they had indeed received the mailer, had read it, were glad to know about it, and even planned to

---

Words That Call for Action

There are certain words and phrases that emphasize the importance of acting immediately. Include ones like these in your offer.

Limited time offer.	Order before _____!
Time is running out!	Introductory offer.
While they last.	Exclusive order.
Limited availability.	Early bird bonus.

These are just a few of the types of phrases that emphasize the need to act quickly. If you couple your main benefit as perceived by the buyer with some form of urgency, you will be more likely to turn a little interest into a solid order.

---

attend "some time." Obviously his mailing had grabbed attention, but it had failed to elicit any action. There was no incentive, no sense of urgency for them to come to the particular seminar he was promoting.

Dr. Allen learned someone receiving a direct-mail piece will do one of three things with it:

1. Throw it away immediately.
2. Put it aside for further consideration.
3. Fill out the order form and call, fax, or mail it immediately.

There is no question that you have lost a sale if your mailer is thrown out. And while people may save it for a later response, don't count on it. Although you might yet reach those customers with a second mailing or a follow-up call at some future time, once a piece of information goes into a file or is put aside, ultimately it will usually get tossed in the trash. So to focus your direct-mail efforts on getting an immediate response, include action words that will make the sale right away.

Dispelling Direct-Mail Myths

Here are some additional points to consider in preparing your mailing.

1. Color is not always more effective than black and white. Sometimes a high-contrast, dramatic black-and-white piece is far more effective than a lovely four-color photograph. The overall design is the key factor.

2. Short is not always better than long. There is more involved in writing a direct-response piece than just keeping it short, even when you are sending out a letter-style promotion. In some cases a rambling, personal style will work better than a brisk business manner. Any letter needs to be long enough to answer all the questions you are likely to be asked if you were there in person. The better you know your customers and what they will want to know before they act, the better your response will be.

3. Your paper choice can make or break your piece. Studies done over the years to test the likelihood of a letter reaching an executive's desk show that paper selection is important. Not only the look of a piece but also the feel of it made a substantial difference. Depending on your target market, you may want to consider one of the recycled papers that allows you to use the recycled logo on your piece, showing that you are environmentally aware, or a rag-content sheet that appears to be more a business letter than a mass mailing. A special weight, texture, or color can add substance and a solid appearance—or it can make your product appear too expensive. A special envelope size, texture, or color can make the piece appear to be social in nature and thus enhance its pull potential, or it can work in reverse. Again, you must match your choices to your market.

4. Messages on the envelope are not always helpful. The direct-mail marketing experts often recommend a teaser on the envelope—such as "Open Immediately," "Confidential," "A personal invitation from Joe Blow," or "A special message from John Doe"—that appears to be handwritten. Sometimes the first couple of lines from the piece itself are used on the envelope, followed by "(continued inside)." These phrases can be useful, but they can just as easily work against you. They will alert the recipients that a sales pitch is coming and give them the chance to toss it out unopened. Certainly an expensive professional or business mailing should never utilize a teaser; on the other hand, a mailing that is promoting a contest or a sweepstakes may find it helpful.

5. Using third-class mail doesn't always save you money. Whether to use first- or third-class mail depends on the type of people you are mailing to, the nature and size of the mailing piece, the list you are using, and the timeliness of your offer. If you decide that first class is the way to go, do not use a postage meter, which will negate the appearance of personalization first-class postage can give your piece. Instead use the most attractive stamps you can find.

Testing Your Piece

If you are in doubt about the best choice for any of the above issues and plan to do a large mailing to thousands, plan to test your direct-mail piece with a small list before you spend huge amounts on a larger mailing to determine whether it works.

Testing is particularly useful when you are sending several items in an envelope. By placing your coupon or special offer in various locations in the mailing and tracking which placements draw the most responses, you can test how the envelope is likely to be opened and the order in which its contents are removed. Then, with your full mailing, you can make sure your major punch is out in front. If the primary piece isn't immediately apparent, people will probably trash the whole mailing before they even know what it is about.

One last piece of advice: don't include glitter or confetti in your mailer unless you want the recipient to curse you loudly. Your mailer will be noticed, but it will also most likely do a great job of unselling your product or service.

Ultimately, the best way to make sure your direct-mail is opened and read is to send it to people who are interested in or in need of what you have to offer and to have a sufficiently high and positive profile for your company that people recognize it and therefore *want* to open mail from you.

Finding a List

Since the way to maximize your response rate is to attempt to reach enough of the right people in the first place, the appropriateness and accuracy of your list will, in great part, determine your response rate. Finding a good list is not as simple as it seems. According to the American Management Association, the overall average response rate to direct-mail advertising is one response from a thousand (.1 percent) pieces sent. Based on this statistic, the average sender gets only one customer from every thousand pieces of mail sent. The minimum cost of postage alone for those pieces is approximately $185. Unless your product or service costs more than that, one response won't even pay the postage. At this rate, even if you got one response for every five hundred mailings, you could fail royally while getting a better-than-average response!

Direct-mail professionals, however, claim an average response rate of one in one hundred, or 1 percent. But here again, the postage costs alone for those hundred mailings will run in the neighborhood of $18, which is precisely why some businesses conclude they can't afford direct mail. With the right list, however, coupled with the right piece, you should do much better than that.

Of course, few lists can meet all these criteria: the goal in building or finding a list should be to come as close to them as possible. The list that comes closest to meeting all these criteria is your own mailing list of satisfied customers. Presuming your product or service is one your customers can use again, or that you can provide some new product or service they need, this list should get far better than a one-in-a-thousand response rate. To draw in new business, however, there are three ways to find a good list: locate and rent one, use a list broker to find one for you to rent, or build your own list.

The Ideal Direct-Mail List

The ideal list would have these characteristics:

1. The names and addresses are accurate and current. (Many lists have 20-percent inaccuracy).
2. These prospects need your product or service.
3. They can afford to buy your product or service.
4. They know or have heard of you, your company, your product, or your service.
5. They have a positive regard for you, your product, or your service.

Renting a List

To begin your search, consider which organizations or groups would have a list of your prospective customers. Is there a civic, trade, or professional association to which they belong? Is there a magazine or newsletter to which they subscribe? Is there a manufacturer or retailer who is already serving them? Each of these sources may be willing to rent you their mailing list. For example, a company that runs a referral service via a computer bulletin board could approach modem manufacturers and rent the names of people in their geographical area who have purchased modems. Someone who has a mail-order catalog of garden accessories could rent lists from gardening magazines. Or a sales trainer wanting to market to book publishers could investigate renting a list from the American Booksellers Association.

Sometimes you can simply contact such groups yourself, ask for their marketing department, and inquire about renting their mailing list. They will either give you the information or refer you to the list broker who handles their list.

The Standard Rate and Data Service, available in many public libraries, is a good resource for identifying lists. Depending on what group of people you want to reach, you can refer to the *Consumer Magazine Rates and Data*, the *Business Publications Rates and Data*, or the *Direct Mail Lists Rates and Data*. The last one profiles over 12,500 mailing lists available for rental, is updated bimonthly, is arranged by market classification, and describes the lists, rental rates, labeling methods, and related information.

A list that is qualified for people who have recently responded to mail will be three to five times as effective as an ordinary list. Of course, you pay more for such a list. Before renting one, determine whether the responses were purchases or simply responses to surveys or offers of free publications. *Responders* are not always *buyers*. When you rent a list, it will be sent to you on mailing labels that can be used only once. (For the legal ramifications of reusing a list, see page 172.)

Using a List Broker

If your target market is relatively easy to identify by a specific set of characteristics (age, sex, zip code, income, purchase profile, and so forth), then a list broker is ideal. A list broker will do the research, compile your list from various sources if necessary, and handle the negotiations of renting it for you. These brokers can be found in the local yellow pages under a heading such as "Mailing List Services."

Most list brokers operate in a manner similar to that of an advertising agency. If the list is already prepared and is acquired from a single source, the broker bills you at the rate posted by the source of the list but receives a discount from that source. Most lists rent for between $45 and $100 per thousand names and are guaranteed for 95-percent accuracy—that is, only 5 percent returns or undeliverables. Brokers also build custom lists, negotiating special fees for preparation services in advance.

Also be sure—especially if you are renting several lists, such as credit-card holders and trade-publication subscribers, that your broker does what is known as a *merge-purge* on the lists to help eliminate costly duplications.

Buying Mailing Lists Through the Mail

We regularly receive direct-mail catalogs that sell mailing lists of names for everything from accountants to zoos. Apparently, more than one large list broker has decided that since direct mail works for many other businesses, mailing lists can be sold by direct mail too. These catalogs include such demographics as age, income, and geography, as well as format options, terms, conditions, guarantees, and pricing. You will be amazed at how specialized these lists can be, with markets as diverse as volleyball professionals, emblem manufacturers and wholesalers, theater specialists for children, and concrete-breaking services.

Questions to Ask in Selecting a List Broker

1. What sources do you use for your lists?
2. Why do you use these particular sources?
3. How often do you use them?
4. What accuracy rate do you guarantee?
5. How often are your lists updated and corrected?
6. How long have you been in business?
7. Are your lists qualified; that is, have the people on them bought similar services or products by mail?
8. Can any of my criteria not be met by your lists? Which ones?

Building Your Own List

If your budget doesn't cover the cost of renting a list or if you are seeking a new, unusual, or highly specialized group of people, you can build your own list starting with responses to the other advertising methods you are using. There are no better prospects than those who have purchased from you before. You can add to your own list by visiting your public library, which stocks volumes of *Who's Who* for almost every industry. There are also all sorts of other directories that list trade personnel at a variety of levels.

Another way to build a list is to take a booth at a trade show and collect names of interested individuals. To boost the number of names you can collect, hold a drawing. Still another approach is to run a contest as part of your radio advertising. However, be sure drawing or contest prizes are something that only your market would want so that you don't get a lot of useless names. For a low-cost way to run such a contest, you can offer your product or service as a free prize to a radio station for their promotions or to a community event in exchange for receiving a copy of the mailing list the contest produces. Or you can contribute a free article to a publication and

---

Direct-Mail Catalogs

American Business Directories
5711 South 86th Circle
P.O. Box 27347
Omaha, NE 68127

They publish:

American Consumer Lists: 82 million households, 4.5 million high-income Americans; available for specified geographical areas.

Lists of 9 Million Businesses, compiled from the yellow pages.

Online Information Network, which allows downloading of lists using a personal computer.

Nationwide Directory of Business: 1,200 titles compiled from the yellow pages; printed directories from which you can create your own mailing labels and use indefinitely. Phone numbers are included.

Dun's National Business List
Dun's Marketing Services
49 Old Bloomfield Avenue
Mt. Lakes Corporate Center II
Mt. Lakes, NJ 07046
(201) 299-0181
Covers 8,500,000 American businesses.

The Hugo Dunhill Mailing List Catalog
630 Third Avenue
New York, NY 10017
(800) 223-6454

The Polk Mailing List Catalog
R. L. Polk & Co.
6400 Monroe Boulevard
Taylor, MI 48180
(313) 292-3200
Provides over 1,000 indexed complete national lists.

---

offer to send some specialized information or a small item to interested readers. If you have selected the right publication and offered the right gift, you will get lots of responses.

Building a good list of your own may take time, perhaps even years, but in doing so through your other advertising and promotional activity you will find these names can be an invaluable resource. For example, Steve Bean, who operates a mail-order software business, over a six-year period found that renting lists produced no results, even though the people on the lists were similar to those who responded to his magazine ads. However, when he built his own list from the names in the latter group, he got a profitable 1-percent response in actual sales.

If you use your own list, be sure to keep it up to date. Send out at least one mailing quarterly, purging the names that are not current and adding new names regularly. Have an address-correction request printed on the envelope. For each address correction, the post office will charge you thirty cents at current rates; and when you mail first class, it will return undeliverable envelopes to you for no additional charge. Mailing-list software makes list maintenance a much simpler task than ever before. But if you find list maintenance too time consuming, you can hire a small or home-based mailing-list management service to keep your list fresh.

One added advantage of building and maintaining your own list is that you can rent your list to other noncompetitive businesses. Take a cue from the major players and salt your list each time you rent it with dummy names and your address or those of friends. However, keep in mind that some of the people on your list may not be eager to get additional direct-mail, particularly if the mailings they receive are not of high interest or potential value to them. All they have to do is call the mailer to find out how their name was obtained.

What You Can Reasonably Expect from Direct Mail

Every direct-mail piece is mailed with great expectations. But in reality, the best expectations are realistic ones. With rare exceptions, the vast majority of whatever you send will end up in a trash can without being opened, so be aware of that before you begin.

Again, keep in mind that the current overall average response rate for direct-mail is one-tenth of one percent, so to get one order, you would have to send out one thousand pieces. Of course, if your product or service is appropriate for direct-mail and you have been using the methods recommended in this book for designing a creative promotional piece and finding a perfectly tailored list, you could reach a response rate of 30 percent or higher, but that is the exception, not the rule. You will be lucky under any circumstances if your response rate reaches the 5-percent mark, which translates to one hundred orders for every two thousand mailings. So do not expect to slay Goliath with a single mailing.

You should not base your expectations or cost estimates on projections of the highest possible return. You will be much safer and more satisfied if you base both on the lowest probable response. Remember that the vast majority of the best potential customers will not do business with someone they have never heard of. Your mailing has merely introduced you to them.

Expecting too much from a single mailing with no other promotional support only leads to disappointment, especially if you have invested your entire promotion budget in that one mailing. When you have met all other criteria and still don't get the response you need, you should consider a program of multiple mailings rather than expecting a single effort to achieve your goal. Or plan to do a mailing in combination with other advertising and promotional methods. Such a multipronged approach is particularly valuable when your product or service is a new one that people don't know about. By introducing yourself through advertising and promotion, you may improve the response to your mailings.

Direct-mail, like advertising, must be thought of as part of a campaign— not as a single technique. With rare exceptions, a single ad in a single publication will bring you little but bills; so it is with direct-mail. Sometimes direct-mail can be even more expensive than advertising. If your budget will not permit a campaign approach or if your break-even point requires a higher response rate than you can reasonably expect, you need to rethink the applicability of direct-mail. You may choose, instead, to use other forms of promotion until you build your business to a point at which you can reduce the risks of direct-mail.

Four Technical Direct-Mail Decisions

In addition to the variables discussed above, there are certain specific decisions you will need to make in planning your direct-mail campaign. Among these decisions are how to time your mailing, how to follow legal regulations, how to choose which carrier and type of postage to use, and whether or not to test your mailing.

Timing Your Direct-Mail Campaign

As with any business, some times of the year are more conducive to pulling a good response rate than others. For mass-market consumer items, pre-Christmas mailers pull the greatest response rates. However, if your product is geared to gardens or water recreation, for example, spring or early summer mailings are more successful. Similarly, the best season for any product or service geared to income taxes is January 15 through April 15. And late summer seems to be a slow time for most industries. So before you do a mailing, consider when people are most likely to be eager to see it.

An alternative approach is to target your mailing specifically to arrive at a

Six Ways to Personalize Your Mailing

1. Use first-class mail or, to save money, a precanceled third-class stamp, not a postage meter.
2. Use your personal or business stationery.
3. Print the address directly on the envelope or use a window envelope. To save money, use clear labels now available for laser printers; they are more effective than white labels and will more than pay for their extra cost in results.
4. Address the envelope to each individual by name, not "Current Resident," "Occupant," or "Owner."
5. Use the person's name and address on the letter and personalize the letter itself in some way by using a mailing-list service or mail-merge software.
6. Follow up with a personal call.

different time from everyone else's, when you have less competition. Someone offering tutoring to children, for example, might have a special promotion during the summer, or a ski school might do a promotion in the summer to sign up early for winter lessons. Reward those who plan ahead with discounts, free gifts, or special offers.

An additional factor of timing has to do with the number of mailings you plan. Most specialists in the field recommend a standard of three. However, the optimal number depends on what you are offering, to whom, how you are offering it, and how much it costs. The three-mailing standard is often effective when seeking new clients or customers, especially those who have never heard of you or your company. Your current client list should be contacted on a regular basis by postcard, letter, a simple flyer, or a newsletter, perhaps presenting a special offer or promotion. For example, Mike Chlanda, who provides business-support services from his home in Yellow Springs, Ohio, sends out monthly postcards to his customers, each featuring a different service he provides.

Legalities

There are several legal safeguards you should take in using direct-mail. First, make sure you are buying a legitimate list. Work only with a legitimate list broker or publication or develop your own list only from legitimate sources. If you are offered a list on the quick take—even if it is your greatly coveted competitor's list—walk away. All lists are salted with dummy names, to prevent you from using a single rental list more than once. Any mailing received by those dummy names opens you up to additional charges at best or even a lawsuit. In some states, theft of a mailing list constitutes a criminal act for which you could pay heavy fines and even go to jail.

Be sure to get copies of all materials about direct-mail regulations from the U.S. Postal Service. Some materials pertain to the regulations on what you may send at third-class rates; others, to business-reply card/envelope requirements. In some cases, the post-office department handling such matters in your area may require you to submit your mechanicals for approval. They are not interested in approving your design; they need only confirm that their machines will be able to read your codes properly.

There are also regulations as to the content and types of items you can and cannot send through the mails. Other regulations apply to how third-class mail must be sorted and to weight, size, design restrictions, and quantities. Be sure you are familiar with all such regulations. Post-office personnel can provide you with the information you need. However, regulations change constantly and not always logically. Do some homework before each mailing or deal with a printer or lettershop that works with direct marketers regularly.

If you quote from other publications in your mailing piece, be sure that appropriate credit is given. If you use more than a simple quotation, get the appropriate permissions required by the copyright laws. Contact your lawyer when in doubt about what is needed. If you include testimonials of any kind, be sure you have a written release or signed permission slip in your files.

Postage Choice

Despite rate increases, the cost of sending your mailing third class is a little more than half the rate of sending it first class. Thus you can mail nearly twice as many pieces for the same postage cost, or you can simply save the difference.

Of course, sending mail first class does increase the likelihood of its getting read, so many businesses use this service for mailing to smaller lists. Not all third-class mail has to look like your standard idea of bulk mail, however. You do not have to print a permit number in a box where the stamp should be, use precanceled stamps instead.

Beyond budget advantages, the primary issue in choosing between third-class and first-class handling is timing. If your promotion is time-dated and cannot survive a delay, do not use third class.

You also have other mailing options. Not all direct-mail is sent through the U.S. Postal Service. Some direct marketers use overnight companies such as Federal Express, Airborne Express, or UPS; others use a messenger service or even their own employees for hand delivery. Your choice depends on your market, what you are sending, and what you are trying to sell.

Testing the List

Technically, direct-marketing specialists claim that to test a direct-mail concept you must use twenty-five thousand to forty thousand names and, to test a list, a minimum of five thousand names. This is fine if you are using direct-mail to approach potentially hundreds of thousands of mass-market consumer prospects. However, the vast majority of small businesses have a targeted market niche that may include fewer than five thousand names.

If you plan to send out only a few hundred pieces, your mailing will itself be a test. As with any other marketing media, direct-mail begins as an experiment, although, hopefully, a well thought-out one. You can learn a great deal from each mailing you do about the list, the design elements, and the copy that works best for your business. But if you plan to send out thousands of pieces, a test of between one thousand and two thousand pieces is advisable and may be sufficient. You can test other things at the same time, breaking your test group into segments and offering alternative lead points or sizes, or layouts, length, or approaches. Rather than trying to test too many things at once, however, let testing answer only major questions you have.

Direct-Mail Multipliers

There are a variety of ways you can multiply your direct-mail response. Using prepaid response cards can help dramatically, as can following up either with an additional mailing or a phone call. This is particularly true in doing business-to-business mailings or in using a list of individuals you know.

Including a Prepaid Response Card

When Heidi Waldmann used a double postcard for the successful mailing that launched her desktop publishing company in Minneapolis, half the card was designed so that anyone interested in her business could tear it off and return it after checking one of the following: "(a) send us more information," "(b) call us with information or to set up an appointment," or "(c) we have no need at the time." Space was provided for them to write their name, address, and phone number, along with any comments. Using such a card can increase the responses and help you follow up more effectively. When you do a large mailing that includes such cards, you can save money by arranging with the U.S. Post Office for a business-reply-mail (BRM) permit so you will pay only for those cards that are actually returned. The post office will usually even supply you with a template to use in printing your cards.

Using Follow-Up Mailings

When using additional mailings as follow-up, be sure to purge those who have placed orders from the list to be used for subsequent mailings covering the same special promotion. There is nothing more aggravating for a customer than to place an order for an item and then continue to receive mailings about it. The customer begins to equate your lack of care in this matter with your overall service approach and becomes reluctant to order again.

Using the Phone to Increase Your Direct Response

The most effective results from direct mail come from combining it with a follow-up telephone call. Obviously this is feasible only when what you are selling is priced high enough that you can afford to invest the time in making phone calls. In fact, the more expensive or customized the product or service, the more likely you will need to combine your direct mail with a phone call and perhaps a personal sales call as well.

There is a rule of thumb in marketing that claims it takes seven contacts to produce a sale. The more expensive the product or service, the more likely this rule of thumb is to apply. Suppose, for example, you are selling a $450 seminar or a $5,000 consulting program. Perhaps some people will call or write to order from your mail piece, but you will get a much higher response if you call first to tell them you will be sending the material and then call to follow up on whether they received it.

Recently Howard Shenson reported in *The Professional Consultant and Information Marketing Report* that a survey of three hundred chief executive officers found that they expect a follow-up to a letter or brochure by either mail or phone. He also reports response rates three to seven times higher when direct mail is followed up by a phone call.

When you call to see whether a mailing was received, often people will not

---

Telephone Follow-Up Step by Step

1. Ask to speak directly to the individual to whom you sent your mailing.
2. If that person is not available, find out a good time to call again. Do not leave a message for the person to call you.
3. If you cannot reach the person, elicit the help of his or her secretary. A secretary can become your greatest ally.
4. When you do reach the person, ask whether your mailer was received.
5. If it was received, ask whether it was of interest and if it was not received, whether it might be of interest.
6. If the response is negative, state briefly why you thought the mailing would be of interest, emphasizing the most important benefits to your listener. Listen carefully to his or her response.
7. If any interest is expressed, offer to send additional information or set up an appointment.
8. Even if your listener is not interested, always thank him or her for the time and offer to be of help any time in the future.

remember receiving it. It probably ended up in the wastebasket or in a pile somewhere. Your follow-up call, however, may elicit enough interest that you can offer to send a replacement, after which you can follow up with a second call.

Following Up Fast

If your direct-marketing efforts are aimed at finding sales leads or are promoting a service, which usually requires that the customer's response involve a request for further information, make sure you make your next contact quickly. If the customer needs additional literature, it should be on its way to him or her within forty-eight hours after receiving the request. If the prospect expects to be contacted personally, the same forty-eight-hour rule applies. As with everything else in marketing, you need to strike when the iron is hot.

Once you have prospects interested, don't waste time in getting back to them. Here again, delay shows a lack of interest or suggests less-than-top-notch organization on your part. And that is the fastest way not only to lose a sale but to lose a customer, permanently.

Tracking Your Results

Whether or not to track a particular direct-marketing promotion should be determined by whatever testing procedures you have already used. If you do not test, consider tracking as a means of preparing your future approaches. Your criteria for tracking could range from whether the list reaches the right people to whether you used benefits that are important to your customers.

For example, suppose you have purchased lists from two diverse trade publications and one credit-card company, each with its own code incorporated in the label. If you make sure to get that code number in your response, the response rate per list can be separated and ranked. Or suppose you wish to experiment with two totally different approaches, but your list is too small for a full-scale testing procedure. You can simply create your own short code to add to the label or to another easy-to-find portion of the return order form. For example, one address could include "Dept. D" and the other, "Dept. K," or, if the headlines are different, you can use the first four letters of each headline as your code.

To make such tracking information as accurate as possible, make sure your printed pieces are alternated one-for-one before labels are placed on them. This will insure the randomness of the distribution among the ZIP Codes to which you are mailing. Here again, your response rate for each code will tell you a great deal about how the two approaches were received.

Since tracking is such a simple process for direct marketers, it is foolish not to gather the information available even if it does not interest you right now. That way it will be at hand when you do need it.

Finally, when using direct mail, remember to keep your expectations within in reason to avoid disappointment. A direct-mail piece is little more than a traveling billboard. A billboard can only sell something to someone who is ready to buy. Do whatever is necessary to send your piece to the right people; focus on the benefits to the customer rather than the features you are proud of; be as creative as your product or service allows; make it easy for a customer to respond; and follow up on every contact or request. Do all these things and your return will exceed your expectations.

Marketing Technique Measure-of-Success Probability Chart

⊕ Greatest probability of success   ◑ Less probability of success

◐ Good probability of success   ● Least probability of success

○ Medium probability of success   — Not applicable

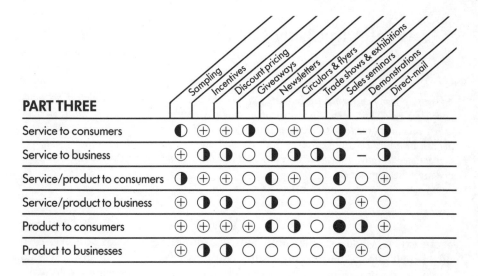

PART THREE

	Sampling	Incentives	Discount pricing	Giveaways	Newsletters	Circulars & flyers	Trade shows & exhibitions	Sales seminars	Demonstrations	Direct-mail
Service to consumers	◐	⊕	⊕	◐	○	⊕	○	◐	—	◐
Service to business	⊕	◐	◐	○	◐	◐	◐	◐	—	◐
Service/product to consumers	◐	⊕	⊕	○	◐	⊕	○	◐	○	⊕
Service/product to business	⊕	◐	◐	○	◐	○	○	◐	⊕	○
Product to consumers	⊕	⊕	⊕	⊕	◐	◐	○	●	◐	⊕
Product to businesses	⊕	◐	◐	○	○	○	○	◐	⊕	○

*Inventive Advertising:
Cementing Your Name in Their Brains
So You're the One They Want*

CHAPTER
ELEVEN

■ ■

What Advertising Can and Can't Do for You

Advertising is one of the most misunderstood and misused of all marketing activities for small and home-based businesses. The unfortunate result is that many who use it waste precious money and time expecting it to be their primary source of business. But used properly, advertising can be a very effective tool. As with direct-mail, success in advertising lies in being able to step outside the costly methods traditionally used and instead find more customized, personalized, and inventive approaches.

We have heard many frightful stories about expensive advertising campaigns that produced no leads and extensive direct-mail efforts that got no results. We have even watched businesses go down the drain pumping more and more money into advertising while waiting anxiously for the phone to ring.

On the other hand, we have also heard glowing accounts of advertising being a trustworthy source of steady business. Advertising is especially effective when you are selling a product to the general public, such as soap or potato chips. For a consumer product, advertising is the most efficient method for reaching the largest number of people. Since most self-employed individuals are selling more specialized products and services, however, using a mass-market advertising approach to getting business is like using a forklift to pick up a toaster. A small or home-based business must determine whether advertising can be a medium for reaching its targeted market.

For example, Judy Wunderlich, who runs a temporary agency for graphic designers in Schaumberg, Illinois, gets all her business by using direct mail to firms that are too small to have an in-house graphic-design staff. Cheryl Myer, who runs Word Processed Pages from her home in Algonquin, Illinois, gets most of her business from the yellow pages, and Roland Sutton of Conway, South Carolina gets the majority of his parking-lot-maintenance service from sending out his own newsletters. These businesses have several aspects in common that make them good candidates for advertising:

- Each provides a service or product that people know they need.
- There is an immediate demand for each of their services or products.
- Each product or service is relatively clear-cut and easy to understand.
- The quality of each product or service is relatively easy to measure.

Despite these apparent similarities, only one of these businesses has chosen advertising as its primary promotional technique. Each has selected the marketing method that is best suited to the nature of its particular business.

Since Judy's company is the first in the Chicago area to offer a service providing temporary personnel in the graphics field, people aren't apt to look for it in the yellow pages, nor would the brevity essential to any advertising medium be conducive to explaining her unique service. Thus advertising would not be a cost-effective selection for her, whereas a mail campaign sent directly to businesses who need such services works well. On the other hand, everyone in business today knows about word-processing services, so they are apt to turn straight to the yellow pages when they need one. Thus, this form of advertising is effective for Cheryl. But since parking-lot maintenance is a highly competitive field, Roland needs some means for distinguishing himself from his competitors. A newsletter provides him with ample space to inform, educate, and sell, which would be too expensive to accomplish through an ad.

The first secret to making advertising work is knowing whether your business is one that is suited to it and, if so, selecting advertising vehicles that are right for you.

Five Common Myths about Advertising

The next two chapters will introduce you to a variety of vehicles that have worked well for others. First, however, we want to clear up five of the most common misconceptions we have encountered about advertising and outline what advertising can and cannot do.

Myth 1: Advertising is what you have to do to get business. Fact: advertising is only one of many ways to get business. Advertising is simply the purchase of time or space in order to promote a product or service. It is only one of many ways to get business. There are many other marketing methods available to you that do not involve buying time or space, some of which might be better for you than the purchase of any kind of advertising. On the other hand, advertising may be the best method for you.

Myth 2: Advertising is too expensive for small businesses. Fact: Advertising doesn't have to break your budget. The high cost of most traditional advertising has actually opened the door for many less costly avenues and techniques that can be just as effective for small businesses. Additionally, there are many creative promotional alternatives, some using techniques similar to advertising.

Myth 3: There is one best advertising method. Fact: Advertising always begins as an experiment. Because most individuals who are in business for themselves don't have a lot of money to spend, too often they begin by putting it all into one approach to advertising that they heard worked well for someone else, hoping it will provide the business they need. In actuality, finding the right advertising medium for your business is similar to concocting a new recipe by trial and error.

Marketing consultant Cork Platt claims that success as a marketer lies in how much you fail. He cautions start-up sole proprietors to avoid the trap of using one advertising approach or outlet at a time, urging instead that they sample several approaches or outlets on a small scale simultaneously. Unless you try combinations until you find the right formula, he warns, you are apt to run out of money before finding the one or two avenues or techniques that will work for you.

Not realizing this nearly put Bobby and Jody Feinstein out of business. When they opened a referral service for household help, on the advice of a business consultant they spent every penny they had on a massive print-ad campaign. They hired an advertising consultant and an excellent designer, carefully selected targeted newspapers and magazines, and blanketed the area with their top-notch ads. You can imagine their horror when virtually no one called from these ads. They later discovered that when people pay for a referral, they want to know the person making it. Ultimately, the Feinsteins discovered they could get an excellent response at trade shows, but they went seriously in debt before doing so. In hindsight, they realized they should have put a little of their money into testing the responses to a variety of marketing approaches, perhaps by starting with a few classified ads while simultaneously experimenting with trade shows or networking. By using such a shotgun approach they would have found out what worked in less time and avoided a near disaster. So avoid the temptation to put all your advertising eggs in one basket until you know from experience what the right basket is.

Myth 4: One shot will do it. Fact: Advertising requires repetition. The fourth misconception about advertising is that a little dab will do you. Advertising is an investment that takes time and repetition. The average

American is exposed to hundreds if not thousands of promotional messages every day. As a result, people have learned to screen out all but those messages that effectively claim their attention. This makes advertising a challenge for any business that is operating on a shoestring. Advertising works on what is called the Rule of Seven, which asserts that a message typically needs to be noticed by any given customer seven times before he or she will take action. The corollary to the rule is that it takes an average of three tries to get noticed once. That means you have to expose a potential customer to your products an average of twenty-one times before he or she is likely to call, come in, or place an order.

For small and home-based businesses with limited advertising budgets, scrounging up the dollars to advertise once can be challenge enough, let alone doing it twenty-one times. However, money spent on hit-and-miss exposures is usually money wasted. For example, when Doris Kay began offering pick-up and delivery services to recharge laser cartridges for downtown offices, she decided to spend her limited advertising funds for a half-page ad in a local business journal with a large monthly circulation. She spent her remaining money to buy a thirty-minute block of time on a small-business-focused talk-radio station. The results from both were poor: she got no calls from the magazine ad and only three from the radio show, and no one actually signed up for the service. Following the Rule of Seven, Doris would have been wiser to invest the same amount of money in a small classified ad in a daily or weekly publication and in shorter radio spots that would run repeatedly over as many weeks as possible. These ads could have been supported by public-relations and promotional activities.

No matter what your business is, if you have the budget to keep doing it, advertising can help. In most cases, however, when advertising funds are limited, you have to be selective and creative to obtain a sufficient number of exposures to get results.

Myth 5: Advertising does the work for you. Fact: You can't sit back and wait. The fifth most common misconception about advertising is that it is a totally passive way to get business. Many people think they can simply put some ads in the proper place and sit back and wait for the business to come rolling in. Rarely does that happen.

While advertising can be marketing while you are working, it also demands that you engage in a highly active and interactive process with the prospective clients or customers it reaches. The more active you are in promoting yourself through a variety of marketing activities, the better results you will get from any advertising you do. All your promotional efforts will greatly increase the chances that people will respond to your advertising. And once they do respond, usually you will have to do more than simply take their order. With the exception of direct-response advertising to which people respond by sending in the money with their order, most ads produce leads— people who are interested. Occasionally they will simply want you to write up the sale, but most of the time you will at least have to close the sale.

For example, Dr. John Grable hired a writer to create an ad promoting his new stress-reduction classes. He ran the ad daily for two weeks in the local newspaper. The first day the ad ran, he forgot to tell the secretary about it, and she told the people who called that they must have the wrong number. After this embarrassing episode, the secretary was well prepared the next day to sign people up for the workshop. Unfortunately, however, they were calling to get more information so they could decide whether to sign up. The secretary didn't know anything about what the seminar covered, so she placed the stack of calls on the doctor's desk to be returned sometime during the day. By now Dr. Grable was very frustrated. The first class was approaching and his advertising had become a headache instead of a route to new business. Fortunately, he had prepared a flyer about the classes to hand out to patients in the office, so he had his secretary mail a flyer to everyone who had called. There were a total of twenty-six calls during the two weeks, but not one person called to enroll after receiving the flyer. Dr. Grable concluded that advertising was just a waste of time and money.

Had he been aware that advertising is not simply a passive order-taking medium, Dr. Grable could have turned these calls into profits. For example, he could have planned to have someone with sales skills take the calls or make follow-up calls after the mailings went out. He could have arranged to have everyone who called for more information visit his office at one set time for a preview, where they could talk with him first hand and register for the classes. Since many of the people attending his classes ultimately come to him for treatment, his advertising would have paid off again and again.

While advertising can and often does produce some rapid sales, if you need immediate business, you are best advised to use promotional techniques such as those discussed in Chapter 9 instead. Research shows that advertising does a better job of stimulating more business from your existing customers than it does of getting new ones.

Choosing Among Eight Inventive Advertising Options

In the following chapters we will primarily explore eight inventive advertising options:

- classified ads
- the yellow pages
- business directories
- newsletters
- radio
- cable TV
- electronic media
- direct-response advertising

When a Small Business Should Advertise

The primary reasons to use advertising are to create awareness of your business and knowledge of what you offer, highlight why someone should select you over others who offer something similar, create a favorable emotional reaction to your product or service, remind people to buy, and stimulate impulse purchases.

When a Small Business Should Advertise	When a Small Business Should Not Advertise
1. When your target market is the mass-market consumer	1. When there is no medium that reaches your market directly
2. When your target market is reachable by one or more particular media	2. When it is not cost effective
3. When there is no other method of reaching your prospect	3. When your budget will not permit proper coverage or repetition
4. When awareness of your company's existence is an essential preliminary to approaching your target market	4. When you expect advertising to bring in customers in droves
5. When you are expanding your line or moving into a new market	5. When there is no way to sell your product or service without one-on-one contact
6. When your budget permits	6. When advertising would be your only method of reaching your market
7. When you can reach the most people who can and will buy your product or service cost effectively through advertising	7. When your advertising cannot compete with that of your competition
8. When most of your competition advertises	8. When you cannot afford to have the preparation done properly
9. When none of your competition advertises	9. When you cannot express the essence of your product's or service's benefits briefly and dynamically

Which advertising media to choose among the wealth of options available is a matter of matching your budget with the ability of each medium to reach the greatest number of people who will buy your products or services. For this reason, people who sell advertising space and ad time talk in terms of cost per thousand, abbreviated as C/M, meaning the actual dollar amount you spend in relation to the number of readers, viewers, or listeners the particular medium claims you reach. Cost per thousand is not a bad way to make comparisons among various media, but be sure that those costs are comparable.

Although any medium will give you a C/M number based on its particular audience, it may or may not give you specific demographic information on that audience. For example, suppose the price of a half-page ad in Publication A is $1,350, whereas the price of the same-size ad in Publication B is $1,475. Publication A has a total circulation of ten thousand people, making their claimed C/M $135; Publication B has a total circulation of six thousand, with an apparent C/M of $246. The natural assumption would be that Publication A would be the better buy.

However, a closer look at the circulation figures shows that of Publication A's ten thousand subscribers, six thousand are age twenty-one to thirty-five, two thousand are thirty-five to fifty, and two thousand are fifty and above. In contrast, Publication B's six thousand subscribers break down into five thousand age thirty-five to fifty and one thousand over fifty, with none under thirty-five. If you are looking for potential customers only between the ages of thirty-five and fifty, the original C/M figures change radically. Publication A's effective C/M is $675, while Publication B's becomes $295, and their value to you is reversed.

So here are several other factors to take into consideration whenever possible when making your advertising choices.

Getting the Most Reach for Your Money

1. Verify the claim. Find out whether a medium's claimed audience is audited or unaudited. If they are audited, the numbers were confirmed by an independent entity; if unaudited, they come from the medium's management and may not be accurate.

2. Get a breakdown of the audience. Carefully investigate the specific demographics of the medium's audience. Determine the categories that might truly be potential customers, and work your cost per thousand based on those numbers.

3. Calculate the total cost. In calculating the cost per thousand, be sure to include total costs, including amortization of your production costs over the span of the advertising period.

4. Track your response. Once you have run some advertising, despite the inherent difficulties and probable inaccuracies, try to determine approximately how many responses or reactions you got. This information will tell you whether an ad is paying for itself and which ads are bringing in the most business.

5. Set a budget. Set up an advertising budget based on the percentage of your gross sales that come from advertising; then don't exceed that budget. For example, if your gross monthly income is $10,000, $4,000 of which comes from referrals or networking and $6,000 from advertising, it is sensible to set aside 60 percent of your marketing funds to invest in advertising. So if you have $1,000 to spend on marketing each month, $600 a month will go to advertising and $400 to various networking activities.

When Do You Need an Advertising Agency?

The decision to hire an advertising agency depends to a great extent on how much advertising you think you will be doing. If your advertising will primarily be limited to the yellow pages, a regularly repeated ad in trade journals, and a few classifieds, involving an agency would probably waste your money and their time.

However, if the best access to your market is through ongoing advertising in a variety of print and broadcast media, you can save time and money hiring an agency to provide a coherent campaign approach to the development and placement of advertising. Keep in mind, though, that most full-service agencies will not give you the time of day unless you expect to have an advertising budget of at least $50,000 a year. The exception would be a young and hungry agency with whom you can grow or a one-person agency who will work with small accounts.

The usual method of compensating an ad agency is to pay 15 percent of the gross amount you spend on preparation and media, which actually works out to 17.65 percent of the net. To illustrate how this works, if a newspaper charged $100 for an ad, the agency would bill you for the $100 and pay the newspaper $85. The fifteen-dollar difference pays the agency. This $150 is 15 percent of the gross, but it is also 17.65 percent of the $85. By the same token, if a printer produces two thousand brochures for you as a client of the agency and bills the agency for $1,000 for those brochures, the agency will bill you $1,176.50, or $1,000 plus 17.65 percent. The extra $176.50 is 15 percent of the $1,176.50. Media and some suppliers do, however, offer a 2-percent discount for payment within ten days of invoicing. So if you pay promptly, the agency should pass that discount along to you. In selecting an agency, take into account:

- the questions they ask you. An agency should want to know a great deal about your business, plans, and expectations.
- the responses you get to your questions. A good agency will be candid about what they can and cannot do and how they charge for services.
- the samples of the agency's recent work. Expect first-class work.
- the results of advertising they have done for other clients. Request and review such data.

For businesses that do not have the size of budget appealing to an agency but still needing professional help, hiring a free-lance designer or copywriter or using a media-buying service can get you both professional service and save you money.

Of course, whether you do it yourself or get help, you need to give your advertising time to produce for you. Remember the Rule of Seven: you need at least twenty-one exposures to get a true test of the results. That is why you need to be particularly inventive in getting the most exposure for the least money. There is no sense advertising unless you can do it long enough and regularly enough for it to have a chance to work.

CHAPTER
TWELVE
■■■■■■■■■■■■■■■■■■■■■■

Using Traditional Print Advertising
Alternatives in Inventive Ways

Advertising in newspapers, magazines, and other print media is often referred to as the "Great Mother" of advertising, because it has provided a forum to advertisers of all sizes, shapes, types, and budgets for hundreds of years. The advantage of print advertising is the wide selection of possible publications you can advertise in and their ability to reach either a broad or a highly targeted base of people.

Traditionally, print advertising refers to buying a portion of a page in the newspaper or magazine of your choice and displaying your ad there. Such display advertising is costly, however, because you are not only paying dearly for the space but must also pay dearly to design the attractive and effective layout and camera-ready art required for your ad.

Therefore, instead of making the investment in such display advertising, many successful small and home-based businesses are using more cost-effective methods of print advertising, such as classified advertising, yellow-page listings, and directory advertising. Then, when they get a particularly strong response from a particular publication, they may purchase a display ad in that publication.

Using Classified Advertising

For many small businesses, the best entry into the realm of advertising is through the classifieds. For example, when Lynn Frances started her cleaning service, she knew her best customers would come from the exclusive community of San Marino, California, so she ran a classified ad in the local San Marino paper. That listing turned out to be her primary source of business— so much so that she continued to run the ad every day of the year.

Classified advertising can serve as a bridge between the more costly display advertising found in most media and the simple listings found in all varieties of directories. Newspapers and most consumer magazines, business and trade journals, and even small association newsletters have classified sections where individuals and businesses can advertise products and services for a minimal fee.

The term *classified* refers to the fact that the ads in this section are placed within categories, according to the type of product or service being offered or the type of purchaser sought. Examples from three different classified advertising sections are reproduced on the next page.

Whether your product or service is suited to *Architectural Digest* or *Video Review,* the local American Red Cross newsletter or a specialized business journal, you will usually find a classified section in which to advertise. Classified sections often consist of the standard "words-only"—no graphics— listings seen in your local newspaper mixed in with varying sizes of display advertising. Other sections consist almost exclusively of mini-display ads, such as those in the Marketplace section at the rear of *PC Magazine.*

Classifieds are most often utilized by people who are already interested in locating a particular type of product or service. For these people, skimming the classifieds is as important as reading the editorial areas.

Classified advertising is usually purchased in one of three forms: by the word, by the line, or by the column inch. Each publication has its own methods of pricing, so check with the particular publication to find out its policies. As with display advertising, there is usually a discount when you repeat an ad several times. Since advertising is a repetitive medium, you should take full advantage of such discounting.

At Home Professions of Garden Grove, California, a business that trains

---

When to Use Classified Advertising

■ When you are beginning an advertising campaign and want to test whether a particular publication will draw for you before you invest in more expensive advertising

■ When you need to advertise consistently in a publication in which you can't afford a more costly ad

■ When you want to compare the response from a variety of publications in preparation for display advertising

■ When you want to launch almost any mail-order business

Deadlines: September/October - July 27 ····· November/December - September 15 ·················· **EF**

M
A
R
K
E
T
P
L
A
C
E

Sample classified ads.

people to become notereader-scopists and medical transcriptionists from home, has built a successful business by placing classified ads in neighborhood shoppers. They use the ads to attract interested individuals to attend free seminars at which they find out about these two high-demand occupations.

To place classifieds in such shoppers on a nationwide basis, you can contact the National Classified Network. (See Resources.) NCN is a media-buying service that specializes in placing nationwide classified ads at substantial savings—as much as 65 percent—in time and money to the advertiser.

In order to take the greatest advantage of classifieds, you must remember that, as in any ad, you have only fractions of a second to grab the reader's attention. Since you have even less space in order to do this, your copy must be even more arresting than that in a display ad.

Some publications permit artwork, some allow headlines, some permit the first few words to be boldface, and still others allow nothing but straight copy. Before you write your ad, be sure to investigate the requirements of the publication in which you are interested in addition to looking at the publication itself. When such enhancements are permissible, there is most likely an additional charge for their use. If they fit within your budget, use whatever enhancements are allowed. Even if most enhancements are not available to you, you may be able to use all caps on the first few words or the entire first line. If none of these embellishments are permitted, you will have to rely exclusively on your choice of words to attract attention.

No matter what your design choices are, your choice of words is critical. Unlike display advertising, all classified advertising focuses directly on selling instead of creating an image or providing information. You must select one point, hit it, and hit it hard again. Make your point without using adjectives or qualifiers that will dilute the message. You must have something specific to offer—a specific product, a specific service, a specific discount, a specific gift, or a specific point.

The first word in your ad, especially if you cannot use a headline, is the most important. Skim through *Words That Sell* by Richard Bayan and select the most powerful word that is applicable to what you are selling. Words such as free, discount, profit, urgent, daring, elite, bold, sparkling, speedy, revitalize, secure, and guarantee all evoke an immediate image in the mind of the reader. They are strong, dynamic words and pull the eye to the next word. Avoid indefinite words like *can, might,* or *may* and impact-losing words such as *the, an, if, a* or any other article. Think of verbally yanking the reader up by the collar.

Look at the classified ads in publications like those you will be selecting for your ad and ask yourself the following questions:

- Do any of the ads catch my attention?
- Which ones?
- Why?
- Is there something in those ads I can apply directly to my advertising?

You will notice immediately that the best ads focus primarily on one point. If someone is offering a disk copy service, that point comprises the bulk of the copy. That a catalog of diskettes and supplies is also offered may be mentioned, but only briefly.

If you have more than one point to sell, buy more than one classified ad. Instead of trying to crowd all your information into a single ad, think about dividing it and placing two or more smaller ads, each with its own set of power words.

As with any other forms of advertising, you must take note of what your competitors are doing in the classified section. If they are all inserting display classifieds, you must consider using the same tactics. However, if you have no competitors using the classifieds, don't automatically assume that they know something you do not. For a nominal amount of money you can begin to establish an advertising presence and test a medium's ability to draw. You may discover something your competitors never thought about, opening a whole new avenue for getting your message to prospects. In fact, in his book *Guerrilla Marketing,* Jay Levinson states that sometimes a classified ad will outdraw a more expensive ad in the same publication.

Where to Place Classified Ads

One of the more crucial decisions you will make will be your choice of media among the four principal outlets for classified advertising: newspapers, consumer magazines, business and trade publications, and independent newsletters.

Newspapers. Local newspapers provide the greatest access to the broadest consumer market in a given area. They usually bridge all gaps of social, economic, professional, and ethnic background within the region they cover. This means that if the only common ground your potential customers have is $10 in their pockets, the newspaper is the best and most cost-effective advertising medium you will find. It is the safest and probably the least expensive medium for broad-based retail advertising.

The primary focus and benefit of newspaper advertising is to sell to individual consumers, not to other businesses. If you are providing a service such as medical transcription or bookkeeping, newspaper advertising is probably not your best bet, but if you provide a babysitting referral service, plumbing services, catering, or dog grooming, it might work well for you.

Consumer magazines. Like newspapers, magazines reach the consumer directly, but unlike them—with the exception of a few general-interest magazines such as *Life* and *People*—these periodicals are targeted to highly specific markets. Whether your potential customer is interested in home improvement *(Home Mechanix)*, motorcycles *(American Motorcyclist)*, travel *(Travel & Leisure)*, fishing *(Fishing World)*, computers *(Home Of5ce Computing)*, or almost any other area, there is probably at least one consumer magazine published on the subject.

The second major difference between advertising in newspapers and in magazines is the frequency with which they are issued. Although some magazines are issued weekly, quarterly, or even annually, the majority of consumer magazines are published monthly.

There is one other major difference. Because of their format, their orientation, and the fact that they are usually printed on coated paper and saddle-stitched or perfect-bound, magazines have a more upscale appearance, resulting in a readership on a slightly higher socio-economic level.

Business and trade publications. Almost without exception, every type of business has at least one major publication dedicated to professionals in that field. For example, there are industry magazines similar to the consumer publications we listed: *Builder, Motor Cycle Industry Magazine, Travel Agent, Action Sports Retailer,* and *Computer Dealer Magazine.*

If your primary clients or customers are other businesses or business people, trade publications should probably be your primary advertising medium. The business decision-makers you want to reach turn to these publications as their main source for industry news, resources, and other educational material. These publications are considered necessary reading for any individual to function efficiently in his or her particular field. Therefore everyone with responsibility in a given industry avidly devours the information in their trade journals.

You don't have to advertise in your own industry publications; instead you may want to place ads in those of your customers or clients. If, for example, you are a computer consultant specializing in developing systems for tool-and-die manufacturers, it would be a waste of time and money to advertise in computer magazines. Your best avenue would be to advertise in the journals and publications produced for the tool-and-die industry.

Independent newsletters. Small special-interest newsletters are a burgeoning avenue for advertising in the 1990s. Some of these newsletters are highly targeted to a specific market. Others are produced by companies to add to their customer contact; therefore, the market base can be very broad. For example, AT&T has a newsletter it sends to a mailing list of 800,000 home-business customers. Often special-interest organizations and associations produce either local or national newsletters, and some publish both. Many of these newsletters accept advertising.

Since most newsletters are very specialized and some have small subscriber lists, however, they can be difficult to locate. Begin your search by checking all the mail you receive. If you belong to a special-interest group or club, you probably receive a newsletter from that organization. If others in that group would benefit from your product or service, see whether the newsletter accepts advertising. Even if it has not done so in the past, it might start taking ads as a way of increasing revenues or offsetting its costs. It is a lot easier to get people to take your money than you might think.

If you don't find appropriate newsletters in your own mailbox, there are directories of newsletters in the public library to investigate. The key is digging to locate a newsletter that reaches the exact people you want to reach and then getting short-term contracts. Since organizations start up and abandon newsletter production on a regular basis, never pay for advertising space more than one issue in advance unless the newsletter is one of long standing.

If your product or service complements your customers' businesses, advertise in newsletters they produce for their customers. For example, if you do word processing or bookkeeping for a legal firm that specializes in corporate law, you can advertise in the monthly newsletter the law firm sends to its corporate clients. Your business does not compete with theirs, and the clients would be a market you might not otherwise be able to reach.

If you produce a product that your customers resell in some form and they produce a newsletter, what better way to assist your customers and build your relationship than to buy advertising in their newsletter?

The primary source of information about all types of print media is the *Standard Rate & Data Service* (SRDS), which comes out in monthly volumes from Wilmette, Illinois. SRDS has separate volumes entitled *Newspapers, Consumer Magazines, Business Publications, Direct Mail,* as well as other print media. To begin the process of deciding on specific print media, visit your local

Newspaper Advertising

Pros

- Reaches a large audience (mostly 35+) in a single exposure.
- Specific sections (beauty, sports, auto, food) target specific customers.
- Reaches a specific geographical area from which a service business draws its customers.
- Small ads can be placed at low cost.
- Couponing and inserts are available.
- Has credibility and wide acceptance and can be read by more than one person.

Cons

- No single paper will reach the entire market. Additionally, very few readers read the entire paper every day.
- Many ads reduce the impact of your ad.
- Deadlines restrict your flexibility.
- As a passive medium, it won't create demand. Best when customer is already in the market to buy.
- Newspapers are usually thrown out each day. People don't refer back to them or pass them from one person to another.

library and review what is available in SRDS. There you will find which publications serve your market, how many people they reach, whom to contact, what their rates are, the deadlines involved, preparation of materials, and other valuable information.

Advertising and Listing in Directories

The one directory that comes immediately to mind is the yellow pages. However, it is not the only directory worth considering when creating and placing directory advertising.

Directories differ from other forms of print advertising in the following ways:

1. Directories are usually more tightly controlled in terms of who can advertise and the format that can be used than other forms of print advertising.
2. Directories are kept close at hand for extended periods of time.
3. Directories place the seller in contact with buyers who are actively seeking products and services.

Consumer Magazine Advertising

Pros	Cons
▪ Readership generally has a higher average income and more discretionary income than newspaper readership.	▪ Specialized circulation can miss most of the target market.
▪ Most magazine readers read them to find resources. Ads can be as important as the articles.	▪ Cost of space is usually much higher than in other print media.
▪ Most magazines cover a greater geographical area than newspapers.	▪ Production lead time means ads must be prepared long before publication.
▪ Far more time is spent reading magazines than reading any other single consumer-based print medium.	▪ Ad clutter means low recall; the average magazine is 50 percent advertising.
▪ Magazines are kept, read repeatedly, and passed from person to person.	▪ Magazine producers usually do not offer the creative or production assistance that most newspapers do.

Other than the yellow pages there are two primary types of directories: trade directories and specialty information directories.

Yellow-Page Advertising

If you have a business telephone line, you already may have been or will be contacted to buy a yellow-page listing. One basic listing comes with your business telephone line. However, the free listing you are entitled to is so minimal that if you intend to use the yellow pages as a means for getting business, you must consider other possibilities.

First, you must decide whether advertising—as opposed to just being listed in the yellow pages will be worth your while. The strongest argument in favor of the yellow pages is that approximately three out of four people who look something up there will follow up with a telephone call. However, about half the people who start out looking for a specific company are attracted to someone else instead, either because they can't find the listing or because someone else has a better ad. That better ad can be yours. The most important variable in deciding whether yellow-page advertising will benefit you is whether or not people turn to the yellow-pages when they buy what you have to sell.

There are many products and services for which people customarily shop through the yellow pages. Word processing, housecleaning, rug cleaning, plumbing, repair services, window washing, extermination, and notary publics are a few examples of such businesses. There are other businesses that people virtually never shop for this way. For example, a management consultant who relies on yellow-page listings for business will be lonelier than the Maytag repairman, and record companies would not turn to the yellow pages to find a songwriter. A corporate executive probably would not seek a freelance urban planner or an architectural design firm in the yellow pages. And of course, if your business offers a new product or service that very few people are aware of, the yellow pages will be of little use to you; no one reads them to find out what's new.

Most businesses, however, lie somewhere in between these two extremes. On certain occasions, some people might turn to the yellow pages to find a product or service that other potential clients would never think to look for there. For example, as a general rule of thumb, in seeking specialized personal and business services such as public relations or marriage and family counseling, most people will look to referrals from other professionals, colleagues, or friends. Yet some people will look for these services in the yellow pages.

To help determine whether your business is one people will turn to the yellow pages to find, see whether there is a category listing there that describes what you do. Then check to see whether most of your successful competitors are there. Contact some of those who have listed to find out what kind of results they have had.

Many home-based businesses have used yellow-page advertising effectively.

Kenneth McKethan, who operates Techni-Lingua LTD, a translation service based in Dunn, North Carolina, uses yellow-page ads to attract business from several cities. Charlotte Mitchell, who operates Notary On Wheels in San Diego, gets a substantial portion of her business from her yellow pages ad. The turning point for Patricia Plake's photography studio in Overland Park, Kansas, came when she improved her yellow pages ad. C. Thomas Fitzwilliam of Arlington, Texas, has had success advertising in an alternative yellow-pages directory for his landscape and irrigation business.

If you think you will benefit from advertising in the yellow pages, keep in mind that they aren't a single directory: yellow pages is a generic term for a variety of often competing advertising books. Within a given region, several companies may produce yellow-page directories that vie with one another for your advertising dollar. In addition to the standard metropolitan-area yellow pages in most cities, you will often find separate suburban editions. You also may find as many as three competing yellow-pages companies covering the entire metropolitan area. Sometimes there are also special neighborhood or business-to-business editions and a variety of specialty yellow pages, such as the Women's Yellow Pages or the Christian Yellow Pages.

In recent years various telephone companies such as GTE, NYNEX, and Southwestern Bell have expanded their yellow pages market into regions their telephone service does not include. In other cases a metropolitan region may split among as many as three local telephone companies, each with its own yellow-pages edition, or contract with the Donnelly Directory to produce both a print and a talking version of the yellow pages. Increasing the confusion, any one telephone company may produce as many as four different types of directories: core, overlay, neigborhood, and specialty. According to Bell Atlantic, the core is the principal book of your local phone company, its territory approximately matching that of the telephone company; the overlay book generally consists of one or more core books and is used to expand the area covered; neighborhood books cover individual market areas such as separate suburbs; and specialty books cover either specific areas of interest or specific portions of the population.

So if you wish to use yellow-page advertising, you first must decide which yellow pages to advertise in and whether to advertise in one or more of the supplemental directories. Complicating the decision, since each of these directories is produced and assembled separately, often each will have different closing dates. Therefore, it is more difficult to determine from the lumped charges on your telephone bill what each is going to cost.

Do not let this situation stymie you, however, or intimidate you into purchasing more advertising than you need. Your choice of how many and which yellow-pages editions to advertise in should depend exclusively on your target market, its location, and its likelihood of using the yellow-pages to find businesses like yours.

In dealing with this proliferation of directories, the prospective advertiser must be fearless in demanding answers from yellow-pages ad-space sales representatives. You also must be just as wary about paying a bill for ad space or production costs. Some directories even send out solicitations for business that look like invoices, and too often these get paid without question.

Part of any decision you make about yellow-page advertising will be based on simply looking through the directory you are considering. However, your sales rep should have some hard figures about what markets the books reach.

Writing and designing your yellow-page ad. There is one reality in yellow-page advertising that separates it from all other advertising with the possible exception of classified ads: when turning to the yellow pages the buyer is actively seeking the seller. For this reason, you cannot use the same advertising copy for the yellow pages that you use elsewhere.

Questions to Ask in Selecting a Yellow-Page Listing

Here are fifteen questions you should ask any space-sales representative before deciding whether his or her book is the right yellow pages for you:

1. Which company sponsors this book? Is it the phone company serving the area in which the book is distributed?
2. How long has this particular book been published?
3. What is the geographical area served by this book?
4. Is this the primary book for the total geographical area your business covers?
5. How many copies were circulated in the past year? (Watch out! Some reps will try to give you the number of books printed rather than those distributed. Also, check to be sure that circulation figures are not inflated by the number of household members instead of the number of books or by huge numbers of employees expected to use one or two directories.)
6. Who gets the directory?
7. How many are provided to each household? Each business location?
8. How often is the directory revised?
9. How is it distributed?
10. How many times per week do people refer to this directory?
11. How many dollars are spent weekly in purchases from this directory?
12. How many of my competitors are in the book already?
13. What kinds of promotions does the publisher use to encourage people to use the directory?
14. What is the publisher's policy concerning rebates for ad production problems such as typographical errors and inaccuracies?
15. How will my ad be billed to me?

In yellow-page ads, you do not have to sell the buyer on the product or service you offer, but you do have to sell the buyer on doing business with you instead of with anyone else listed in the same section.

Sadly, despite the facts that yellow-page advertising is the only viable avenue for many businesses and that it can be an effective medium for many not yet utilizing it, far too many businesses do little to get the most from this medium. Many who do use the yellow pages simply purchase a standard ad, developed on the spur of the moment over the phone, and then just renew it

---

The Four Types of Yellow-Page Ads

There are four types of ads available to yellow-page advertisers:

Listings. The single listing is your basic, nondescript yellow-page ad, which is usually free. If you want your company name in all caps, you pay extra. You also pay extra if you want your company name and phone number in boldface type, if you want your listing in red instead of black, if you want to be listed under additional categories, or if you want to list additional information such as a second number or description.

Trademark listings. The trademark listing is a group of dealers, distributors, and others associated with a particular brand name, listed under that brand name. Usually the parent company pays for the master "Authorized Sales and Service" listing along with some promotional copy. Each affiliate decides whether it wants to pay to be listed under the master. This could apply to home-based franchises in a given metropolitan area, as well as to distributors and direct-sales organizations. *(If this is applicable to your business, this is the one place you should definitely be listed!)*

Space ads. The space ad is an expansion of the basic alphabetical listing. It ranges in size from one-half inch to two inches, is one column wide, and is limited to a hairline border and, usually, eighteen-point type. The company name is printed in all caps, and both it and the phone number are set in boldface. If you want to use a company or industry logo and/or a combination of red and black inks, you pay extra.

Display ads. The display ad is available in sizes ranging from one-quarter of a column (which is usually laid out in a format just shy of 2½ inches deep, one column wide) to a full page. Some directories limit the size of ads to a quarter-page in order to protect the smaller advertisers, but in many major metropolitan areas it is not at all uncommon to see page after page of half- or full-page ads. Most phone directories offer a bonus to display advertisers in the form of a booster to their regular listing that indicates the position of the display ad, such as "See our display ad on page _____." Red ink is available for an additional charge.

automatically every year when a salesperson calls, without investigating the response rate their current ad is generating to determine whether it is working.

Usually the yellow pages are filled with flat, bland advertising that's isn't geared to sell. Yet it is a fiercely competitive medium. The only possible advantage to appearing in the yellow pages lies in being able to win a direct, head-on battle to outsell the competing ads in your section, so a little dynamism in your yellow-page ad will go a long way toward making it more effective.

When placing your yellow-page ad, you may run into major restrictions in regard to what you want to put in your ad and what you want it to look like. There are some companies that place strict and somewhat arbitrary limitations on the design. Some directories also place restrictions on type size, artwork, and punctuation. Copy limitations often include a ban on any comparative statements (no matter how true the claim might be), unsupported superlatives, and guarantee specifications. However, these limits are not universal, even within the same edition. For the most part you will find few absolute controls in design, layout, or typeface in display ads other than those imposed by the size, readability, and appeal of the ad.

Companies publishing yellow pages offer free assistance in the development of copy, design, and layout. This is helpful as long as you don't allow the salesperson to sell you on a weak, boring ad that won't sell, which unfortunately is highly probable. Remember, the salesperson has to turn out a dozen or so ads every week in addition to doing his or her main job of selling the ads.

The yellow pages is a fiercely competitive medium. In order to be even slightly effective, you have to put punch into your ad. In writing it, review the list of phrases in the first copywriting test in Chapter 14 and make sure you eliminate every one of them or anything that vaguely resembles them. Look through a copy of the yellow pages for the strongest ads you can find and emulate those.

In designing the ad, limit yourself to a maximum of one typeface and three type sizes in addition to your logo or company identification. Don't waste space by stating the obvious, such as repeating what you are if that is the same as your company name or heading. Don't crowd the space with extra type or unnecessary artwork; make the ad easy to read. Use only artwork that enhances your sales message. But do use bullets to set off different points. Also, research shows an eighth-page display ad will triple the number of calls produced from an in-column space ad with a trademark.

As with any other print advertising, your headline and layout are the most important aspects to work out—they have to draw the reader's eye to your ad and away from all others. Once you have the reader's attention, your copy has to sell. The briefer and more to the point it is, the better, so use as few words and lines as possible. This will allow you to use larger type. The final most important eye-catchers are your company name and address and, even more important, your telephone number. Make these as prominent as your headline.

Yellow Pages: Pros and Cons

Pros	Cons
■ Reaches consumers who are ready to buy now.	■ Copy is revised just once a year.
■ Almost every household or business has a yellow pages.	■ Your ad appears next to those of your competitors.
■ People expect certain types of businesses to be listed and look there first.	■ There may be copy restrictions.
■ Display ads can include the key information someone needs to make a choice.	■ Because it is all advertising, people will see your ad only if they are actively shopping for what you offer.
	■ People don't look in the yellow pages for some types of businesses.

Don't hesitate to reject a design or layout that doesn't work, even if the deadline is fast approaching. Of course, it is always best to allow yourself plenty of time to plan your ad well ahead of the closing date. That way you have the time to throw out as many unacceptable layouts as you must in order to get a good ad for your investment.

Trade Directories

Trade directories offer an avenue for highly tailored business-to-business advertising. Some of these directories are published as an adjunct to a major trade paper or magazine. Often in such cases, those who advertise in the paper or magazine are offered a free listing.

If your business is primarily geared toward a narrow business market, advertising in the appropriate trade directory is far more important than advertising in a standard yellow pages, although listing in a business-to-business yellow pages may be equally essential. The right trade-directory listing can be a source of prospects for your company because the readers are already looking for a supplier when they use a directory. And, sometimes of equal importance, just being listed in a directory can confirm that you are who you say you are. Therefore it is definitely worth seeking out these directories and selecting those that will give you the best potential response.

Your best sources for information on such directories once again are your library and SRDS. All questions recommended in the yellow-page section on page 197 should be asked of the sales rep for each trade directory in order to help determine which ones will best promote your product or service. Then, in placing your ad, the focus needs to be on what makes you different from all your competitors and on conveying this unique advantage in your directory listing.

Specialty Information Directories

Also in most local libraries are a variety of specialized directories, some of which accept advertising but many of which do not. In fact, there is a *Directory of Directories*, published by Gale Research. Perusing this directory will help you identify other directories to consider, and reviewing those directories will tell you whether they accept advertising and are apt to meet your needs.

Unless it is geared toward a very specific market, advertising in one of these directories will probably not be the most cost-effective use of a small advertising budget. Listing in them, however, can add substantially to a small company's credibility.

Some of these directories have very strict criteria that limit those who may be listed. If these criteria are not stated clearly in the directory itself, a call to the publisher or sponsoring organization will get you this information. At least an equal number of specialty directories are interested in getting whatever listings they can; these often charge for a listing. The price of the listing may be that of subscription to the directory, which can range from a few to many hundreds of dollars. Many other special directories, however, are completely accessible to small businesses, and some simply require an application in order to be listed. It is worth the effort to seek them out and get whatever listing you can.

Every trade and professional association has a membership directory, which may take advertising in addition to listing its members. For example, *The National Speakers Association Membership Directory* is not only a membership directory; it is also a resource for any organization seeking to hire a professional speaker. So in addition to a listing, some speakers will take out ads featuring their programs. In addition, other companies will advertise their services to the speakers themselves. This year's directory includes ads by printers, cassette-production companies, training firms, publishers, and other support services for professional speakers. The *American Marketing Association International Membership Directory and Marketing Services Guide* operates similarly; in addition to being a membership directory, it is a resource for companies who need to hire marketing firms, so some members take out ads and other companies advertise to sell their services to the marketing firms themselves.

To determine whether listing in a directory will be worth your time, money, and energy, see who lists in the directories you are considering and phone them to find out whether their listing has helped them and how.

Although print advertising is certainly the type of advertising we are most familiar with, it is by far not the only advertising technique open to you. The next chapter will examine other inventive advertising avenues.

CHAPTER
THIRTEEN

■■■■■■■■■■■■■■■■■■■■■■■

Other Creative Advertising Alternatives

There are a variety of less-well-known, relatively low-cost creative advertising opportunities that some resourceful home-based businesses are using successfully. One that is used often is posting information on bulletin boards; others involve use of cable television and radio. Another method that holds untapped potential for home businesses is using various types of electronic media. And finally there is direct-response advertising, which includes any form of advertising that calls for the viewer, reader, or listener to act immediately with an order or inquiry.

Bulletin Board Announcements and Tear Pads

While free advertising is the exception, bulletin boards are one such exception. Consider how many times you have seen bulletin boards in laundromats, print shops, grocery stores, banks, bookstores, employee lounges, and libraries. Perhaps you have even located goods or services advertised on them.

Wayne Orth has found bulletin boards the best way to sell his self-published book, using 8½" × 11" signs. Some bulletin boards, however, limit entries almost to the size of an index card. That limitation didn't stop Peggy Glenn, who pinned index cards on university bulletin boards to announce her typing service. It was the only advertising she did at first, yet within three months she was earning more than she had as a secretary for the same university. So even with its limitations, bulletin boards have provided essential initial customers to new businesses.

The key is to locate bulletin boards where your potential customers and clients go. For example, the bulletin boards of college campuses and state unemployment offices are ideal places for a résumé service to let people know what it does; print shops, another common spot for bulletin boards, are ideal for a graphic designer or desktop publisher's card or tear pad.

A tear pad can range from a simple flyer with tear-off numbers along the bottom to a well-produced placard to which is attached a pad of informational slips or requests. Use a tear pad in place of a simple flyer or index card on bulletin boards to make sure your phone number is retained. The tear-off slip might even be a coupon good for a 10-percent discount on their first job or order.

Using bright yellow paper stock for your announcement will help it stand out from the rest, and desktop-publishing or word-processing software can also help you create a more interesting sign. Bulletin boards are so popular that there are now companies that make a business out of posting other people's announcements on them.

Broadcast Advertising

Small and home-based businesses often don't consider advertising on radio and television, making the assumption that these media are far too expensive to fit into a small advertising budget. With network television, this is invariably true. However, there are three areas of broadcast that should be considered for some small businesses: radio, independent television, and cable television.

Having Your Own Radio Show

An unusual way to buy radio advertising that can be valuable to professional and personal service businesses is to buy what is called brokered time for your own weekly half-hour or hour-long radio show. Marriage and family counselor Dr. Barbara De Angeles of Los Angeles used such a program to build her now nationally known Making Love Work seminars for couples. From that show she has gone on to become a best-selling author and network-television commentator. Dr. Murray Susser, who broadcasts via telephone from his office, has such a show to promote his medical practice. Public-relations consultant Ann Schmidt has a show that features her clients, successful business people, authors, or artists. Stockbroker Brian Sheen has a popular investment program in Florida. Dr. Nancy Bonus fills her nondiet weight-loss classes from her show "The Psychology of Weight Loss."

Each of these businesses is professional and information-intensive and focuses on an issue nearly everyone is interested in: health, relationships, money, or weight loss. The more educated a person is about the complex subject matter these businesses address and the unique approach these professionals offer, the more likely he or she is to purchase the product or service. Hence a large block of time to explain and teach on the air is good for such businesses.

Nancy Bonus expresses it this way: "My competitors are the national weight-loss programs. They have big advertising budgets for national television and major newspapers. As a sole practitioner I can't meet them in that arena. But a weekly radio show provides me with high local visibility for my program. Also, my approach to weight-loss requires that people give up dieting totally forever. This is a new concept. People find it hard to believe at first and so a thirty-second spot or a little print ad can't give enough information to convince them to try something so revolutionary. But my show gives them a chance to hear the whole story. And then they want to try it."

If having your own radio show would fit your business and appeals to you, contact local stations and ask whether they broker time. Then proceed as you would in evaluating any advertising purchase. You will probably have to submit a proposal outlining the nature of your show and sign a contract agreeing to adhere to certain guidelines. One added advantage of advertising in this way is that you often have the option of recovering your advertising costs by selling advertising spots on your show to your suppliers or to other compatible businesses.

If you don't want the responsibility of a full-blown weekly show but believe you could benefit from having a regular radio presence, consider purchasing time from someone else's show. For example, financial consultant Dan Silverman ran a regular twelve-minute weekly feature for a year on insurance and investments for small businesses on the *Here's to Success* program in Los Angeles; veterinarian Jeffrey Werber had a daily three-minute spot on pet care on another local program.

Having Your Own Television Show

If your business is highly visual in nature, you might consider having a show of your own on either cable or independent local stations. This is not as extravagant as it may seem. For approximately six times the cost of one minute of time, you can buy an entire half hour on a local broadcast or cable station. If you were, for example, a caterer, you could use each show to develop a theme; prepare foods that carry out that theme; give out recipes; interview florists, decorators, or location owners; and show how to produce a small party from start to clean-up.

The basic sets you will need probably can be rented as part of studio time along with a crew and equipment. Production will be expensive, but if you are good at planning and selling, you can get sponsors from other businesses involved in activities that complement yours. The companies a caterer might approach include florists, party-equipment rental companies, tent rental

---

Radio: Pros and Cons

Pros	Cons
■ Ninety-nine percent of all households have radios. Adults eighteen and older spend more than three hours a day with radio.	■ Getting sufficient exposure at the prime listening drive-time hours on the popular stations can be expensive.
■ Radio goes everywhere. Ninety-five percent of all cars have radios.	■ Ads are limited to what can be conveyed by sound. There is no visual element to the message.
■ Radio can create a demand for what you offer, because someone who is listening is going to hear it.	■ Often listeners can't respond immediately, because half of all radio listeners are in cars.
■ Radio programs are simple to produce and can be done in a variety of commercial lengths.	■ Phone numbers heard while driving may be forgotten or written down hurriedly and misplaced.
■ Radio is a highly personal medium.	■ Listeners jump from station to station.
■ It can help establish you as an authority "as heard on . . . radio".	■ Radio, while reaching a specific audience, may reach too broad an audience for specialized businesses.
■ The auditory nature of radio makes a message more easily remembered.	

---

companies, cleaning services, printers specializing in invitations, party-list services, costume shops, bridal shops, boutiques, china and gift shops. By purchasing a ten-, twenty-, or thirty-second spot, these sponsors can cover the costs for air time and production. And if you are really good at lining up such sponsors, you might even make some money on your show.

Once you make the decision to do a show of your own, whether on radio or television, it is wise to hire a consultant to help you plan and even produce the show. You do need a producer other than yourself, as someone needs to be available to make decisions while you are on camera. This consultant can also keep you from making expensive mistakes and help your show gain professional polish. According to broadcast-media consultant Alan Lawrence of Talco Productions, "Nobody wants to hire an amateur for any business. And if your presentation looks amateurish, you will be thought to be an amateur."

What you fill your time with is important as well. If you want to reap the full benefits of a radio or TV program of your own, make your sell subtle. Use the show to establish yourself as an authority or expert in your field. Of course, there is always time to mention your company name and phone number or to display it prominently on the set.

Another low-cost alternative is public-access programming. Local cable stations often have a public-access channel on which they air local programming, which is sometimes referred to as local origination. Usually this channel is distinct from an educational or governmental channel on which city council or community-college programming appears. Time on public-access cable is free or very low cost and includes all production, which is done by the cable station. Therefore you don't need to hire a producer. Applicants usually need to submit proposals for the shows they want to produce, and sometimes the cable company requires that you attend a free seminar on how to produce your own shows. A public-access show cannot be a commercial, but usually at the end of the show you can give out your name, telephone number, and address.

Whether you choose a local independent station, cable, or public access, if your business is highly visual in nature and you have a broad consumer market, having such a show could work well for you. For example, hair stylist Ed Salazar has a weekly cable show that keeps his appointment book filled, and yoga teacher Louise Dianna has such a show to promote her classes and private sessions. Other businesses that may do well with television shows are make-up artists, public-relations firms (which could book their clients on their show), organizers, image consultants, cooking instructors, sales trainers, and caterers. Watch the various local, cable, and public-access stations in your area to see whether you can imagine yourself doing such a show.

Cable Television: Pros and Cons

Pros

- TV targets groups by program interest.

- Cable is relatively low cost—very low if you choose public access.

- TV can show off a highly visible business like nothing else.

- TV allows for a high degree of creativity.

- Being on television can give you a glamorous image and high visibility.

Cons

- Cable must compete with network TV for viewers.

- Cable audiences are growing, but are still apt to be limited.

- Production can be time-consuming if not costly. When not done professionally, you and what you offer look amateurish

- Often little is known about who is watching.

- Public-access cable may not allow you to actually sell on the air, so you have to be subtle.

Electronic Media

As we approach the close of the century, an entirely new realm of communication is opening for advertising and promotion: the world of electronic media. At the moment, the electronic media are still young. But as fast as new media opportunities arise, open-minded individuals are jumping in to make use of them, so some doors of opportunity close about as quickly as they open. Only time will determine the future value to you of these new media, which include online services and facsimile, or fax.

Online Computer Services

Online services are accessed via one's computer using an electronic device called a modem. Some of these services are geared toward research and provide extensive information databases; others are dedicated to a specific company or point of focus, such as Dow Jones News Retrieval or the other major newswires, including AP and Reuters.

The online services most affecting smaller businesses, however, are the major utilities, such as Compuserve Information Service and Genie, and local special-interest bulletin boards. Each of these companies provides the opportunity to acquire information and assistance and—more to the point—by participating, establish an international reputation and generate sales leads.

Although each service has its own rules and regulations in regard to posting advertising on its respective electronic bulletin board, there are options to explore that allow you to post information about your product or service in various databases. Additionally, for product-oriented businesses, you can even establish—for a fee—your own direct outlet in the shopping area of such services. Phillip and Lesley Schier are a good example. They operate a mail-order business doing several million dollars a year in sales from their home, selling computer software, accessories, and books. They run their businesses on CompuServe's Electronic Mall and have now expanded to other computer networks.

If you have a computer and a modem, it is worth your time to explore each of the available services to discover its applicability to your business. To locate major information services, refer to *The Complete Handbook of Personal Communications* by Alfred Glossbrenner or *The Cuadra Directory.*

Fax

Facsimile, or fax, is one of the newest avenues for advertising, and it is currently fraught with controversy. Increasing numbers of states are passing laws prohibiting the transmission of unsolicited facsimile, or "junk fax," and national legislation is pending.

However, all facsimile advertising does not have to be unsolicited. Several companies are currently conducting feasibility studies on fax-transmitted newsletter subscriptions, some of which would be heavily supported by advertising. By the time you read this, there may be an entirely new market opening up that could provide highly targeted advertising media to key business markets with minimal production requirements.

All in all, this is an exciting time to be in business. There are new advertising avenues created all the time. To explore some of these new electronic media, you need to do some research and turn on your imagination.

Direct-Response Advertising

When you see an ad in a magazine or newspaper or hear a radio or television spot that incorporates a coupon, a postcard or fill-in-the-blank, words to the effect of "Tell them you saw it here and receive an additional 10-percent discount," or even a telephone order number, you are looking at some form of direct-response advertising.

The value of this form of advertising lies in its ability to generate not only inquiries but also sales. The purpose is to push the reader to take immediate action. An additional value of direct response advertising is that it provides the advertiser with one of the most accurate tracking techniques available. If you use the same ad in two different publications and receive two hundred responses from one and ten from the other, you can determine that it might not be worthwhile continuing to advertise in the lower-response medium. Unless those ten inquiries lead to high-dollar, high-profit sales, the response is probably not paying the cost of the ad.

When a direct-response ad is placed in any print medium, the same rules apply to it as to any other print advertising. The only real difference is the inclusion of some means by which the reader can make a direct response. Usually this is simply a box that allows readers to fill in their name, address, and other pertinent information. Providing a telephone number, especially an 800 number, for information or ordering will increase your response and is becoming increasing important, since people are coming to expect this convenience. Today 800 numbers are highly affordable and easy to get. They are offered by all major long-distance carriers. The 800 number can ring directly into your existing telephone line and cost only a few dollars a month, depending on the number of calls you receive.

Another type of direct-response advertising uses magazine inserts. Inserts are full pages that are printed by the advertiser and provided to the publication to be tipped in—that is bound in—with the rest of the publication. In most cases all printing costs of the insert are borne by the advertiser, with the publication charging for the inclusion. Sometimes, an insert can be more effective than a print ad.

There is a trick, however, to getting a good response from inserts of which most advertisers are apparently unaware, and that is to simply request—and, if necessary, negotiate—to be the first insert in the publication. Research indicates that results decrease with each succeeding insert within a publication. Therefore, you are more likely to pull a strong response if your insert is first.

Other forms of direct-response advertising include the packets of similarly oriented postcards, called card decks, that are sent in wrappers to large groups of possibly interested individuals. These postcards do not generally solicit orders; instead they solicit inquiries for product and service information.

For additional information about card decks, refer to Part III of *Business Publication Rates and Data* from SRDS. There you will find an entire section listing the publishers of card decks. In running through the card-deck information you will find single ad rates ranging from just under $1,000 to around $2,700, with the bulk in the area of $1,500 to $2,000 for black and white. Most publishers of card decks offer discounts or lower rates for multiple insertions.

Card Decks: Pros and Cons

Pros

- They produce genuinely interested sales leads.
- If someone takes the time to fill out one of these cards, chances of a sale are good.
- The cards provide ample space to describe and sell your service.
- It is easy to track exactly where the sales came from.

Cons

- They have limited space to get your message across, which limits selling pizazz.
- They are crowded with similar and possibly competing products and services.
- Cards often stick together.
- There is no control over who receives the cards and little control over production.

Marketing Technique Measure-of-Success Probability Chart

⊕ Greatest probability of success   ◑ Less probability of success

◐ Good probability of success   ● Least probability of success

○ Medium probability of success   — Not applicable

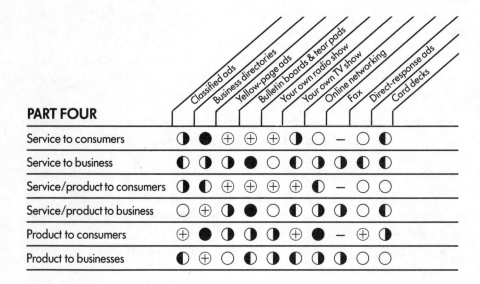

PART FOUR	Classified ads	Business directories	Yellow-page ads	Bulletin boards & tear pads	Your own radio show	Your own TV show	Online networking	Fax	Direct-response ads	Card decks
Service to consumers	◐	●	⊕	⊕	⊕	◑	○	—	○	◐
Service to business	◐	◑	◐	●	○	◐	◑	◐	◑	◐
Service/product to consumers	◑	◐	⊕	⊕	⊕	⊕	◐	—	○	○
Service/product to business	○	⊕	◐	●	○	◐	◑	◐	○	◐
Product to consumers	⊕	●	◐	◑	◐	⊕	●	—	⊕	◐
Product to businesses	◐	⊕	○	◑	◐	◐	◑	◐	○	○

PART FIVE

The Technicalities of Producing
Your Marketing Materials

CHAPTER
FOURTEEN
■■■■■■■■■■■■■■■■■■■■

Writing and Designing Materials That Sell

As a small or home-based business, you most likely will be preparing most of your own materials—at least at the outset. This means you will not only be selecting where those materials go but will also probably develop your own promotional campaign theme and the concepts and design for each individual piece, whether it is the simplest letterhead (and coordinating business card) or the most elaborate brochure, catalog, or direct-mail package. In this section we will outline basic guidelines for creating your own successful marketing tools.

Even in writing and designing your materials, it is important to keep in mind the fundamental rule of marketing success:

> The measure of a successful marketing campaign is the extent to which it reaches, at the lowest possible cost, the greatest number of people who can and will buy your product or service.

This rule not only applies to where you use your materials but to the appeal you make. You want to appeal to the people who need, can afford, and will buy what you have to offer. Although many people may find a message interesting, the only ones you really need to reach are those who truly need your product or service and are willing to pay for it. The following guidelines all stem from this single basic rule.

Twelve Guidelines for Creating
Successful Marketing Materials

1. Think in terms of a marketing campaign, not single pieces. Every promotional item and every selling activity should reinforce the premise and the goals of your marketing campaign.

Each item you use is similar to a play in a football game. As the head coach of your promotional campaign, you cannot simply plan one play at a time; you must look ahead and develop an overall strategy and a framework of plays for the entire game. Even if you are simply developing a display ad for the yellow pages, you should approach the task as part of your entire marketing effort. You get the best results when every technique you use is coordinated to complement and enhance the others.

2. Aim your message directly at the people who can benefit from your product or service and at those who are in a position to buy. Don't try to please everybody, and don't waste time and effort trying to reach only a tiny segment of your market with general advertising unless your budget is astronomical. Gear your messages and your methods directly to those who can and/or do use your product or service.

3. Put yourself in the position of your prospect—the person receiving your message. Any promotional copy you write must be prepared from the point of view of the potential customer. If you must write copy that shows off your brilliance, enjoy the exercise and then throw it in the trash. The only things of importance to the customers you hope to attract are the advantages to them of purchasing your product or service.

4. The amount of money spent on a particular piece of promotional material has absolutely no relation to the ability of that piece to accomplish its objective. In this sense, having a small promotion budget becomes an advantage. In fact, often the less money spent, the more successful the promotion, because there was no money to waste on ego-boosting material or production values that don't produce sales. Also, with a smaller budget more time and energy is focused on creating the most effective promotion possible.

A few years ago, Great American Soups spent an incredible fortune on an advertising campaign that created mini Busby Berkeley movies starring dancer Ann Miller. Each of these spots cost in excess of a million dollars, but unfortunately they didn't sell soup. No matter how charming or witty an ad campaign is and no matter how highly produced, if ten minutes later no one remembers the name of the advertiser, it is a flop even if everyone can describe the ad vividly.

5. The goal is not to create a memorable promotional piece, but to create a piece that makes your product or service memorable. A promotion piece may become a hot topic of conversation, but if it doesn't sell the product or service for which it is created, it hasn't done the job. Throughout the history of promotion there have been dozens of wonderful campaigns, especially in the realm of advertising, that have provided great entertainment for millions of people without doing the job they were created to do: sell the products or services.

Thirty years ago, when Mike Nichols and Elaine May were still young stand-up comics, there was a brewery that hired the witty team to work on some radio and television commercials for Jax Beer. These commercials have gone down in history as some of the funniest, most whimsical, and most entertaining broadcast moments of all time. They were quoted every day in offices and shopping areas around the country, with the punch lines repeated over and over. But they did not sell Jax Beer. So make your message the thing to remember, not how cleverly it was said.

6. *Being clever just for the sake of being clever is a dangerous game.* Just because you think something is cute or witty doesn't mean that anyone else will, or that they will even understand your ingenious creation. This does not mean you should never use humor or wit in promotion, rather that you use it sparingly and in such a way that there is no chance of making the audience feel stupid. A good example of the positive use of humor are the highly popular and very successful television commercials for Hefty Garbage Bags. The "Hefty! Hefty! Hefty! Wimpy. Wimpy. Wimpy." campaign not only made the audience laugh, it remained in their minds when they arrived at the store. An important point is that the slogan contained the name of the product, so if you remembered the ad, you also remembered the product.

7. *Aim for an immediate impact!* Whether you are using print, broadcast, direct mail, or any other form of promotion, you have to remember that you have only one or two seconds to get the attention of your prospect. You want to use copy that grabs the spotlight, visuals that arrest attention, or even sounds that stop people cold. Select whatever you use carefully to make sure it has immediate impact.

8. *Less is usually more.* Avoid clutter. As with most other endeavors, the less you try to say in any single promotional piece, the more impact what you do say will have. If any part of your piece doesn't reinforce your message, throw it out.

9. *Limit each piece to a single objective.* The more points you try to make, the more you dilute the effectiveness of any single point. Having more than one theme per piece will only net you a confused audience, whereas a single objective will permit you to focus directly on one aspect and sell it thoroughly.

10. *Whether in print, on radio, or on television, limit the emphasis used throughout the particular promotion.* If you accentuate too much, you will end up accentuating nothing. For example, take a look at almost any ad—especially a print ad. An advertiser has a great many important things to say. A common mistake is to use the same type size for each point in the hope that none of these points gets lost. Whether that size is large or small, its sameness makes all the copy run together, so nothing ends up seeming important. The same thing can happen when a message is offered on radio or television. When you are selling, make your most important point stand out from everything else.

11. Always call for action.   A promotional piece should not only appeal to and interest the audience, it should attempt to rouse them to action. To get people to act, it is helpful to lead them by stating clearly what action you wish them to take. Tell them to write for, call for, look for, or remember your product.

12. Before making any absolute claims about your product or service, any comparative claims over that of your competitors, or any special offers to various customers, and before sending any form of promotion through the mail or having any direct communication with a competitor, be sure you are aware of all of the laws that might affect you, your promotion, and your actions.   Chances are you are unfamiliar with the Robinson-Patman Act, which, among other provisions, forbids unequal treatment of customers. For example, you can't give a discount to one customer and not to another who buys the same quantities under the same conditions. And you probably haven't heard of the Moss-Magnuson Bill, which permits the Federal Trade Commission to haul advertisers into court without prior hearings and binds all competitors to a consent order signed by any one of them, thereby making all guilty if any one admits guilt. Nor are you likely to know about the various FTC regulations regarding proof in advertising or the postal regulations or even the FCC regulations concerning claims made over the telephone. We certainly were not aware of the many legal issues related to advertising and promotion when we went out on our own. But as long as you are using the mail, the public airways, the print media, or telephone lines, such fraud statutes apply to you.

Some of these regulations might seem to be unreasonable and arbitrary. However, they are designed to protect consumers from patently false and/or dangerous claims. And because you are bound by these restrictions the moment you promote or advertise, you must be aware of them in order to ensure that your promotional efforts and advertising conform to ethical standards. Since your competitors may not be any more aware of these regulations than you are, you can't rely on what they are doing as a guideline for protecting yourself. Therefore we recommend that you discuss your planned promotion campaign with your attorney before you implement it, to assure you are in compliance.

Creating Your Promotional Concept

As you set out to write your copy, begin by deciding what approach you want to use to reach your customer or client. For best results, you will want to put forth a well-thought-out concept that is consistent with the overall guiding theme for all your marketing activities. Each time you use a particular marketing tool to further that overriding concept, you will be adding a powerful building block to your business presence.

Not only is each marketing tool—in this case a piece of promotion—a part of the whole, it is also a single, unique experience for the potential customer or client, and therefore it must also stand alone with a distinct concept of its own. So if you cannot state in one or two sentences the underlying concept of each ad you prepare, each brochure you create, or each gift you hand out, you need to start again.

Selecting Among Four Basic Promotion Appeals

Most promotion appeals fall into one of four types: comparisons, demonstrations, advantages, and fear.

1. Comparing yourself favorably.   Making a positive comparison of your product or service to those of others is the most popular method of appeal. Comparison ads are used in all media. Even most brochures imply a comparison with competitors. The comparison you make may be stated outright, as in asserting that your product or service is better than another, or all others. This is usually done with words like *better, best, faster,* and *greater.* A comparison approach may also simply be implied, by using such statements as "Only _____ does it right."

This is a particularly good appeal when you have well-known competition from whom you need to distinguish yourself. To experiment with this approach, compare your product or service to that of your competition. How are you better? What do you offer that they don't? These comparisons could become the basic appeal for your marketing pieces. Be sure to discuss any planned comparisons with an attorney, however, before making them the heart of your marketing concept.

2. Demonstrating what you can do.   A demonstration or presentation of what your product or service does is the second popular appeal you can use. Nutritionist Ken Yasney is using testimonials, for example, as the heart of his advertising campaign. He asked several of his highly satisfied clients to tell him in their words what his service had done for them, and their quotes appear in his ads. Private-practice consultant Gene Call uses the same approach in direct-mail packages to promote his training programs for professionals on how to market their businesses. He quotes people who explain how dramatically their practices have grown after taking his Word of Mouth training. Susan Page, owner of Freeze Frame Photography, shows before and after pictures in her ads. And, of course, weight-loss programs are notorious for demonstrating the results of their products with before and after shots.

Demonstration is an excellent appeal to make when you are selling something with tangible, observable, or easily describable results. To experiment with using this approach in your promotional campaign, think about how you could show off the results of what you do.

3. Highlighting your advantage. Another common form of promotion appeal is to focus on a major benefit of purchasing or using your product or service. Yellow-page ads for word-processing services, for example, often focus on several advantages, such as fast turnaround, pickup and delivery service, and accuracy. The most popular form of the advantage appeal is to feature low prices, special sales, or discounts.

Appeals that focus on the positive and negative emotions involved with a product or service also fall into this category. An ad for a tutoring service that shows a child crying while his parents look at his report card is one example. The headline copy reads, "Help him make the grade." A different piece with the same appeal might show the child running into the kitchen with a big grin on his face, eagerly showing his report card to his mother, beneath a headline that reads, "Grade card day can be a time of celebration." Our research shows that promotional pieces that appeal to positive, desired outcomes are generally more effective than those appealing to the negative effects one wants to escape, so we would advise the owner of the tutoring service to select the concept with the happy child over the one with the crying child.

To experiment with writing copy using an advantage appeal, list all the major benefits your clients receive from buying your product or service and ask yourself how you could feature these in a promotional piece.

4. Fear. Fear-based promotion is far more prevalent than one might expect. Although such an appeal could be classified under the emotional area of the advantage appeal, it is usually recognized as a slightly separate promotional approach.

When an airline touts its safety record, it is in essence saying, "Fly us or you'll die." A BMW television ad showing a near accident avoided by the car's maneuverability is another fear-based appeal. Still others include the Michelin tire ads that show babies sitting on the tires and the DuPont brochures for Stainmaster® that shows kids dropping messy food on a new carpet. More subtle fear-based approaches with which we are all familiar are found in commercials for mouthwash to avoid the embarrassment of bad breath, toothpaste to avoid trips to the dentist, buffered aspirin or aspirin alternatives to avoid aspirin-induced stomach problems, and laundry sprays that promise to alleviate the humiliation of static cling.

Appealing to fear is a good approach to use when what you are urging people to buy is not that attractive, but the consequences of not buying it are even less attractive. For example, insurance is a product that is often sold with an appeal to fear. Who looks forward to spending hundreds of dollars on insurance? But the results of not spending it can be even less appealing. Chartered financial consultant Dan Silverman points out in his successful radio ads that less than 5 percent of Americans are financially independent at the age of sixty-five, but that by doing some financial planning now, you can be among the top 10 percent.

To investigate using this appeal in your promotion, identify what happens to people if they don't use your product or service. Would fear of the consequences be enough to motivate them to buy? Experiment with making these consequences the focus of a possible appeal.

We suggest experimenting with a variety of appeals and selecting the one you believe will draw the best results. Here are several ways to begin:

Talk to your clients and customers. If you have clients or customers now, ask them what appealed to them about your business. Why did they select you? If there is a strong pattern among their answers, it may indicate your best appeal.

Examine the competition. Notice what your competition is appealing to and which of your competitors attracts the most business. You might also take note of what your competition is not claiming. Perhaps you offer an advantage they can't, such as pickup and delivery.

Be willing to test. Ultimately, however, remember that promotion, like all marketing, is an experiment. If an ad doesn't draw good results or a brochure ends up in the trash, it may not be that you chose the wrong medium or the wrong person; you may be making the wrong appeal. You may have to try several appeals before you hit the target.

Study other marketing materials. Before actually preparing your own promotion, look through several magazines, newspapers, and other publications, watch television commercials, and listen to radio spots. Read every piece of junk mail that comes to you and study every flyer and brochure handed to you. Tear out and make notes on all promotional materials that grab your attention. Try to determine—over and above any personal interest you might have in the product or service—what it is that hooked you. Keep in mind each of the characteristics of the appeals mentioned above.

You will notice that even if several features are covered in the pieces you like, the focus will be on one overriding point, which is made quickly and reinforced consistently with whatever copy, artwork, and production is used.

This is the concept, which should be clearly and concisely stated.

In the advertisement "75 Reasons to Buy Soft Type" above, you will notice that the concept is stated very clearly at the top of the ad. Although a great deal of copy follows, it all reinforces that initial concept. This is clearly a benefit-oriented piece. It lists seventy-five reasons to buy in a numerical form that appears to involve much less copy than it actually does. If you have even a fleeting interest in software-based typefaces, you will read this ad thoroughly.

In contrast, look at the ad above for a similar product, Publisher's Power-pak. The headline reads "Great Faces" followed by "from your dot matrix printer." Although the name of the product is prominently displayed in the center of the page, neither it nor the headline nor the artwork strongly indicate what the product is. Even "Typefaces" is contradicted by the artwork which implies human faces. The attempt to be witty and humorous confuses the concept. Whatever the intended appeal, it got lost in the morass of clever ways aspiring to attract attention. Unless you are grabbed by the prominently mentioned price, you most likely will not take the time to read the rest of this ad.

We have used print ads to illustrate these points because they contain in microcosm all the elements necessary for any piece of promotional material.

The Basic Steps to Writing Copy That Sells

Although many experts would disagree, we believe that anyone can write a competent, creditable promotional piece by following the twelve guidelines outlined earlier. The key factors are concentration, effort, and following the steps outlined below. But first read the eleven basic psychological principles of copywriting listed in the box on the following page.

Step 1. Think before you write. Analyze your product or service carefully. List every feature it has to offer, both tangible and intangible.

Step 2. Translate features into benefits. Put yourself in your prospective clients' or customers' shoes or find someone who can do so. Evaluate each of the features on your list in relation to its specific benefits to the user by determining how each feature will improve the user's life or business.

Step 3. Arrange the benefits in order of importance to the user. Rewrite your benefits in order of importance not to you, but to the user. You may need outside help for this, as it is sometimes difficult to separate yourself from your own views. You might even ask a group of actual or potential users to rank the list for you.

Step 4: Select those benefits that are unique to your company. All companies are going to promote low prices, top quality, and good service. What you need to find are those benefits that your customers can expect to receive from you alone. If there are none, you have to identify the unique manner in which you approach the benefits. This is your unique selling point, and it will be your most valuable promotion asset.

Step 5. Use your unique selling point or number-one user benefit for your headline or primary copy. State this benefit in the briefest, most succinct manner possible. Your only other safe alternative is to use a one-liner to introduce a group of benefits with a phrase such as "5 Ways To . . . ," or "25 Reasons To. . . ." The use of a dramatic number—even an implied one—gets attention.

Eleven Psychological Principles of Copywriting

1. If a potential buyer is involved in a conflict between his or her emotions and his or her intellect, the emotions will win. It is your job as copywriter either to make this principle work for you or to avoid such a conflict.
2. People tend to seek easy formulas that simplify complexity. Any factor—benefit, feature, or otherwise—that creates confusion should be dropped from awareness, no matter how great it seems. This applies to selling as well as nonselling factors.
3. Negative ideas can be misunderstood and take longer to interpret. Avoid negatives, and don't introduce problems that don't already exist in the user's mind, even if you see your product or service as a solution to it. That will also create confusion, and it can unsell what you may already have sold.
4. People's responses are usually in direct proportion to that with which they personally identify. Don't assume that just because you know something about your product or service, your user will too. By the same token, don't assume your prospects know nothing—never talk down to them.
5. Concrete words and ideas are more easily remembered, understood, and recalled than abstractions. The more specific and concrete you can be, the better. Solid facts will outsell generalizations, truisms, and clichés every time.
6. People hear, read, and more clearly understand words they are familiar with. Simple, common, and familiar words will get a better response than clever, different, and unusual ones. As Winston Churchill said, "Old words are good, simple words are best." Use words like *clean, easy, find, good, guarantee, love, life, money, proven, results, save,* and *you.*
7. People feel more comfortable if they know they are doing what others have done. Testimonials add credibility to your cause.
8. People respond best under the pressure of deadlines, therefore, promotions that create a sense of urgency will get a better response.
9. People don't pay 100-percent attention to what they see, hear, and read. For example, they glance instead of read, generalizing from fragments of information. Their attention spans are very short—ten to twenty seconds at best, according to Freelance Writers' Report. You have to capture people's attention within the first three seconds. Messages need to be conveyed simply and quickly with metaphors, slogans, or jingles.
10. People doubt assertions of perfection. Don't make absolute claims that seem too good to be true.
11. Most people prefer gradual improvements to either major changes or no change at all. Focus on how what you offer is better or makes things better.

Step 6. Use the headline to get attention and the body of the copy to sell. Don't try to do too much in the headline. You want it to exemplify your concept clearly or draw the prospect directly to it, but it does not need to contain everything you want to say about your product or service. The purpose of a headline is to get the viewer to stop and read further.

Step 7. Don't try to sell every benefit in a single promotional piece—even a direct-mail package—unless that is likely to be the only one the prospect will ever see. Don't overburden the body copy. Use a few of the most important benefits to reinforce the impact of your headline, and limit yourself to those benefits alone.

Step 8. Keep your copy lean and mean. Use the shortest words possible and avoid extra syllables and words. Do not use odd tenses. Use *can* instead of *are able; go* instead of *are going.* Limit paragraphs to seven lines or under.

Step 9. Avoid meaningless phrases. Don't waste space or time with meaningless phrases such as "fast service," "top quality," or "leader in the field." If you cannot be more specific, omit the idea.

Step 10. Don't offend, even unintentionally. Check and recheck your copy, and have several people with varying perspectives and backgrounds read it. Unintended innuendoes, accidental idiocies, and potentially offensive images can destroy good copy without your even being aware they are there. And sometimes you will be surprised at what someone else thinks you've said!

Step 11. Use humor cautiously. Humor can be very effective, but in more cases than not it accidentally backfires. Just because you understand a certain joke doesn't mean the reader will or that he or she will think it funny. If your readers don't appreciate your humor, your entire piece is usually wasted. Also, the injudicious use of humor almost always violates Step 9.

Look at the piece of advertising on the following page in light of the above suggestions. Decide whether this ad would get your attention and interest you enough to read further.

If you said this is a great headline and a pretty darn good ad, we agree. The bold headline appeals to every single one of us—we are always looking for someone with all the answers. But if that were all that was said, the normal reaction would be serious skepticism, and rightly so. Yet just below the arresting headline is a block of whimsical and intriguing questions and the implication that CompuServe can answer them. Then, the third copy block supports the claim in the headline.

This ad also uses the most modest production techniques of all: one color, one typeface (with three fonts), and a logo. You can't get any simpler or any more effective.

Finally, Somebody With All The Answers.

Why is the sky blue? How much does Isaac Asimov weigh? Why won't my Macintosh talk to my laser printer? How do you fold fitted sheets? How's the weather up there? Who put the bop in the bop-sh-bop-sh-bop? Where can I find the best steak in Chicago? How much is that doggy in the window? How is OS/2 going to affect me? Which hard drive is best for me? Will you marry me?

When you join CompuServe, your computer becomes a communications link between you and more than 500,000 CompuServe members. That's more than a half million different jobs, skills, experiences, interests, senses of humor, hobbies, and interesting peccadillos.

The possibilities are endless. Because CompuServe's communications services include everything from special interest forums to electronic mail and fax services. They let you ask questions (our forums, for instance, can sometimes solve hardware and software problems faster than the manufacturers can), give answers, and make just about any kind of contact you want. (It's true. We've already had several online marriages.)

So become a member of CompuServe. Because let's face it, 500,000 heads are better than one. Any questions?

To join CompuServe, see your computer dealer. To order direct or for more information, call today.

CompuServe®
800 848-8199

Come see us at P.C. Expo, Booth 220, Javits Convention Center, NYC, June 19-21.
CIRCLE READER SERVICE 33

Testing Your Copywriting I.Q.

Every phrase and sentence on the following list came from a real ad. Put a check next to those phrases or headlines you think are good marketing copy.

_____ For all your _____ needs.

_____ Quality _____ supplies.

_____ Quality work.

_____ All work done by skilled professionals.

_____ Quality quickly.

_____ The name you can trust.

_____ Where caring makes the difference.

_____ The future . . . here today."

_____ No job too large or too small.

_____ Our people make the difference.

_____ Full service.

_____ Dependable, courteous service.

_____ Professionally designed and supervised.

_____ Workmanship of superior quality.

_____ Expert installation.

_____ The perfect gift for any occasion.

_____ Modernize to economize.

_____ A tradition in downtown _____.

_____ Latest models.

_____ For the discriminating homeowner who wants the very best at an affordable price.

_____ The special place for special people.

_____ You've got to see it to believe it.

_____ It's our service that makes the difference.

_____ Prompt service.

_____ We will not be undersold.

_____ We're the problem solvers.

_____ The only name you need to know.

_____ Individual attention.

_____ Call us first.

_____ Commitment to Quality

_____ Save cash.

_____ You can depend on us.

_____ The "No Nonsense Agencies."

_____ Call and compare.

_____ Setting the new standards . . .

_____ We add Tender Loving Care.

_____ Where decorating ideas begin.

_____ Your best bet.

_____ Low prices.

_____ Custom designed to your perfection.

_____ We make owning a home so easy.

_____ Where you're somebody special.

_____ . . . Tailored to your budget.

_____ See what you've been missing.

How many of these phrases did you check? Whether slogan, headline, or even part of body copy, not one of the above focuses on a single unique selling point or number-one user benefit. Nor do they relate to the rest of any copy you would want to feature. They simply take up precious space.

The correct answer to this test is NONE. Think of this entire list as mistakes you can avoid. If you checked any of the items, go back and study the Basic Steps to Writing Copy That Sells, and be sure to eliminate such dead weight from your copywriting efforts.

Copywriting Do's and Don'ts

DO talk directly to your prospect in your copy. Use words such as *you* or *your* freely.

DO use straightforward language. You are having a conversation with your prospect. Write the way you would talk.

DO get straight to the point. Say what you have to say and keep it short.

DO use action words or "grabbers."

DO be enthusiastic. Enthusiasm is contagious.

DO be realistic and accurate.

DO use specifics whenever possible.

DO talk about your problem-solving track record, not your credentials.

DO make your copy progress directly and inexorably to a single, specific conclusion.

DO call for action NOW!

DO revise your copy with each reprint.

DON'T use language that has no meaning for your prospect, even if it looks great.

DON'T waste space with nice or cute turns of phrase.

DON'T use excessive adjectives.

DON'T make wild overstatements or vague claims and comparisons.

DON'T try to cover every possible feature and benefit you can think of.

DON'T go into complex technical details and descriptions.

DON'T discuss your formal degrees and credentials.

DON'T use meaningless clichés and trite phrases.

DON'T use cynicism and sarcasm unless you are extremely sure of your market. That appeal rarely succeeds.

DON'T criticize your prospect's lifestyle, taste, family, or previous choices.

Retesting Your Copy Writing I.Q.

The following phrases and sentences are also from existing advertising. Check the ones you think are good.

_____ Even at 250 mph, a _____ wears out slower than everybody else.

_____ Next time your mind wanders, follow it.

_____ A truly great ship is something of a destination in itself.

_____ Unique sanctuary.

_____ Appreciate music in a whole new light. (windows)

_____ Sherle Wagner replaces the silver spoon. (pictured with baby)

_____ Ooops.

_____ Romantic legends.

_____ Furniture that's soft, sculptured, sensuous.

_____ The flat earth, oat bran and Polish vodka.

_____ An automobile that says you've arrived but weren't affected by the trip.

_____ How to correct the excesses of the fast track.

_____ Sometimes luxury is better measured in hours than in dollars.

_____ New color portfolio.

_____ Foreign car specialists.

_____ Factory trained.

The correct answer is ALL. You will notice, however, that this is a much shorter list. Examples of good copy are far fewer than they should be. This is not because good copy is so hard to write, but because two things are involved in creating bad copy: egos and laziness.

Since you don't have a reason to relax and be lazy, the only thing you really have to worry about is ego—yours or that of whoever is writing the copy. If you always put yourself in the shoes of the customer, you'll find it a lot easier to write copy—and a lot easier to sell that customer.

Designing Effective Visuals

Once you have your headline and copy, it is time to take a look at all the visual elements of laying out the promotional piece itself. In most cases—whether print, broadcast, or even direct mail—promotion is a medium that makes use of the eyes. Therefore, the creation of a promotional piece is directly concerned with what we call the visuals.

Notice that we did not use the more common word _artwork_. The visuals in a promotion piece are far more than the artwork. They are all the elements of the complete layout or production, including the way in which you block the copy and use the white space around the print; how you use the performers, guests, set pieces, and props in television; and how you use the voices, silence, pacing, and sound effects in radio.

Because of the high budget and specialized expertise required in most television promotional techniques, however, we will confine our discussion of visuals to the print media. If television is a viable option for you, you would be wise to consider working with a consultant, agency, or production company skilled in the preparation of video for the television media.

Designing the visuals for your promotional pieces is actually easier than it might appear. Although you will find below some do's and don'ts for creating visuals, few of these are absolute. However, if you are a novice, treat them as hard-and-fast rules at first. As you become more experienced and have a larger budget, you may explore breaking some of them. It takes experience to know when to crowd the space in your brochure, ad, or flyer and when to leave it bare, when to use a photograph instead of a line drawing, or when to use nothing but well-arranged copy blocks.

Look again at the CompuServe ad on page 223. It is simple, clean, and uncluttered, with three obvious blocks of copy neatly separated by white space. A single typeface was used throughout the ad, but it was rendered in three fonts: the huge bold headline, the screened middle-sized questions block (if you use a magnifying glass you can actually see the dots), and the small support copy at the bottom. The only thing that matches the weight of the headline is the CompuServe registered trademark.

This arrangement of copy, artwork, and white space is called *layout*. In designing any layout you will be choosing a variety of elements. If you have never designed marketing materials, you may have taken these elements for granted, but each involves choosing from among many alternatives. In designing your piece, you must select:

1. The typeface. This refers to the shape or style of the letters, numbers, and symbols you use. A typeface may be serif (with little tails), sans serif (without little tails), Roman (upright), Italic (slanted slightly to the right), or headline (with fancy designs for special use).

Each manufacturer of typefaces has its own names for the individual typefaces. However, these are usually easily recognized from one manufacturer to another because the choice of names is often similar. Such names as Times, Helvetica, Futura, Park Avenue, Garamond, and Century Schoolbook each indicate different typefaces.

2. The font. This refers to a single height, width, or other adornment of the basic typeface. The height is measured in point sizes, each point equaling 1/72 inch. The width refers to how close or far apart the individual letters are from one another and how narrow or wide each letter is. It includes such classifications as Condensed (including Medium and Extra Condensed), Wide, Extended, Expanded, and Open. The weight refers to the thickness of the strokes of the letters; it can be Light, Medium, Demibold, Bold, Extra Bold, Black, and Ultrabold. Other adornments might include shadow effects, outlines, shadings, and screens.

3. The photographs. Photos are reproduced in one-color halftone, duotone, or four-color process. Sometimes the halftone is printed on a screen of a color to give the impression of a duotone.

4. Line art. When a photograph is either not available or not affordable, line art can prove equally illustrative. In many cases line art can be superior in selling punch to a photograph, and it doesn't require using halftones.

5. The color. One to four colors are available on standard presses. Colors can be used as pure ink tones with a variety of screens that reduce the value of each color, or each color may be used in concert with others to create any color under the sun in what is called process color.

6. White space. Just as important as any other element in a layout is the area in which there is nothing. White space allows you to direct the viewer's eye to the important elements of your piece.

There is no sure-fire formula for selecting from among these elements to design a piece of promotion. If there were, design would no longer be a creative art and every letterhead, flyer, brochure, ad, and catalog would look alike. The effectiveness of any piece lies in creatively combining these elements in a unique way that impacts the viewer. The only true teacher for developing effective visuals is experience.

Since you probably don't have a lot of experience designing visuals, you should increase your experience in looking at them. Become aware of your reaction to the promotional pieces you read, see, and hear. Tear out any ad that affects you either positively or negatively, and write down what it is that you are reacting to. Is the ad hard or easy to read? Does it make its point, and does that point leap off the page at you? How much of the copy did you read,

---

Do-It-Yourself Layout Tools

Whether you are promoting a service business or a product, designing attractive layouts improves your print promotion. If hiring an artist or photographer to create original art is beyond your budget, try these do-it-yourself layout tools:

1. Stock shops. Stock shops maintain huge libraries of photographs and/or line art, and there is at least one in most cities. Usually you rent the particular piece of artwork you want to use on a one-time basis. Each stock shop has its own particular contracts and rules for renting their artwork. Familiarize yourself with their policies before agreeing to rent, particularly if you plan to use your layout in several different promotional pieces.

2. Desktop publishing software. Pagemaker or Ventura for MS-DOS computers, or QuarkXPress or Pagemaker for Macintosh, can help you produce interesting layouts. A software package such as Bannermania by Broderbund can provide a wide variety of typefaces and fonts with which you can experiment for effect.

3. Clip art. Various software packages, such as *Metro ImageBase*, provide clip art that can be used with most desktop publishing software. Local art-supply stores also carry books of clip art and cartoons.

4. Press-on letters. Also available from your local art-supply store are sheets of press-on type in various faces and fonts as well as borders and clip-art-type designs. Although these are somewhat difficult to use until you develop a good eye and steady hand, they do provide you with access to sizes and styles otherwise available only with full typesetting.

and what got you to read that much? Did it arouse your interest or your annoyance? Why? Do the same for letterheads, business cards, flyers, circulars, brochures, catalogs, and direct-mail packages.

Make a file for good pieces and another for not-so-good pieces. Keep these samples in your files and look at them from time to time. When you are ready to design your own layout, take out only the good file to review. Then go to work with your own creativity, keeping in mind the positive aspects of those samples. Try to apply the principles you have observed to your own work. When you have finished, take a look at your not-so-good file to make sure you haven't fallen into some hidden trap.

A trick for developing your first layout is to select two or three samples from your good sample file. Determine which of the sample layouts best suits your copy and artwork, and use that layout with your material.

The purpose of any layout is to reinforce visually what you are trying to say with words. Don't use artwork and other design elements to simply fill up space. They must contribute to the impact of your presentation.

Producing Marketing Materials

How you produce your finished layout depends entirely on how you are planning to use it and where you are going to place it. Many publications, including newspapers and some trade publications, will paste up your ad and prepare the camera-ready art for you. This camera-ready art is called a mechanical. Usually there will be an additional fee for this service, so be sure to find out what it is up front. When using such a service, all you need is a rough layout with the headline sketched in, boxes to show where artwork goes, and lines representing body copy, as shown in sketches on the following page.

How People Read Ads

Research by Gallup Applied Science into how people read advertising and other promotional material provides valuable insights into what draws and keeps their attention. They found that the respondents in their sample:

1. look at the product, the headline, and the coupon in that order. They don't read any of the small type.
2. usually read from top to bottom. They prefer the offer at the top, the product in the middle, and the coupon at the bottom.
3. skim from the right side of the page to the left.
4. are attracted to the word *free*. They seem to find it even if smaller than other elements.
5. focus on the coupon longer if there is a picture on it.

If you plan to use your layout for more than one purpose, however, it is probably worth the expense to hire a professional to prepare the mechanical. This can include typesetting, halftone preparation, color separation, line art, paste-up, and other services. The master for the layout will be yours to keep and use for any other promotional material as well. You can, of course, try creating your own mechanical. If so, you need a steady hand, an excellent eye, a large, flat surface, and a T-square.

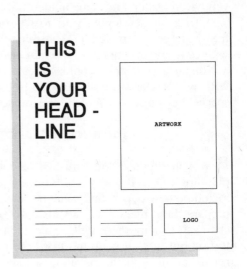

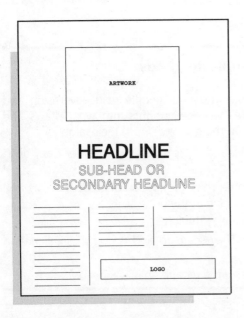

Do's and Don'ts for Creating Your Visuals

DO think in terms of thirds. Most visuals work better if the focus of the page is divided visually into three equal sections.

DO avoid dividing any page into halves either vertically or horizontally.

DO balance the weight of the visual elements. In the sample layout, the visual weight of the artwork balances that of the headline. If the artwork is dark and heavy, you might want the typeface of the headline to be bold and heavy.

DO make your headline readable.

DO separate your headline clearly from the rest of your copy and your artwork.

DO limit yourself to three fonts (one typeface, preferably a Roman face) per page, with the single exception of your logo or trademark.

DO consider placement carefully.

DO use a professional typesetter if you are providing mechanicals unless you have exceptional desktop publishing capabilities. You may, of course, use a 300 dpi laser printer to produce working type for layout tests.

DON'T let the message get buried in the medium. You are not creating a great work of art; you are creating something that will SELL!

DON'T let the visuals take over the point you want to make. They exist only to enhance the impact of the idea.

DON'T let clever graphics distract the viewer from your message. A clever visual is clever only if the reader grasps it instantly.

DON'T use more than one reverse. If you do, your ad will start to look hokey and overdone.

DON'T change your ad regularly unless each ad is part of a series that maintains the same layout and look.

DON'T get so cute with fonts that the reader has to work to decipher what the words are.

DON'T use humor unless it contributes to the memorability of the product or service. Usually humor calls attention only to itself, in which case it will be little help in selling your product or service.

Before making any preparations, be sure to ask your printer or the medium that will produce your piece what form they require to meet your specifications. Certain types of design or printing require more extensive assembly of art and copy elements, and each element must be handled separately.

Tracking Your Marketing Results

Once your promotional piece is out in the marketplace, you will be eager to know whether it is producing the results you want. Yet one of the most difficult tasks marketeers have is tracking the results from the money they have invested. Arrange a way to determine what business a particular brochure, direct-mail package, flyer, ad, or medium has brought in, because this information will be a great help in planning where to place future promotion dollars. There are several ways you can do this.

1. *Judge from overall response.* In some cases you have to rely on the overall response to your entire promotion campaign. If business is good, your campaign must be working.

2. *Keep records of how you get business.* Make it a policy to inquire as to how a client or customer heard about you. Include such a question in answering all phone inquiries and on all intake or order forms. Have a tally posted in a convenient location so you can compare the draw of your various efforts. Remember the rule of seven, however, and don't become discouraged if your marketing efforts don't result in immediate business. The effects of promotion are cumulative and may develop weeks and months later. This applies to all the methods we have discussed; even networking takes time to produce results.

3. *Use direct response to test.* If there is any reason to question a particular promotion piece, try a period of running a special offer with it as a direct-response piece to check the results. Place the same offer in approximately the same location in each of your test markets. Code the address of each coupon or reply card or the portion that is to be returned. If a prospect calls with an inquiry, request and record the code of the particular piece he or she received.

4. *Look at sales, not just inquiries.* The number of inquiries you get is not nearly as important as the number of actual sales made. In advertising, a publication that pulls five hundred inquiries and results in three $100 sales may not be as valuable a promotional avenue as, say, one that pulls twenty-five inquiries that produce fifteen $1,000 sales. So track the number of inquiries that turn into sales by their source. And if you find a low rate of converting inquiries to sales, be sure to find out why.

Keep Marketing No Matter What

If you keep promoting and advertising and trying a variety of methods, two things will happen: first, you will begin to find the concepts and methods that pull consistently for you and can invest more in these avenues; and second, you will develop a marketing momentum. Your various promotional and advertising efforts will begin reinforcing each other. People will recognize you from your promotion and ads and will think about you whenever the need for your product or service arises.

Above all else, remember that promotion does not make good customers; good products and business relationships do that. Promotion can only get people interested in you. Then, you must see to it that they become customers and that they come back again and again.

CHAPTER
FIFTEEN

■■■■■■■■■■■■■■■■■■■■■■

Turning Interest into Business Again and Again

Suppose someone you meet at a networking function is interested in talking with you further about what you do. You give her your card and ask her to call you at the office tomorrow, but she never calls. Or perhaps a man comes up after a speech you have given, wanting to find out more about your business. He begins describing a problem he is having, implying that perhaps you can help. You set up a lunch to discuss it further, but an emergency arises and he has to cancel the lunch. By the time you reach him on the phone, you discover he has hired someone else.

If either of these situations sounds all too familiar, you are not alone in leaving valuable business on the table. Chances are, more business would be yours for the taking if you recognized that the majority of the marketing activities you undertake, including advertising, will go no further than to bring a prospect to you or make the person receptive to your next contact.

Whenever anyone contacts you expressing any degree of interest, this is evidence that your marketing efforts are working. Each such contact represents potential business. However, that usually is as far as your marketing effort can go. When people respond favorably to any marketing effort, they seldom are sold; they are ready to be sold. They are waiting for the details of how much your product or service costs, how it works, and whether you can do it another way; they may also want to know whether you have another color, who else has done what you have, what results you have had, and how your product or service can be suited to their specific needs. Sometimes people will ask you these questions directly, making your job easier; more often than not, however, they don't know what questions to ask, so they simply let you know they are interested and wait for you to take over from there. If your marketing has truly caught their interest, they want you to convince them that, indeed, you do have what they need. They are hoping you do, but they want reassurance.

Once your marketing has developed this positive interest, you must convert that interest into a decision to buy. As sales trainer Joel Weldon says, "Cows don't give milk; you have to take it from them every day." So it is with marketing. Marketing produces the interest; now you have to turn that interest to your advantage. This process is called *closing the sale.*

If, like many others, you dread the word *sale,* keep in mind that your marketing effort has done the most time-consuming and unpleasant parts of making the sale. You won't need to be cold calling strangers. Your marketing has found the potential customer; it has qualified the customer to make sure he or she is interested, and it has even made the initial sales presentation. All that remains for you to do once interest is expressed is close the sale.

Closing a sale is	**Closing a sale is not**
■ discovering how you can best meet someone else's needs	■ doing a slick con job
■ providing additional information	■ pushing products or services onto someone who doesn't want them
■ clarifying concerns	■ using high-pressure techniques
■ working toward a win-win agreement	■ engaging in a win/lose contest
■ establishing or building a relationship	■ glad-handing and backslapping
■ forming a mutually beneficial partnership	■ putting one over on the client
	■ manipulating someone against his or her will

Fifteen Secrets to Closing a Sale

Turning interest into business is essentially a matter of recognizing and responding positively to someone's desire. Someone has a need that you may be able to meet. Your goal is never to coerce people into buying something from you or even to convince them to buy; it is simply to discover whether in fact you can meet their need. If you are convinced you can do so and can convince them too, they will buy.

Here are specific steps you can take to make sure the interest you have generated through your marketing doesn't slip away.

1. Take the initiative to make a follow-up contact. Respond immediately to any signal of interest by proposing that you get back to the interested person by phone. Do not try to close a sale at some meeting or event; you want your customer's full attention without interruption or distraction. If you have been called already, so much the better. Provide whatever information is requested and proceed to set up a further contact or close the sale. But never wait for people to call you back. They probably won't, so why take the chance?

2. Determine whether a phone or personal meeting is called for. The more complex the decision involved in buying your product or service and the higher your price, the more likely your follow-up call should be to schedule a personal meeting. In such situations, you will want to turn phone inquiries into personal appointments as well.

3. When you call, make sure it is a good time for the person to talk. If it is not, schedule a more appropriate time. Even when you are calling to set up a personal meeting, your caller may have a variety of preliminary questions that need to be answered before he or she can decide to meet with you. Respond as clearly as you can, but do not try to go into complicated material by phone. Certainly don't quote a price over the phone when you need to meet to determine exactly what will be involved. Emphasize that you will be able to explain everything in more detail when you speak in person.

The Best Time to Phone

Avoid the busy hours of the day for the business you are calling.

Business	Hour to Call
Bankers	Before or after banking hours
Dentists	Before their appointments begin, usually about 9:30 A.M.
Doctors	After morning hospital rounds and before they begin seeing patients, usually about 9:00 A.M.
Executives	Before the secretary arrives or after he or she has left for the day, or late morning after startup tasks are completed, usually around 10:30.
Trial lawyers	During the noon recess, which may run from late morning to about 2:00 P.M.
Salaried workers	At home after dinner but before prime-time TV
Stockbrokers	Before or after the closing of the stock exchange (open 10:00 A.M.–3:00 P.M. EST)
Teachers and Professors	In the late afternoon at home or after 6:00 P.M.

Following Up on Interest

Tips for Follow-Up Meetings

- Bring a brochure or packet of material to leave with customers. Make sure you bring enough for everyone.
- Use visual aids when possible, such as product samples, a video, photos, or a flip pad.
- Have everything you need in a case with you. Know where each item is for immediate access.
- Make sure everything you will be using is in working order before you leave your own place of business.
- Be flexible. Invite questions. Make the meeting a dialogue, not a monologue.
- Keep subtle control of the meeting. Gently bring it back to the decisions at hand when needed.
- Never run over the agreed time for the meeting. Schedule a next appointment if you need to.
- Don't give out information no one needs. Let the questions you are asked guide the focus of the meeting.
- Dress slightly more conservatively than whose with whom you will be talking.

Tips for Follow-Up Phone Calls

- Make the most of your voice. It is the only channel of communication you have on the phone.
- Be pleasant, authoritative, and confident.
- Smile before you dial or pick up the phone. The smile will automatically translate to your voice.
- Always confirm that it is a good time to talk.
- Never read a script, but do write out key words and phrases for the main points you want to make.
- Prioritize your points so that you have a short list of those you *must* make.
- Subtly guide the discussion to cover those main points.
- Have all the information you need at your fingertips; including price sheets, specifications, and resources.
- Place sales calls on a line without call waiting. You don't want to be interrupted at crucial moments.
- Listen for what is being said between the lines and respond directly to that.

4. Think service, not sales. Once you are meeting with someone, whether in person or by phone, focus your attention on finding out what your potential client needs and determining whether it is something you can supply. Find out as much as you can about the results the person is seeking and what interested him or her in your product or service.

5. Welcome all questions. In contacting you for further information, potential buyers want to determine whether you know enough about how your product or service would relate to their particular business, their life, and their needs. They may ask you questions that were clearly answered in the ad, your speech, or other literature; perhaps the information didn't register, or perhaps they need reassurance. They may even ask you the same question several times.

Ultimately, the reason someone chooses your product or company probably isn't because of *what* your product or service provides; someone else almost certainly provides it, too. People will buy from you because of *how* you do whatever you are selling. Particularly when you have an information or service business, the primary reason people do business with you is, in fact, *you.*

In selecting your product or service, buyers must put some aspect of their company in your hands. Therefore they must trust that you truly represent something they can rely on and whatever happens, you will act in their interest and give them straight answers. With most people such trust does not come automatically. Often, all the questions, delays, doubts and hemming and

---

Sources of Market Data to Help You Close Sales

1. **Be a secret shopper.** Interview or visit your competitors as if you were a potential customer. Observe them at work when possible, noting your reactions and those of others. Attend their events.

2. **Review market data available from the industry.** Most trade associations have statistics on average prices, average income, means of advertising, and other such areas.

3. **Provide a sample of what you offer and observe the response.** Place items on consignment in several local stores, offer a service to members of a specific organization, or exhibit at a trade show. Watch the reactions to what you offer, and get feedback.

4. **Hold an informal focus group.** Invite a group of individuals to meet with you to react to your product, service, or marketing piece.

5. **Use an informal questionnaire or survey.** Distribute a written questionnaire for individuals from your market to fill out and return, or conduct an informal survey in person or by phone.

6. **Read trade magazines and newsletters.** The trade papers, as these are sometimes called, will give you an idea of the most pressing issues and concerns of your clients and customers.

hawing you encounter are part of the process a person needs to go through to determine whether you are someone he or she can trust. This is the main reason that on average it can take at least seven contacts to make a sale.

6. Understand before you answer. Although buyers may ask questions about your academic preparation or background or the details relating to your product or service, they are usually not interested in that information per se; they are seeking evidence that you know about, understand, and can do something about what they need. So don't just start answering questions by plunging into a lot of details. If you don't find out everything you can about a person's needs before you answer, you may unwittingly unsell yourself.

For example, suppose you offer a bookkeeping service and someone calls to find out about it. The caller asks how many years you have been in business, what you charge to do a general ledger, and whether you do the work on site. Instead of jumping in with price information, we suggest answering the first and third questions and then asking questions of your own to determine the person's needs, such as "What type of business do you have?" "How are you handling your bookkeeping now?" and "How many active accounts do you have each month?" By requesting this information, you have conveyed that you are interested in the caller's needs and, once you have the crucial information you need to answer the caller's questions from an informed position, you can demonstrate how you would tailor your work to meet those needs. You won't be shooting in the dark or hoping your answers are heading in the right direction.

7. Know your competition. Be prepared not only to address questions about your product or service specifically, but to demonstrate how it compares to others, what trends it reflects in the field, what research shows relative to the issues involved, and how people similar to your prospect are using what you offer.

8. Exude confidence in your skills and in your knowledge. In order for others to trust that your product can handle the work they need done, they first need to believe that you are convinced you can do it. So once you have enough information to know that you can handle the work, assert confidently how you will proceed and the benefits that will result.

Never try to act as though you know about something when you don't. Instead, offer to get back to your questioner with additional information. If you try bluffing your way through, you run a high risk of displaying your ignorance and lessen your ability to inspire the necessary trust.

One of the best ways to inspire that necessary trust is to talk about work you have done with similar clients and to offer the names of references your potential client or customer can contact. First, however, be sure to ask questions and listen carefully to the replies so you are certain to be addressing the person's actual needs. Another way to boost your authority is to hold informal surveys or focus groups with potential customers to find out as many of

Gathering Low-Cost Market Research

When to use do-it-yourself market research

- When you want to know which features will appeal most to prospective clients.
- When you are wondering how effective your marketing is.
- When your business isn't thriving and you need to find out why.

Do-it-yourself focus groups

- Invite seven to ten individuals from your market whom you don't know to an informal meeting.
- Ask them to respond to your product or service or your marketing piece.
- Prepare a list of specific questions to which you want answers, such as:
  Would you use the product or service?
  Why wouldn't you use it?
  What are you using now?
  What are you satisfied with?
  What are you dissatisfied with?
  How much would you pay?
- Encourage all comments. Show no preference or bias.
- Watch body language. It can be more revealing than what people say.
- Tape-record the meeting so you can thoroughly review the feedback.
- Offer a gift or fee to those who attend.

Do-it-yourself surveys

- Be sure the questions are clear and mean the same thing to everyone.
- Keep instructions and questions simple. Keep the survey short.
- Keep all your personal opinions and preferences out of the questions.
- Make the survey visually attractive and easy to read.
- Begin with questions that screen for those actually in your market.
- Use primarily multiple-choice and forced-choice answers, which can be quantified, such as: Rank on a scale of 1 to 10. Check those that apply to you. Write *true* or *false*. Write *yes* or *no*.
- Have at least one open-ended question that allows people to comment freely. Leave room for additional comments.
- Test the questionnaire first with several people to be sure it is understandable and provides the information you need.
- If mailed, enclose a stamped, self-addressed envelope.
- To increase participation, hold a drawing or offer a small gift to respondents.

the concerns, questions, and issues that will arise when you talk with potential buyers. You can also hire someone to conduct these for you, or you might want to hire a market-research consultant to review the questions you plan to ask to make sure you are likely to draw meaningful responses. Having such first-hand information will prepare you for objections and provide you with insights into the issues someone may be facing so that you can respond more knowledgeably.

9. If possible, offer some type of guarantee. Offering a guarantee—of satisfaction, parts, or accuracy—will short-circuit many objections and serve as proof that you believe in your product. While a photographer can't guarantee that her customers will get a photo they will love and a therapist can't guarantee that his patients will be cured, there is usually some type of guarantee you can offer, even in a service business. The photographer, for example, can guarantee proofs will be returned within three days, and the therapist can guarantee that every phone call will be returned within two hours.

Among the guarantees that work well for service businesses, Roger Lane promises that unless students attending his finance course double their income in six weeks, they can continue in the course free of charge until they

---

When and How to Ask for the Order

- **The time to ask** for the order is when the buyer doesn't have more questions and you don't have any more information to provide.
- **Ask directly.** Say something like "We can get started tomorrow. Shall I come by in the morning?" or "All that's required is a check. Do you want me to bill you?"
- **Offer to make a proposal, bid, or estimate.** If what you are selling is complex, offering to provide a proposal, bid, or estimate will give the prospective client time to look over what you can do. (See the Resource List to locate further information on how to develop a proposal.)
- **Follow up on the proposal** by asking how it seems to the buyer. If the response is positive, all you have to do is say, "Okay, when do we start?" or "How many would you like?" or "When would you like your first shipment?"
- **If the person can't give you an answer,** you may not be talking to the decision-maker. In that case, ask what you can do to make the job easier. For example, you can offer to provide additional information for the decision-makers or join in making a presentation to them.
- **If the buyer is stalling,** you can always ask the one question that usually makes people take notice: "What will it take to get your business?" You are really asking, is what the real problem is and, if there isn't one, that the sale be completed.

---

do. Word processor Camella Cortez guarantees a 10 percent discount if the customer finds any typing errors and of course, that she will correct them. And hairstylist Shannon King offers to take back any beauty-care product that doesn't make a noticeable difference. In each of these cases, rarely does anyone actually take the offerer up on the guarantee. Instead, people get hooked on the service.

10. Welcome and respond to objections. Often people dread hearing any fussing, griping or grumbling, complaints, criticisms, negative comparisons, excuses, or other general reasons someone doesn't seem to want to buy. All such reactions are referred to in sales parlance as objections. However, you should be delighted when you hear them, for several reasons.

First, if someone is raising an objection, this is a sign that they are still interested but that some concern is preventing them from acting. No one will take the time to raise objections who doesn't retain some interest. Second, these objections can be viewed as someone's internal dialogue that they have decided to voice to you. This gives you a chance to see whether you can help the person get past these concerns.

Objections are the best way for you to know and then to get around any resistances someone has to buying. Think of objections as stated questions. Someone who says, "That's an awful lot of money" is essentially asking, "Will this really be worth that much to me?" And "But I need this by Wednesday" means that someone is asking whether they can get it sooner. So whenever you hear an objection, consider how you can answer the question that underlies it. People rarely say what they mean when they object; the objection is a sign of uncertainty. This is why objecting to price is so common. Your job is to draw the buyer out to discover the real problem behind the objection. You may find that it is a very real concern that you can take care of, or you may find out that the concern is based on inaccurate information.

Finally, objections are the best way for you to determine whether you can actually meet someone's needs. And if you can't, the sooner you find that out, the better.

11. Find out whether the person is ready to make a buying decision. Once you have addressed the major concerns, ask a question to test whether the person you're talking with is ready to buy. Having explained how your service works, for example, you might ask, "Does that sound like something you want to do?" or "So would you like to make an appointment? Asking such questions will bring out any remaining objections for you to respond to. If the person no longer seems interested, point out a benefit that originally had appeal one more time just to be sure your assessment is accurate.

12. Walk the person step by step through what is involved in buying. As you sense someone's interest growing, explain step by step how to order and get the service underway. The more graphically you can describe how

How to Handle the Most Common Objections

Business-to-business

Your price is too high.

- "What exactly are we comparing it to?"
- "Let me show you how we can be more cost effective for you."
- "Have you considered the following benefits?"
- "What we offer differs from our competition in the following ways. Which of these differences might be important to you or your company?"

We can't afford such a product or service.

- "Let me show you how we can actually save you money over your current methods."
- "You have acknowledged the potential value to you, perhaps you can't afford *not* to take advantage of the benefits."

We can't afford it right now.

- "We can make special billing arrangements to suit your needs."
- "With references we would be happy to open an account for you."
- "The sooner you take advantage of the benefits, the sooner you can reap the rewards."

It won't work for us.

- "Let me show you how it will fit into your current operation."
- "We will be happy to tailor it to your specifications."
- "Let me show you how it has worked for others in your situation."

We need it in another form.

- "Exactly what changes would be suitable for you?"
- "We will be happy to work with you to suit your needs."

I don't have time to discuss it right now.

- "Your time is very valuable. Let me show you, very briefly, how we can save you time as well as money."
- "Of course, you are busy. When would be a good time to show you how we can save you both time and money?"
- "I know your time is pressing, but I do want you to know about this limited offer."

I'll think about it.

- "Do so. I know you will find it of great advantage to you. I will contact you early next week to see if you need any further information."
- "What questions are in the back of your mind right now?"
- "What additional information would be of help to you in your considerations?"

Thanks. We'll call you.

- "I will give you a call next week to see if you need any further information."
- "Let me ask you honestly: What will it take to get your business?"

How to Handle the Most Common Objections

Business-to-consumers

I can get it cheaper elsewhere.
- "Can you also get the following advantages?"
- "Are you actually getting the same thing elsewhere?"
- "Have you considered the following benefits that are available only through us?"

I can't afford it.
- "Let me show you how it will save you time and money now and in the future."
- "Let me show you how it will pay for itself in _____ weeks/months."
- "We do offer special discounts under the following circumstances."
- "Let me show you how it would be far less expensive than the alternatives you are considering."
- "You realize that you will be missing out on _____?"

I can't afford it right now.
- "We would be happy to accept your credit card."
- "We do offer the following credit program."
- "The sooner you make the purchase, the sooner you can start enjoying the benefits."
- "You might want to consider that there will be a price increase as of _____."
- "We do offer discounts or special prices under the following conditions that apply to you."
- "Let me show you how it can start paying for itself right away."

It won't work for me.
- "Tell me a little more about what it is you need."
- "Why do you feel it won't work?"
- "Let me tell you about others who found it solved similar needs."
- "What if I guarantee that I will refund your money if you are not happy with it?"

I don't like the _____ (feature or aspect such as color or location).
- "What is it about that feature or aspect that is not suitable for you?"
- "What feature or aspect would be more suitable for you? Perhaps we can adapt it to meet your needs."
- "That particular feature or aspect does not interfere in any way with the major advantages it will provide you. Let me show you why."

I'll have to think about it.
- "What additional information will you need to help you decide?"
- "Why not try this sample to show you how it would work for you."
- "We are currently offering a special promotion for a limited time."
- "Are there any questions at all that you still have, even in the back of your mind?"

simple it is and how soon the customer will have the desired outcome, the better. Such a description enables the person to imagine going through the steps and enjoying the results.

*13. **Ask for the order.*** People often will not actually reach a decision without your requesting them to do so. Mistaking this hesitancy for reluctance, the novice at closing sales may give up on the sale, propose speaking again some other time, or invite the person to think the offer over and talk later. Even sales professionals sometimes miss the sale by not actually asking for the order. In a recent study of professional sales reps during a monitored call situation only approximately 10 percent of the reps asked for the order. Even when the reps were told that the buyer would be placing an order, still only 17 percent asked for it. The rest didn't and lost the sale.

Don't make this mistake. If there is one thing that will increase your ability to turn interest into business, it is asking for the order. So don't balk when it comes down to the nitty-gritty of asking for business. Before you hang up the phone or walk out of the office, ask for the sale directly.

*14. **Get the money.*** No deal is truly complete until the money is in hand or the contract is signed. Spell out and tie down all the financial terms at the time of the sale, and get the full amount or a down payment whenever possible. If you must bill or extend credit, establish the terms of the payment and get what you have agreed to in writing either in the form of a simple contract, a signed purchase order, or a letter of agreement. Don't do any work or turn over any product until such an agreement is in place. Be sure you have your customer's authorized signature on some form of agreement that states clearly what is being purchased and under what terms.

Spelling out all terms clearly in a proposal makes this process easier. It is simple for the customer either to sign the proposal form as is or to transfer that information to a purchase order. If the information is transferred to a purchase order, contract, or letter of agreement, be sure it is transferred accurately and that no alterations are made either in substance or appearance.

You can have your attorney draw up a standard contract with blanks for the date and cost figures, or you can write a contract yourself using a form book from a law library or by using such computer software as Venture by Star Software, which provides simple pro forma contracts. These can be tailored to your needs. However, be sure to have your attorney review what you create. You are not a lawyer and, even when using standard forms, there may be special laws or circumstances in your state that are not accounted for.

When extending credit, check a new customer's credit rating and/or references thoroughly before you start working or ship a single item. You can locate credit-reporting agencies in the yellow pages or use a computer-based service such as Newsnet, available through CompuServe's IQUEST, which provides TRW credit reports. From a business you also want to request a credit application. The customer's bank and at least three credit references

---

Basic Questions to Ask Credit References

- How long has the applicant been a customer?
- What is the applicant's highest credit allowed?
- How quickly does the applicant usually pay his or her bills? (30 days? Slow 30? 60 days? Slow 60? Longer?)
- Are there any currently overdue invoices?

---

may be your most valuable sources of credit information. Just be sure you ask the right questions and read carefully between the lines of the answers.

Before deciding what approach you will take when negotiating any of the above financial agreements, find out what the normal practices are in your field. Nothing can make you appear to be more of an amateur than not knowing how the money is handled.

One last point: there will be those few times when you have to assume the unpleasant task of collections. If a customer does not pay you within the time allotted by your agreement (usually thirty days), request payment with a cordial phone call. If you still have not received payment by the forty-five day mark, call again, firmly but politely making it very clear that the customer will receive no more merchandise or work until the bill is paid. Once they have passed the sixty-day mark, with rare exceptions, customers should be placed on a C.O.D. basis only.

One of the greatest mistakes small businesses make is relying on a few very large customers instead of maintaining a broader base of medium-sized customers. If a company that gives you thousands of dollars worth of business doesn't pay for it and on time, you lose money. In addition to the lost payment for your product or service, there are dozens of hidden costs and, therefore, losses in dealing with slow-paying companies. You cannot afford that kind of customer. Make sure people pay on time or put them on C.O.D. Losing a non-paying customer is no loss.

15. Always leave the door open for the next contact. Should you not be able to close a sale, you need to determine whether there is sufficient interest to suggest a next step. For example, if a person explains that he or she is moving and unable to make a commitment, you can offer to call again in two weeks. If a company is in the middle of a contract and cannot change suppliers, take advantage of the time to prepare creative selling points for the next proposal period and keep in touch with the buyer to impart information and to show continued interest and reliability.

Whenever sufficient interest remains, set up a specific date and time for the next contact. If appropriate, offer to send additional material or a brief proposal and set up your next call or meeting on your calendar. Remember that you need an average of seven solid contacts before a person is ready to buy.

Don't get discouraged. The more work a sale takes, the more committed the eventual buyer will be and the more difficult it will be for someone else to take the client away from you. One company called regularly, though infrequently, on a major wire service for fourteen years, through three different buyers, without completing a deal. But when the wire service finally made the decision to change to the persistent supplier, the deal represented half a million dollars per year in business. Twenty years later they still have the business.

Even when there will definitely be no sale, thank your prospects for their interest, express your pleasure at meeting them, and let them know that you will be happy to serve them anytime in the future should they need your product or service. Keep their names on your mailing list and send materials out at least quarterly so that your name remains in the forefront of their minds.

Communicating Versus Manipulating

Much has been said about sales and manipulation. Some sales trainers point out that most communication we engage in every day is manipulative, because we are trying to get someone else to think or do something we are advocating. Therefore, they suggest, sales is no different, and we need not be concerned about being manipulative. While it may be true that much of our communication is meant to get others to do our bidding, we believe that this argument misses the point.

We have all been pressured at some time into buying something we didn't really want and resented it later. As a result, most people who are new to closing sales feel somewhat self-conscious about selling, wanting to be sure to avoid the discomfort and negative feelings that arise from such manipulation. Manipulation, in this sense, is trying to get someone to buy something they neither want nor need. In the long run, it never pays off. People won't use the unwanted item; they may even feel angry about it and try to return it or back out on the agreement. You lose their future business, and they won't send any more business your way. They may even bad-mouth you to others. Studies show people are more likely to denounce a business than to praise one.

If you have a product or service that people need and it does in fact meet that need, you don't have to be concerned about having to manipulate people into buying it. Your task in closing the sale is to help each person reach a decision. Customers want to be sure what you offer will met their needs before they part with their money, so you must address their concerns and doubts. Helping people get past their concerns is not manipulation; it is helping them get what they want.

Getting Repeat Business

Attracting new business costs at least six times more than retaining existing business, according to Carole Congram, editor of *The American Management Association Handbook of Marketing for Service Industries*. That means the best way to get business to come to you is to get your existing clients to keep coming! But here is a shocking fact: When the Small Business Administration asked businesses why they thought customers stopped doing business with them, most said prices were too high. Yet when the agency surveyed customers to find out why they left to buy elsewhere, only 9 percent cited price. Being treated indifferently was the reason 68 percent left.

Once you have business, the wisest marketing investment you can make is to invest in ensuring that your customers come back again and again. Customer service or customer relations is one area wherein you, as a small business, have the advantage. You can do it better than larger businesses because you can offer the personal touch that will make the difference. Martin Wallach, who operates an advertising agency from his suburban Chicago home, is able to say to prospective clients, "You'll never be dealing with an underling. You'll work with top people all the time."

Using Your Greatest Advantage: The Personal Touch

Large companies today often try to rotate personnel in their purchasing departments to prevent personal relationships from forming with suppliers. These companies are under the impression that business is done between institutions rather than between people. They believe that this detachment best fosters the competition between their suppliers and thereby results in lower prices. What these companies don't realize is that there is far more to a business relationship than price. What often ends up happening in such an impersonal buying arena is that the most reputable companies back out of the bidding war, knowing they cannot and will not compete on price alone. This leaves only the less-than-top-flight vendors as the pool from which many of these companies have to choose.

One thing such companies miss is the assurance of quality. Another is the guarantee that the supplier will still be in business next week. And the most important loss is the service that comes from having a close and strong business relationship. No one is going to stop everything to bail a fickle customer out of a problem or emergency, but most people will go out of their way for someone who has gone out of the way for them again and again.

As a small business, your greatest advantage is that you can provide personal service. Each of your clients is a valued asset, not just another account number. You have the personal touch and can provide service above and beyond that expected. Ultimately, the company with the confidence to stand by its product or service, follow through on day-to-day orders, and assist the buyer if he or she makes a mistake is the company that keeps the business.

The way this trust is developed is by slowly but surely building a history of confidence—a history that shows you will deliver again and again. The more you are able to help someone do his or her job, the more that person will come to rely on you. Part of this trust comes from attention to the details that few others bother with. If you are providing bookkeeping services to the office manager of a law office, for example, the more you apprise that manager of what you are doing, how, and why, the better able the manager is to answer questions from the law partners. Every time a partner asks why the billing was done a particular way, if you have prepared the manager to handle the questions to the partner's satisfaction, he or she looks like a hero to the partner and you are a hero to the office manager.

No matter how long you have had customers, continue to treat each one like a brand-new customer you want to impress. Never take people's business for granted; someone else will most likely be glad to serve them. Impress them again and again.

Seven Ways to Make Sure Your Business Keeps Coming Back

1. Do a great job! Go the extra mile for each customer. Give people more than they expect. Even if you don't make much money on the first job, do it so well they will want to pay more the next time.

2. Deliver on time. Meet your deadlines. Don't promise what you know you can't deliver just to get the business. Make sure the deadlines you promise to meet are realistic ones; then see if you can beat them. Coming in ahead of time will be a delightful surprise.

3. Solicit feedback. Always inquire to make sure the customer is pleased. When possible, check out satisfaction each step along the way, while corrections are easier to make. Let customers know you want to hear any suggestions or complaints.

4. Make it right. Should a problem develop, do whatever is needed to compensate the customer. Reduce the price, redo the job, exchange the item, or throw in something additional of value. Be willing to negotiate, and be flexible and understanding even when the customer created the problem. Don't argue over who caused it; just work to resolve it to everyone's satisfaction.

5. Give preferential treatment. Let your regular customers know that they come first. Give them whatever preferences you can for time slots or discounts. When possible, exclude them from price hikes.

6. Go out of your way to assist your customers' business. If possible, refer business to them or provide them with tips that will aid their success. Introduce them to others who could be of help to them.

7. Answer phone calls and correspondence promptly. Even if this means you need to hire full- or part-time help or work late, make sure you stay current. Whenever possible, phone calls should be returned within two hours, and letters should be answered within the week. Don't be concerned if you have to leave a message. It is less important that you actually reach the customer than that the customer knows you tried to respond swiftly.

Handling an Irate Customer

There is only one way to handle irate customers: agree with them. Agree not that they were wronged by the company, but that they certainly should not have been treated poorly. Empathize with their situation. There is nothing that will take the wind out of the sails of anger more quickly than empathetic agreement.

Sometimes doing this seems difficult, especially if the customer is particularly abusive. But an unhappy customer is a time bomb that can do you damage for years to come if you don't defuse it before it explodes elsewhere. If you handle the situation well,you will at the very least avert disaster and you just might earn a loyal, satisfied customer. The moment you go on the defensive—even if you are right—you have lost not only the battle but the war and the business. If, on the other hand, you offer to investigate the problem and get right back to your customer, not only does the anger fade but confidence in both you and your company increases as well. There are three *nevers* for dealing successfully with angry people:

Never *contradict an angry customer.* If for legal reasons you cannot afford to agree, respond sympathetically and offer to investigate the situation.

Never *lie to an angry customer*—or to any customer, for that matter. You will probably get caught, making a customer angrier, and with good reason. You will succeed much better if, again, you offer to look into the problem.

Never *give an irate customer an immediate answer.* Even if you know exactly what the problem is and how it occurred, tell such customers you will check on it and get right back to them. This gives you a chance to double-check your information and, more important, it gives customers a chance to vent their anger and cool down. Until an irate customer has gotten past the initial fury, he or she is neither interested nor ready to listen.

Sixteen Little Relationship-Building Ideas That Make a Big Difference

Often the little things make the biggest difference. Try some of these to make sure your customers know how much you value their business.

1. Make a record of each customer's birthday and send a card or novelty gift, such as a balloon. You might even consider sending a handmade card.

2. Note each customer's special interests and copy magazine articles pertaining to those interests. Send the articles to customers with a personal note saying that you thought they might enjoy the articles if they haven't already read them.

3. Send a good customer tickets to a favorite sports game or show he or she has been yearning to see.

4. On a special occasion like a company anniversary, send a personalized mug with a note that you will buy the coffee (or tea).

5. As soon as they come out, send a customer a special-interest calendar for the next year.

6. If you know a customer is going through a frantically busy period, send a gourmet picnic lunch or something from his or her favorite restaurant.

7. Everybody goes to lunch. Suggest a power breakfast.

8. If a customer does an exceptional amount of business with you during a specific time, write a thank-you letter.

9. Create a custom T-shirt that reflects your relationship with a customer (World's Greatest Customer!) or a private joke you share.

10. Visit a good customer in the hospital; don't just send flowers.

11. Invite a good customer to your home for dinner.

12. Involve yourself in activities of interest to your customers. (Don't fake an interest, but why not try something new?)

13. Offer to conduct mini-training sessions, if applicable, on your customer's site.

14. Remember a customer's children's birthdays with cards or small gifts.

15. Attend all weddings, funerals, bar mitzvahs, christenings, and other events to which you are invited.

16. Ask customers for suggestions on how you can improve.

Managing a Self-Sustaining Business

As your marketing plan begins drawing people to you and you turn their interest into business with greater regularity, you will find that your business begins to develop a momentum of it own. If all goes well, ultimately, satisfied customers will comprise the bulk of your business. Between their return business and new business they refer to you, it will be self-generating. Marketing for new business will become less important, while the importance of customer relations will increase.

At this point, you can begin shifting your budget allocations from lower-cost time-consuming marketing efforts to smaller amounts of more costly marketing that involves less of your time but continues to provide your business with a high profile within your market. You may choose to do more image-building activities and fewer promotion or less direct-response advertising.

You may also find yourself faced with more business than you can handle, and you will be presented with having to make the enviable choice of expanding or containing your business. You can expand by adding staff to carry out the work and devoting your time to continued marketing and sales efforts, or you may contain by raising your prices and referring out your overload business. Whichever you do, we advise that no matter how busy or successful or comfortable you become, you continue marketing actively to your existing client and referral base and keep up a maintenance level of promotional activity within your specific market.

Building a high profile that will attract business through its own momentum is like following a body-conditioning program. Getting your body in peak condition requires considerable time and energy, but once you have achieved your goal, a maintenance program will keep you there with much less effort. If you stop all workouts, however, your body will revert quickly to its previous state of poor conditioning. So it is with marketing: if you let the excellent program you have developed go, you will quickly lose your market's attention, and others who are marketing aggressively will take your place. Then, should you need to attract more business again, you will have to exert considerable effort to regain a level of recognition that will attract a steady business flow. Supporting a sustained marketing effort, however, takes much less time, energy, and money, and it will enable you to ride out slow periods simply by stepping up your marketing a little.

The more you can incorporate marketing into what you regularly do in the course of offering your product or service through sampling, participating in your community and profession, and providing top-notch customer service, the easier this ongoing process of marketing will be. And you will have become a premier marketeer. You will be among the growing number of Americans who wake up every Monday morning to the freedom of being your own boss without having to give up the security of a regular paycheck, because when you get to your desk, there will be gainful work for you to do.

RESOURCES

■■■■■■■■■■■■■■■■■■■■■■

A guide to some of the best references a fledgling marketeer can use in following the suggestions and advice in this book. We have used an asterisk (*) to tag resources that are usually available through libraries, online services, or 900 services.

Chapter 1

Association Marketing Directory. 1726 M Street N.W., Suite 1002, Washington, D.C. 20036. (800) 541-0663.*

CompuServe Information Service. 5000 Arlington Center Boulevard, P.O. Box 20212, Columbus, OH 43220. (800) 848-8199 or (614) 457-0802.*

GEnie. General Electric Information Service, 401 North Washington Street, Rockville, MD 20850. (301) 340-4494.*

Guerilla Marketing: Secrets for Making Big Profits from Your Small Business, by Jay Conrad Levinson. Boston: Houghton Mifflin, 1985.

Guerilla Marketing Attack, by Jay Conrad Levinson. Boston: Houghton Mifflin, 1989.

Marketing for the Home-Based Business, by Jeffrey P. Davidson. Holbrook, MA: Bob Adams, 1990.

The Marketing Sourcebook for Small Business, by Jeffrey P. Davidson. New York: John Wiley.

Marketing Warfare, by Al Reis and Jack Trout. New York: McGraw-Hill, 1986.

Marketing Without Advertising—Creative Strategies for Small Business Success, by Michael Phillips and Salli Rasberry. Berkeley, CA: Nolo Press, 1986.

Marketing Without A Marketing Budget, by Craig S. Rice, Holbrook, MA: Bob Adams, 1989.

Positioning: The Battle for Your Mind, by Al Reis and Jack Trout. New York: Warner, 1986.

The Small-Business Resource Guide, by Joseph R. Mancuso. Englewood Cliffs, NJ: Prentice Hall, 1989.

Street Smart Marketing, by Jeff Slutsky and Mark Slutsky. New York: John Wiley, 1989.

Thomas Register, Thomas Publishing Co., One Penn Plaza, New York, NY 10119. (800) 222-7900, x200.*

Part 1
Word-of-Mouth Marketing

Dun's Market Identifiers. Available on Dialog Information Services and CompuServe Information Service. Database contains directory information on over 6.7 million U.S. establishments, both public and private. Includes sales figures, number of employees, net worth, date and state of incorporation, and other data.*

How to Get More & Better Referrals: 73 Proven Strategies. Howard L. Shenson, 20750 Ventura Boulevard, Woodland Hills, CA 91364. (818) 703-1415. 1990. Pamphlet.

The Naming Guide: How to Choose a Winning Name for Your Company, Service or Product. The Salinon Corporation, 7430 Greenville Avenue, Dallas, TX 75231. (214) 692-9091. Pamphlet.

The Printing Papers Primer, by Maxwell A. Clampitt. The ADD Group, R.D. 2, Box 175, Laceyville, PA 18623. (717) 833-5164. 1991.

Pocket Pal—A Graphic Arts Production Handbook. International Paper Company, Pocket Pal Books, P.O. Box 100, Church Street Station, New York, NY 10008-0100. (212) 431-5222.

Thomas Register Online. Available on Dialog Information Services and CompuServe Information Service. Database contains information on almost 150,000 U.S. and Canadian manufacturers and service providers and is updated on an annual basis. Includes products and services provided, trade names and descriptions, exporter status, names of parent or subsidiary companies and other data. Also available in print in libraries.*

World Chamber of Commerce Directory. Worldwide Chamber of Commerce Directory, Inc., Loveland, CO. (303) 663-3231. Annual.*

Part 2
Public Relations: Establishing a Reputation
That Means Business

Corporate Meeting Planners. *The Salesman's Guide,* 1140 Broadway, New York, NY 10001. (212) 684-2985.

Bacon's Information, Inc. Bacon Publishing Company, 332 South Michigan Avenue, Suite 1020, Chicago, IL 60604. (312) 922-2400.*

Business Periodical Index. H.W. Wilson Company, Bronx, NY. Annual.*

Directories in Print. Gale Research Inc., Book Tower, Detroit, MI 48226. (313) 961-2242.*

Gale Directory of Publications and Broadcast Media. Gale Research, Inc., Book Tower, Detroit, MI 48226. (313) 961-2242. Annual.*

Gebbie Press All-in-One Directory. Gebbie Press, Box 1000, New Paltz, NY 12561. Annual.*

How to Get Quoted & Talked About by the Press. Howard L. Shenson, 20750 Ventura Boulevard, Woodland Hills, CA 91364. (818) 703-1415.

Lesly's Public Relations Handbook, by Phillip Lesly. Englewood Cliffs, NJ: Prentice Hall, 1983.*

Newsletters in Print. Gale Research, Inc., Book Tower, Detroit, MI 48226. (313) 961-2242.*

Oxbridge Directory of Newsletters: The Most Comprehensive Guide to U.S. and Canadian Newsletters Available. New York, NY. Annual.*

Professional's Guide to Public Relations Services, by Richard Weiner. New York: Public Relations Publishing, 1988.*

Publicity: How to Get It, by Richard O'Brien. New York: Barnes & Nobel, 1977.

Speak and Grow Rich, by Dottie Walters and Lillet Walters. Englewood Cliffs, NJ: Prentice Hall, 1989.

Standard Periodical Directory. Oxbridge Publishing Company, New York, NY. Annual.*

Toastmasters International. P.O. Box 9052, Mission Viejo, CA 92690. (714) 858-8255.

Ulrich's International Periodicals Directory. R.R. Bowker Company, 1180 Avenue of the Americas, New York, NY 10036. Annual with quarterly updates.*

The Unabashed Self-Promoter's Guide: What Every Man, Woman, Child and Organization in America Needs to Know About Getting Ahead, by Jeffrey Lant. Jeffrey Lant Associates, 1983.

Part 3
Direct Marketing: Getting Your Message Across One-on-One.

AT&T Business Toll-Free Directory. (800) 426-8686.

The Complete Direct Mail List Handbook, by Ed Burnett. Englewood Cliffs, NJ: Prentice Hall, 1988.

Corporate Contacts. (Sells internal directories of companies.) (301) 587-1819.

Direct Mail Copy That Sells, by Herschell Gordon Lewis. Englewood Cliffs, NJ: Prentice Hall, 1986.

Directory of Conventions. Successful Meetings, Inc., Bill Communications, Inc., 633 Third Avenue, New York, NY 10017. (212) 986-4100.*

Dun's Electronic Business Directory. Available on Dialog Information Services and CompuServe Information Service. Database contains directory information on over 8.5 million businesses and professionals in the U.S. Includes type of business, SIC code, number of employees, professional's name, Dun's number, industry and city population in addition to other data.*

Encyclopedia of Associations. Gale Research Company, Book Tower, Detroit, MI 48226. (313) 961-2242.*

The Greatest Direct Mail Sales Letters of All Time, by Richard S. Hogson. Chicago: Dartnell Corporation, 1987.

Letters That Sell, by Edward W. Werz. Chicago, IL: Contemporary, 1987.

Mail Order Selling made Easier. John Kremer, Ad-Lib Publications, 51 North Fifth Street, P.O. Box 1102, Fairfield, IA 52556. (800) 669-0773.

National Directory of Addresses and Telephone Numbers. General Information Company, 401 Parkplace, Kirkland, WA 98033. (800) 722-3244.*

PhoneFile. Available on CompuServe Information Service. Database contains consumer data for over 80 million U.S. households. Includes name, address, phone number, and length of residence.*

Style Sheets for Newsletters, by Martha Lubow and Polly Pattison. Thousand Oaks, CA: New Riders, 1988.

Trade Show Bureau. Box 797, East Orleans, MA 02643.

Trade Shows and Professional Exhibits Directory. Gale Research Inc., Book Tower, Detroit, MI 48226. (313) 961-2242.*

Tradeshow Week Data Book. Tradeshow Week, 12233 West Olympic Boulevard, Suite 236, Los Angeles, CA 90064. (800) 521-8110.*

Part 4
Advertising: Cementing Your Name in Their Brains
So You're the One They Want

Arbitron Ratings, Radio, Metro Market Guide. 142 West 57th Street, New York, NY 10019. (212) 887-1300.*

Better Brochures, Catalogs and Mailing Pieces, by Jane Haas. New York: St. Martin's, 1984.

Broadcasting Yearbook. 1705 DeSales Street, N.W., Washington, D.C. 20036. (202) 659-2340.*

Editor & Publisher International Year Book. Editor & Publisher, 850 Third Avenue, New York, NY 10022.*

Getting the Most from Your Yellow Pages Advertising, by Barry Maher. New York: AMACOM, 1988.

Great Promo Pieces, by Herman Holtz. New York, John Wiley, 1989.

Handbook of Advertising Art Production, by Richard M. Schlemmer. Englewood Cliffs, NJ: Prentice Hall, 1990.

How to Make Newsletters, Brochures & Other Good Stuff Without a Computer System, by Helen Gregory. Sedro-Wooley, WA: Pinstripe, 1987.

National Classified Network, 4343 West Northwest Highway, Suite 915, Dallas, TX 75220. (214) 352-0612.

Standard Rate and Data Service. 3004 Glenview Road, Wilmette, IL 60091. (708) 256-6067.*

Successful Direct Marketing Methods, by Robert Stone. Lincolnwood, IL: National Textbook Company, 1990.

Write Great Ads: A Step-by-Step Approach, by Erica Levy Klein. New York: John Wiley, 1990.

Words That Sell, by Richard Bayan. Chicago, IL: Contemporary, 1987.

Conclusion: Turning Those Who Come To You Into Business

American Marketing Association. 250 South Wacker Drive, Chicago, IL 60606. (312) 648-0536.

Birch/Scarborough Research. Coral Gables, FL. (305) 753-6043.

Bureau of the Census. U.S. Department of Commerce, 8903 Presidential Parkway, Washington, D.C. 20230. (202) 523-1221.

clientBase. A total, fully automated computer program for practice marketing and management. Howard L. Shenson, 20750 Ventura Boulevard, Woodland Hills, CA 91364. (818) 703-1415.

Consultant's Guide to Proposal Writing: How to Satisfy Your Clients and Double Your Income, by Herman Holtz. New York: John Wiley, 1986.

The Contract & Fee Setting Guide for Consultants and Professionals, by Howard L. Shenson. New York: John Wiley, 1990.

Direct Marketing Association. 11 West 42nd Street, New York, NY 10036-8096. (212) 768-7277.

Do-It-Yourself Marketing Research, by George Breen and A.B. Blankenship. New York: McGraw Hill, 1989.

The Greatest Salesman in the World, by Og Mandino. New York: Bantam, 1968.

Guideposts for Effective Salesmanship, by Robert R. Blake and Jane Srygley Mouton. New York: McGraw Hill, 1970.

Influencing with Integrity, by Genie Z. Laborde. Palo Alto, CA: Syntony, 1987.

Marketing Manager—The Best 100 Sources for Marketing Information. A supplement to *American Demographics* magazine. American Demographics, Inc., 108 North Cayuga Street, Ithaca, NY 14850. (800) 828-1133.

Marketing News Directory of Software for Marketing Research. In April issue of *Marketing News,* published by the American Marketing Association, 250 South Wacker Drive, Chicago, IL 60606. (312) 648-0536.

Sales and Marketing Management Magazine. Annual survey of buying power. ISE Publications Ltd., Georgian House, 31 Upper George Street, Luton, Beds, LU12RD, England.

The Sales Script Book, by Donald J. Moine, Ph.D., and Gerhard Gschwandtner. Personal Selling Power, P.O. Box 5467, Fredericksburg, VA 22405. 1986.

Shenson on Consulting, by Howard Shenson. New York: John Wiley, 1990.

Successful Telephone Selling in the 90's, by Martin D. Shafiroff and Robert L. Shook. New York: Harper/Collins, 1990.

Think and Grow Rich, by Napoleon Hill. Greenwich, CT: Fawcett, 1960.

To the Letter, A Handbook of Model Letters for the Busy Executive, by Dianne Booher. Lexington, MD: Lexington, 1985.

Unlimited Selling Power, How to Master Hypnotic Selling Skills, by Donald Moine and Kenneth Lloyd. Englewood Cliffs, NJ: Prentice Hall, 1990.

1990 U.S. Industrial Outlook. U.S. Department of Commerce, International Trade Administration. Order from the Superintendent of Documents, Government Printing Office, Washington, D.C. 20402-9325.

INDEX

■ ■

These books are available at your local bookstore or wherever books are sold. Ordering is also easy and convenient. Just call 1-800-631-8571 or send your order to:

Jeremy P. Tarcher, Inc.
Mail Order Department
The Putnam Berkley Group, Inc.
390 Murray Hill Parkway
East Rutherford, NJ 07073-2185

			Price (U.S.)
_____	Working from Home	0-87477-582-5	$14.95
_____	The Best Home Businesses for the 90s	0-87477-633-3	11.95
_____	Making It on Your Own	0-87477-636-8	11.95
_____	Getting Business to Come to You	0-87477-629-5	11.95
_____	Making Money with Your Computer at Home	0-87477-736-4	12.95

Subtotal _____
Shipping and handling* _____
Sales tax (CA, NJ, NY, PA) _____
Total amount due _____

Payable in U.S. funds (no cash orders accepted). $15.00 minimum for credit card orders.
*Shipping and handling: $2.50 for one book, $0.75 for each additional book. Not to exceed $6.50.

Payment method:
☐ Visa ☐ MasterCard ☐ American Express
☐ Check or money order
☐ International money order or bank draft check
Card # _____ Expiration date _____
Signature as on charge card _____
Daytime phone number _____
Name _____
Address _____
City _____ State _____ Zip_____

Please allow six weeks for delivery. Prices subject to change without notice.

Refer to code # WORK